BRITPOP AND ENGLISH MUSIC TR.

CW00922017

Britpop and the English Music Tradition

Edited by

ANDY BENNETT
Griffith University, Australia

JON STRATTON
Curtin University of Technology, Australia

Routledge
Taylor & Francis Group

LONDON AND NEW YORK

First published 2010 by Ashgate Publishing

2 Park Square, Milton Park, Abingdon, Oxon OX14 4RN
711 Third Avenue, New York, NY 10017, USA

Routledge is an imprint of the Taylor & Francis Group, an informa business

First issued in paperback 2016

Copyright © 2010 Andy Bennett and Jon Stratton

Andy Bennett and Jon Stratton have asserted their right under the Copyright, Designs and Patents Act, 1988, to be identified as the editors of this work.

All rights reserved. No part of this book may be reprinted or reproduced or utilised in any form or by any electronic, mechanical, or other means, now known or hereafter invented, including photocopying and recording, or in any information storage or retrieval system, without permission in writing from the publishers.

Notice:
Product or corporate names may be trademarks or registered trademarks, and are used only for identification and explanation without intent to infringe.

British Library Cataloguing in Publication Data
Britpop and the English music tradition. – (Ashgate popular and folk music series)
   1. Alternative rock music – Great Britain – History and criticism. 2. Popular music – 1991–2000 – History and criticism. 3. Popular music – Great Britain – History and criticism. 4. Music – Social aspects – Great Britain – History – 20t h c entury.
   I. Series II. Bennett, Andy, 1963– III. Stratton, Jon.
   781.6'6'0941'09049–dc22

Library of Congress Cataloging-in-Publication Data
Bennett, Andy, 1963–
   Britpop and the English music tradition / Andy Bennett and Jon Stratton.
        p. cm.
   Includes bibliographical references and index.
   ISBN 978-0-7546-6805-3 (hardcover : alk. paper)

   1. Popular music—Great Britain—History and criticism. I. Stratton, Jon. II. Title.

   ML3650.B45 2010
   781.640941—dc22

                                                                            2010008301

ISBN 978-0-7546-6805-3 (hbk)
ISBN 978-1-138-26215-7 (pbk)

Contents

Section 3   Post-Britpop

List of Musical Examples

Notes on Contributors

Andy Bennett is Professor of Cultural Sociology and Director of the Griffith Centre for Cultural Research at Griffith University in Queensland, Australia. He is author and editor of numerous books including *Popular Music and Youth Culture* (Palgrave Macmillan, 2000), *Cultures of Popular Music* (Open University Press, 2001), *Remembering Woodstock* (Ashgate, 2004), and *Music Scenes* (with Richard A. Peterson, Vanderbilt University Press, 2004). He is Editor-in-Chief of the *Journal of Sociology*. He is a Faculty Fellow of the Center for Cultural Sociology, Yale University, an Associate Member of PopuLUs, the Centre for the Study of the World's Popular Musics, Leeds University, and a member of the Advisory Board for the Social Aesthetics Research Unit, Monash University.

Ian Collinson is an Associate Lecturer in Media in the Department of Media, Music, Communications and Cultural Studies at Macquarie University, Sydney, Australia. He teaches mainly media theory and history. Most of Ian's research has concerned the relationship between popular music and identity. He has published on Billy Bragg ('England, half English: the pragmatic patriotism of Billy Bragg', in Ian Collinson and Mark Evans (eds), *Sounds & Selves: a Select Conference Proceedings, IASPM-ANZ international conference, Wellington NZ 2005*, Perfect Beat Publications, 2007), the Asian Dub Foundation's response to 'Cool Britannia' ('Dis is England's New Voice: Anger, Activism and the Asian Dub Foundation', in G. Bloustein et al. (eds), *Sonic Synergies: Music, Identity, Technology*, Ashgate, 2008) and globalization, football 'plainsong' and fan communities in Australia ('Singing Songs, Making Places, Creating Selves': Football Songs & Fan Identity at Sydney FC', *Transformations in Culture 4/1*, 2009). He has also edited two collected conference proceedings for the Australian and New Zealand Branch of IASPM (2007 and 2008).

Stan Hawkins is Professor in the Department of Musicology, University of Oslo. He is author of *Settling the Pop Score: Pop Texts and Identity Politics* (Ashgate, 2002), and *The British Pop Dandy: Music, Masculinity and Culture* (Ashgate, 2009). He is co-editor of *Music, Space and Place* (with Sheila Whiteley and Andy Bennett, Ashgate, 2004), and *Essays in Sound and Vision* (with John Richardson, Helsinki University Press, 2007). His publications also appear in numerous edited books and journals, including *Popular Music, Popular Music and Society* and *Popular Musicology Online*. He is Editor-in-Chief of *Popular Musicology Online*.

Rupa Huq is Senior Lecturer in Sociology at Kingston University. Her research to date has largely been on youth culture and pop as in her latest book *Beyond Subculture* (Routledge, 2006). She is currently working on a book on suburbia and in her spare time has turned her hand to DJing and politics (Deputy Mayoress of London Borough of Ealing, Municipal year 2010–11).

Dave Laing is a Visiting Research Fellow at the University of Liverpool and a freelance researcher, author and editor. He is Associate Editor of the journal *Popular Music History* and the author of *The Sound of Our Time* (Sheed & Ward, 1969), *One Chord Wonders* (Open University Press, 1985) and *Buddy Holly* (Equinox, 2010). He was a co-editor of *The Faber Companion to 20th Century Popular Music* (Faber & Faber, 1990) and the *Continuum Encyclopedia of Popular Music of the World* (Continuum, 2003). He has contributed to several edited collections including *Global Pop, Local Language* (Harris M. Berger and Michael Thomas Carroll (eds), University Press of Mississippi, 2003), *The Popular Music Studies Reader* (Andy Bennett, Barry Shank and Jason Toynbee (eds), Routledge, 2006) and *The Cambridge Companion to The Beatles* (Kenneth Womack (ed.), Cambridge University Press, 2009).

J. Mark Percival is a Lecturer in Media at Queen Margaret University, Edinburgh and lives in Glasgow. His doctoral thesis (*Making Music Radio*, University of Stirling, 2007) focused on the social dynamics of the relationship between record industry pluggers and music radio programmers in the UK. He has recently written about Scottish indie music production in *Popular Music History* (2009), and contributed book chapters about popular music and tartan, (in Ian Brown (ed.), *From Tartan to Tartanry: Scottish Culture, History and Myth*, Edinburgh University Press, 2010), and mediation of popular music (in Hugh Dauncey and Philippe Le Guern, eds, *Stereo: Studying Popular Music in France and Britain*, Ashgate, 2010). Mark has presented papers on local music production and on music radio at many international conferences. Since 2008 he has been chair of the UK and Ireland branch of the International Association for the Study of Popular Music (IASPM). Mark is a member of the Radio Studies Network. Alongside his academic career he has been a Mercury Music Prize judging committee member (1999 and 2000) and a DJ for BBC Radio Scotland (1988–2000), playing alternative, indie and electronica.

Derek B. Scott is Professor of Critical Musicology and Head of the School of Music at the University of Leeds. He researches into music, culture and ideology, and is the author of *The Singing Bourgeois: Songs of the Victorian Drawing Room and Parlour* (2nd edn Ashgate, 2001), *From the Erotic to the Demonic: On Critical Musicology* (Oxford University Press, 2003), and *Sounds of the Metropolis: The 19th-Century Popular Music Revolution in London, New York, Paris, and Vienna* (Oxford University Press, 2008). He is the editor of *Music, Culture, and Society: A Reader* (Oxford University Press, 2000), and *The Ashgate*

Research Companion to Popular Musicology (Ashgate, 2009). He was a founder member of the UK Critical Musicology Group in 1993, and at the forefront in identifying changes of critical perspective in the socio-cultural study of music. He is the General Editor of Ashgate's Popular and Folk Music Series, and Associate Editor of *Popular Musicology Online*. His musical compositions range from music theatre to symphonies for brass band and a concerto for Highland Bagpipe. He has also worked professionally as a singer and pianist in radio, TV, concert hall and theatre.

Jon Stratton is Professor of Cultural Studies at Curtin University of Technology. Jon has published widely in the areas of cultural studies, Australian studies, Jewish studies, race and multiculturalism, and popular music studies. Jon's most recent books are: *Australian Rock: Essays on Popular Music* (Network Books, 2007), *Jewish Identity in Western Pop Culture: The Holocaust and Trauma through Modernity* (Palgrave Macmillan, 2008) and *Jews, Race and Popular Music* (Ashgate, 2009). Reflecting Jon's interest in race, multiculturalism and the plight of asylum seekers, Jon has also co-edited, with Suvendrini Perera, a special issue of *Continuum: Journal of Media and Cultural Studies* titled: *The Border, the Asylum Seeker and the State of Exception* (23/5, 2009). In addition, Jon has recently published articles on race and multiculturalism in Australia in *borderlands e-journal*, *Social Identities* and *Cultural Studies Review*.

Sheila Whiteley is Emeritus Professor of Popular Music at the University of Salford, Greater Manchester. As a feminist musicologist with strong research interests in issues of identity and subjectivity, she is known for her work on gender and sexuality as well as for longstanding interests in popular culture, and the status of women in the cultural industries. She is author of *The Space Between the Notes: Rock and the Counter Culture* (Routledge, 1992), *Women and Popular Music: Popular Music and Gender* (Routledge, 2000) and *Too Much Too Young: Popular Music, Age and Identity* (Routledge, 2005), and editor of *Sexing the Groove: Popular Music and Gender* (Routledge, 1996) and *Christmas, Ideology and Popular Culture* (Edinburgh University Press, 2008). She is co-editor of *Music Space and Place: Popular Music and Cultural Identity* (with Andy Bennett and Stan Hawkins, Ashgate, 2002) and *Queering the Popular Pitch* (with Jennifer Rycenga, Routledge, 2006). She is currently co-editing the OUP Handbook on *Popular Music and Queerness*, with Fred Maus, Sophie Fuller and Rachel Cowgill, and is on the *comité scientifique* for the colloquia 'Genres artistiques, genres sexués' (Paris, September 2011, co-organized by Marie Buscatto, Mary Leontsini and Hyacinthe Ravet). She was Chair of Popular Music at the University of Salford (1999–2006), Visiting Professor at the University of Aarhus, Denmark (2008) and the University of Brighton (2007–9). She has also published a novel, *Mindgames* (available from Amazon) which is based on her experience of being stalked following a conference at Brown University, USA, in 1996.

Nabeel Zuberi is a Senior Lecturer in the Department of Film, Television and Media Studies. His book publications include *Sounds English: Transnational Popular Music* (University of Illinois Press, 2001) and *Media Studies in Aotearoa/ New Zealand 2* (co-edited with Luke Goode, Pearson, 2010). He is completing a monograph on the study of popular music after digitization, *Understanding Popular Music* (Sage, forthcoming). In recent years he has published articles with the journals *Perfect Beat* and *Science Fiction Studies*. His most recent writing includes 'From a whisper to James Brown's scream' for tobias c. van Veen, (ed.), *Afrofuturism: Interstellar Transmissions From Remix Culture* (Wayne State University Press, forthcoming), and 'Guantánamo here we come' for Sean Campbell and Colin Coulter (eds), *The Smiths: Music, Culture, Politics* (Manchester University Press, forthcoming). Nabeel's current research focuses on western Muslims and contemporary media. He has co-hosted The Basement on BASE 107.3 FM Auckland (basefm.co.nz) since 2004.

General Editor's Preface

The upheaval that occurred in musicology during the last two decades of the twentieth century has created a new urgency for the study of popular music alongside the development of new critical and theoretical models. A relativistic outlook has replaced the universal perspective of modernism (the international ambitions of the 12-note style); the grand narrative of the evolution and dissolution of tonality has been challenged, and emphasis has shifted to cultural context, reception and subject position. Together, these have conspired to eat away at the status of canonical composers and categories of high and low in music. A need has arisen, also, to recognize and address the emergence of crossovers, mixed and new genres, to engage in debates concerning the vexed problem of what constitutes authenticity in music and to offer a critique of musical practice as the product of free, individual expression.

Popular musicology is now a vital and exciting area of scholarship, and the *Ashgate Popular and Folk Music Series* presents some of the best research in the field. Authors are concerned with locating musical practices, values and meanings in cultural context, and draw upon methodologies and theories developed in cultural studies, semiotics, poststructuralism, psychology and sociology. The series focuses on popular musics of the twentieth and twenty-first centuries. It is designed to embrace the world's popular musics from Acid Jazz to Zydeco, whether high tech or low tech, commercial or non-commercial, contemporary or traditional.

Professor Derek B. Scott
Professor of Critical Musicology
University of Leeds

Acknowledgements

This book is the product of some two years' work. Andy Bennett would like to thank co-editor Jon Stratton for making this such a pleasurable project to work on. Jon, likewise, would like to thank Andy for the ease and pleasure with which this project has proceeded.

Andy would also like to thank his colleagues at the Centre for Public Culture and the School of Humanities at Griffith University for their help and support with a range of academic and research matters while the hard work of putting this book together was in progress. Finally, Andy acknowledges with deep gratitude the mentorship of friend and colleague Professor Richard 'Pete' Peterson, who sadly passed away while this book was in production.

Collectively, we would like to thank Susan Leong for her work in standardizing the formatting of the chapters and getting them ready for submission to Ashgate. We would also like to thank Mar Bucknell for his work proofing this book.

Thanks must also go the School of Media, Culture and Creative Arts, Curtin University of Technology, for making funds available to pay for Susan's work and the Faculty of Humanities at Curtin for funding the index and the proofing. Jon would also like to thank Associate Professor Steve Mickler, Head of the School of Media, Culture and Creative Arts, for allowing him time away from teaching to work on this project.

Last, but by no means least, we would like to thank the contributors to this collection for their patience and speedy responses to our comments and questions on their chapters.

Introduction

Andy Bennett and Jon Stratton

At the height of the Britpop phenomenon, during the mid-1990s, 'Britpop' was branded by music journalists and critics alike as a critical resurgence of British popular music. Musically and lyrically, Britpop was regarded as a return to form – a brand of characteristically British, or more specifically 'English', popular music that rekindled the spirit of the mid-1960s 'British' invasion of the US by groups such as the Beatles, the Rolling Stones, the Kinks, the Who and the Small Faces. Indeed, a number of these groups, notably the Beatles, the Kinks and the Small Faces, were frequently cited as key musical influences by leading Britpop artists such as Blur and Oasis. The purportedly English qualities of Britpop acquired a currency at a number of levels. From the perspective of the British music industry, Britpop was considered an antidote to the dominance of US-originated musical styles such as rap and grunge (see also Chapters 4 and 8 in this book) whose rapid commercial success and incisive impact on youth audiences around the world had seen Britain lose momentum as a key player in the global popular music industry. Riding on the wave of the indie-guitar scene of the early 1990s, Britpop's merging of indie's guitar-based melodic pop style with a 1960s retro-aesthetic quickly found a niche, both nationally and overseas. The fact that Britpop was considered by the music industry and associated taste-makers as something 'authentically' English was further demonstrated through the speed at which groups such as Blur and Oasis found a place in the English rock/pop canon. In September 1995, one year after the release of Blur's breakthrough album *Parklife*, UK retro music magazine *Mojo* ran an extended feature on the band,[1] referring to their new album *The Great Escape* as 'the most eagerly-awaited long-player of 1995'. The same *Mojo* issue ran a feature in which Blur vocalist Damon Albarn met and interviewed a personal icon, singer-songwriter Ray Davies of the Kinks, further cementing in the popular imagination Britpop links with the Kinks and other 1960s English popular music icons.

That Britpop bands often cited regionality – both real and imagined – as an important aspect of their musical identity was another factor that facilitated opportunistic comparisons with the 1960s from the point of view of the music industry and the music press. For example, the northern roots of Oasis as compared with the London-centric sensibilities of Blur provided endless avenues for comparisons with the Beatles and the Rolling Stones (even when critical points of reference, for example the northern gritty aesthetic of Oasis as compared with

---

[1]   David Cavanagh, 'Blur in the Studio'.

the Art School posturings of Blur, were distinctly problematized when imposed onto the Beatles and the Rolling Stones where such neat distinctions were difficult to apply). However, region and regionality went further in the Britpop discourse. Songs such as Pulp's 'Common People', described in John Dower's 2003 film document *Live Forever* as the defining song of the Britpop sound, transformed kitchen-sink melodrama into a 'warts and all' pop celebration of English working-class life.[2]

Also critical to a contemporary understanding of the Britpop phenomenon is the way in which it was effectively hijacked – or allowed itself to be hijacked – by mainstream politics in the mid-1990s. As future prime minister Tony Blair's New Labour campaign gathered momentum, Britpop and its associations with a young, 'cool' British public presented itself as a crucial and seemingly willing partner in the promotion of a new cultural political discourse – 'Cool Britannia'.[3] The foundations for the Cool Britannia rhetoric, and the role of Britpop within it, had been established through the British popular press that, as early as 1994, had been intimating that the emergence of Britpop defined a new cultural sensibility in the UK, conflating in the process the terms British and English in a way that has continued to problematize Britpop. Thus as Cliff Jones, writer for leading popular culture magazine *The Face*, said of Blur in 1994 in the wake of the success of the group's *Parklife* album:

> By rebelling against th[e] gradual dumbing down of a nation, by openly championing a switched-on, sophisticated Britpop image [Blur have] defined a New Englishness. It's an attitude based not on a nostalgic Carry On Mr Kipling Britain, but a Britain that you will recognise as the one you live in. A place where dressing well and having a good haircut matter.[4]

Despite such bold statements, however, a salient criticism, and one that has been revisited on Britpop many times since, was its overly nostalgic representation of a nation. As Cloonan observes,[5] the Britain and/or England portrayed in much of the Britpop material is ethnically white and appears to be set in an imagined past. Little reference is paid to the ravages of de-industrialization and unemployment or the social unrest created through racism and inequality. Both musically and culturally, it was claimed, Britpop seemed content to airbrush out of existence significant eras of social and cultural change in Britain and England.

The political economy of Britpop was also sharply questioned. Although it was championed in some quarters for allegedly reviving the musical fortunes

---

[2] Andy Bennett, '"Village Greens and Terraced Streets": Britpop and Representations of "Britishness"'.

[3] Martin Cloonan, 'State of the Nation: "Englishness", Pop, and Politics in the mid-1990s'; see also Chapter 6 in this book.

[4] Cliff Jones, 'Looking for a New England', p. 42.

[5] In 'State of the Nation: "Englishness"'.

of a nation, Britpop itself seemed to be a purely 'English' affair. Little or no reference to Scottish, Welsh or Irish bands was or has since been made in relation to Britpop. Indeed, as Mark Percival explains in greater detail in Chapter 8, groups from these countries generally exhibited little interested in being associated with Britpop. In this respect, as in others then, Britpop appeared to be a reaffirmation of long-established status quo. Thus the bands who attracted the attention of the London-based British music press and were readily associated with the Britpop trend tended to be those English bands who were London-based or who were prepared to travel to London for gigs.

The legacy of Britpop continues to impress itself on English popular music. The purpose of this book is to revisit and re-evaluate Britpop as a musical and cultural phenomenon that was both shaped by and has contributed to the shaping of English musical and social institutions. As such, the book is both a historical study and one that brings the Britpop legacy right up to date, with chapters in the latter half of the book considering the impact of Britpop upon the way contemporary English popular music artists are positioned – or position themselves – in the English cultural landscape.

The first section of the book, 'History and Context', maps the musical and cultural influences on Britpop from the mid-nineteenth century to the early 1980s. Dave Laing provides an outline of music hall, discussing its origins and most important artists; he also provides an outline of the debates over the politics of music hall. Discussing the way music hall morphed into variety, Laing emphasizes the importance of the new technology of the microphone. He also discusses the revival of music hall in the 1960s and 1970s, and the importance of BBC television's *The Good Old Days* to that revival. Laing shows some of the continuities in the expression of Englishness between music hall and Britpop. Music hall has been a constant resort for English artists, and Laing shows its centrality to the culture of working-class life in the late nineteenth and early twentieth century. Next, Jon Stratton argues that music hall was the basis of the tradition that was at first swamped by American musical forms but was then reasserted, often in new combinations with American music. Skiffle was one example of an American musical form that was taken up and reworked in the service of English culture. By the mid-1960s, the Beatles and the Kinks were making music that acknowledged the music hall tradition. Even the Rolling Stones, the quintessential English rhythm and blues group, were including elements drawn from music hall and other areas of English culture. Britpop has been considered irremediably male.

In Chapter 4, Sheila Whiteley considers the influences that produced this trend and examines the ways that groups with women in dominant roles, most importantly Echobelly, Elastica and Sleeper, bought into the laddism of Britpop or attempted to carve out a role distinct from the dominant ideology. As Whiteley observes, these groups looked to punk and New Wave to find a ground from which to explore the gender orthodoxy of male-dominated Britpop. Then Andy Bennett considers the ways that groups in the 1970s form a missing link between the assertions of Englishness in the 1960s and the Britpop of the 1990s. To this end Bennett considers groups such as Slade and Cockney Rebel who are usually absent in critical discussions of Englishness. Indeed, as Bennett remarks, the 1970s, before punk, are often noted in histories of Britpop but rarely given the attention they deserve. Bennett considers how these groups worked with an everyday Englishness, often expressed in accent and in a critical consideration of elements of English culture such as the educational system. Madness, with their use of ska and reggae rhythms, pioneered the incorporation of these Jamaican forms into a celebration of white, English working-class life suggesting a complex acknowledgement of Britain's racialized society.

Section 2 examines the Britpop phenomenon itself, from its connections with New Labour through the discourses of genre, style and sexuality associated with Britpop, to the problematic conflation of the terms 'British' and 'English' in the cultural and commercial rhetoric of Britpop. Rupa Huq focuses on the relationship between New Labour and Britpop. Huq considers how New Labour's rhetoric of Cool Britannia drew on Harold Wilson's positioning of Labour in the 1960s as the party to lead Britain into the future and how this nostalgic revisioning of the past was echoed in the ways that Britpop groups looked to the groups of the 1960s for inspiration and validation. As Huq argues, while New Labour wanted to use Britpop for its own purposes, most especially to woo the youth vote, the Britpop groups were quite apolitical. There was, as she notes, no Britpop equivalent of Red Wedge, the 1980s grouping of musicians in support of Labour. At the same time, while new musical forms such as jungle and bhangra were evolving among racialized, marginalized groups, the members of Britpop groups were overwhelmingly white and male. In the end, Huq suggests, 'Britpop can be characterized as a post-ideological soundtrack to post-political times'.

Derek Scott provides a close musical analysis comparing the sounds of the 1960s groups with the sounds of the Britpop groups. He argues that those people who claim that, for example, Oasis sound like the Beatles, have not paid close attention to the music each group was making. He suggests that Britpop 'was made possible ... by the emergence of a rock canon and, consequently, the idea of classic rock'. At the same time, as Scott goes on to detail, the relationship between Oasis and the Beatles, while present, is superficial. Scott's point is that each group is, ultimately, a product of its time. Mark Percival is concerned with that vexed problem of whether Britpop, as a term and as a musical style, covered the whole of Britain, or just England. Percival excludes Northern Ireland from his discussion because of the complexities associated with that region. He considers how Welsh and Scottish groups identified with indie and rejected Britpop as a sell-out from indie values. This took place at the same time that political power was being devolved from Westminster. The Welsh National Assembly and the Scottish Parliament were established after referendums in 1998. At the same time, Percival argues that Welsh and Scottish groups did not perform Welshness or Scottishness. Rather, they asserted their difference through a rejection of the lifestyle associated with Britpop groups and an assertion of values that were claimed to be typically Welsh and Scottish. In addition, in Wales, there has been much debate over whether groups should sing in Welsh. Percival offers a discussion of the different ways that the Stereophonics, Manic Street Preachers and Super Furry Animals have identified their Welshness, and the practical ways that the last group has managed their shift from singing in Welsh to making albums in English.

Finally, in this section, Stan Hawkins looks at the ways that masculinity gets played out in the laddism that was so associated with the Britpop groups. Hawkins is particularly interested in vocal performances. He provides four detailed analyses, of James Dean Bradfield from Manic Street Preachers, Noel Gallagher from Oasis, Damon Albarn from Blur, and Jarvis Cocker from Pulp. Noting Hawkins's use of Manic Street Preachers, whom Percival identifies as a Welsh group antithetical in some ways to Britpop, this is a good moment for us, as editors, to explain that we have deliberately not tried to homogenize the contributions to this collection. While the chapters all cover different aspects of the Britpop phenomenon, and in this sense complement each other, we have allowed them also to express different positions on what Britpop is and which groups might be considered Britpop artists. Hawkins tells us that 'Britpop signalled a distinct reaction to the new trends of masculinity that emerged in the 1980s and the set of liberal politics the New Male upheld'. Through his close analyses of the four singers, Hawkins argues that 'all communicate the normative rules of gendered practice through their performances'. He goes on to consider how the assertion of Britpop, laddist masculinity functions in terms of an anxiety about the performance of heterosexuality brought about by the New Male unsettling of heteronormativity.

Section 3 examines the English music–cultural landscape in a post-Britpop context, considering how the legacy of Britpop has shaped the music and politics of contemporary English guitar bands and more recent English-originated music genres such as grime and dubstep. Ian Collinson's concern is with the new generation of guitar groups in the early 2000s. He chooses three, all of which have achieved great popularity in Britain, for particularly close examination – Kaiser Chiefs, Arctic Monkeys and Bloc Party. He argues that these new guitar groups owe more to the groups of the 1970s than the 1960s. At the same time, there has been little change in the composition of these groups, that is, 'this new wave continues the gender, ethnic and racial exclusivity of Britpop'. In this regard, as Collinson argues, Bloc Party stands out as a racially mixed group. For Collinson, Bloc Party is different in other ways as well. While Kaiser Chiefs and Arctic Monkeys evidence a nostalgia for the 1970s, Bloc Party, Collinson argues, offers a new engagement with 'ideas of Englishness'. Nostalgia is a theme that runs through this collection. The 1960s groups nostalgic for a lost empire and a time before American-driven consumerism; the laddist Britpop groups nostalgic for the 1960s when, apparently, gender roles were clearer and men knew how to be men; and more recently, groups in the 2000s nostalgic for what they think was the simpler nationalism of Britain in the 1970s, a time, perhaps, before devolution and when, only in 1973, Britain finally voted to join what was then the Common Market. Nostalgia, as Collinson quotes Ruth Adams remarking, is 'a constant presence in British culture'. It is a prism through which Britons understand their present and their past. Collinson argues that the generation of guitar groups he is discussing are all concerned with the question of Englishness and that they all, even Bloc Party, which at least identifies some of Britain's social problems in the 2000s, fail to describe what a new Englishness might look like.

Nabeel Zuberi's chapter makes a stimulating comparison with Collinson's. Where Collinson identifies the loss of imagination of the white, male guitar groups in a renewed English future, Zuberi examines what he calls 'some of the black humours in dance music during the last decade'. Zuberi focuses on artists like Dizzee Rascal, Sway and M.I.A. – here is where we find the Asian- and Afro-Caribbean-originated Britons. In this music that explores new soundscapes using new technologies, we find both the expression of anger at Britain's racialized subordination of minority groups and the innovation that generates new musical forms like grime and dubstep that are, inevitably, politically engaged. Zuberi explores the ways that Dizzee Rascal asserts his Englishness that, as a black Briton, he feels he is being denied. He also discusses M.I.A., showing how her popularity has developed virally across the internet, utilizing new digital technologies of reproduction and distribution. The contrast between the white guitar groups that Collinson discusses and the brown and black artists that are Zuberi's focus offers an indictment of a British culture that continues to marginalize people of colour.

Britpop was, and is, often understood as a reassertion of the British popular music tradition in the face of the popularity of grunge. However, Britpop, as the chapters in this book suggest, was simultaneously involved with the assertion of a white, male, heterosexual Englishness. From this point of view, Britpop was a conservative reaction to the changes that were transforming Britain in the 1990s. Among these, this collection identifies the crisis in national identity associated with devolution and the European Community; the political crisis associated with the demise of Thatcherite conservatism and its replacement by New Labour's Cool Britannia in the landslide general election of 1997; the crisis in British whiteness as second- and third-generation people of colour asserted their Britishness and their place in English culture; the crisis in masculinity as the acceptance of the New Male signalled also an unsettling of heteronormativity. Collinson's conclusion that the post-Britpop groups he is discussing can offer no new vision of Englishness, or Britishness, is disturbing. As we have seen, Britpop evolved as a reassertion of a British tradition of popular music that goes back to the beat groups of the 1960s. Britpop's vision was regressive, a reinstatement of traditional race and gender concerns. At the same time, as Percival explains, the aesthetics of Britpop were rejected by Welsh and Scottish groups who remained staunchly indie in their attitudes. Britpop was really Eng-pop.

We also need to remember that Britpop was just one form of music among many in England in the 1990s. From at least the establishment of ska and reggae as indigenous English musical forms in the 1960s and 1970s, popular music across Britain has been a melting pot of diverse sounds. Unlike the United States, where there has been a long tradition of musical segregation, since at least the Equals and the Foundations in the latter half of the 1960s, Britain has had popular mixed-race groups that meld together a wide variety of musical genres. Where the ska influence on the Equals' recordings was subtle, the changes in British musical sensibilities meant that, in 1994, the same year that Oasis released *Definitely Maybe* and Blur released their third album *Parklife*, Pato Banton could have a number 1 hit with a reggaefied version of Eddy Grant's 'Baby Come Back', a 1967 number 1 for the Equals. Bloc Party may have, as Collinson suggests, no musical vision for the present, or the future, but their mixed-race make-up and their dance-genre influences point to a breaking-out of the white, male (and heterosexual) straitjacket that has limited the ability of post-Britpop guitar groups to come to terms with the fundamental changes that have been taking place in British and, especially, English, life. At the same time, Zuberi's analysis of the musical creativity and political engagement of those racialized and marginalized in Britain suggests other possibilities. Grime-influenced artists who have achieved chart success such as Dizzee Rascal and M.I.A. signal the ways that white Britons are adapting to a new multicultural and plural musical mix. In addition, some grime artists have started working with white guitar groups who might have been identified as Britpop but are now more commonly called indie, forming a new hybrid genre which Statik, a grime producer who has been a pioneer in this development, has christened grindie.

SECTION 1
History and Context

Chapter 1

Music Hall and the Commercialization of English Popular Music

Dave Laing

In 2009, the music journalist Paul du Noyer wrote that the Sex Pistols were London's 'last great music hall act'.[1] Other writers have linked such pop and rock acts as the Beatles, the Kinks and Madness with 'music hall'. However, the consensus of historians of popular entertainment is that music hall as an entertainment medium and a song genre was in terminal decline as early as the second decade of the twentieth century. One aim of this chapter is to explain how it has been possible to argue that a defunct area of British popular song can 'live again' in the pop music of the late twentieth century. The other principal aim, to which the first part of the chapter is devoted, is to establish the distinguishing features of music hall as both an entertainment medium and a genre of British song and to analyze its demise as a dominant form of popular culture.

Origins and Development of Music Hall

There is a consensual view of the main elements of the origins of music hall in the literature on nineteenth-century popular music in Britain, for example in the works of Pearsall (1975), Russell (1997), Lee (1982), Kift (1996) and Bailey (1998).[2] According to these authorities, music hall was a form of commercial entertainment for the urban lower classes introduced in the mid-nineteenth century. The forerunner of the music hall was the 'glee' or singing night held in London taverns.[3] It took its name from the specialist venues that were built or adapted to provide an evening's show by up to a dozen separate acts, ranging from singers and dancers to trick cyclists, jugglers, magicians and animal acts. To this extent it was similar to the contemporaneous vaudeville scene in the United States.

---

[1]   Paul du Noyer, *In the City: A Celebration of London Music*, p. 202.

[2]   See Ronald Pearsall, *Edwardian Popular Song*; Dave Russell, *Popular Music in England, 1840–1914: A Social History*; Edward Lee, *Folk Song and Music Hall*; Dagmar Kift, *The Victorian Music Hall: Culture, Class and Conflict*; Peter Bailey, *Popular Culture and Performance in the Victorian City*.

[3]   Laurence Senelick (ed.), *Tavern Singing in Early Victorian London: The Diaries of Charles Rice for 1840 and 1841*.

The consensus was summarized neatly by Jeffrey Richards in a book dealing only in passing with the music-hall system:

> The music hall became the prototype of the modern entertainment industry, rapidly commercialized as capital was invested, advertising techniques were developed to promote stars and a hierarchy of stars and supporting acts was evolved. By the 1870s many music halls were mounting shows twice-nightly to maximise returns on investment. Initially, music halls were independent operations, normally set up locally by enterprising publicans. But the railway system made touring possible and circuits developed with artists touring regularly. By the 1880s and 1890s there were several nationwide circuits.[4]

Music Hall as a Song Genre

Jeffrey Richards, again, provides a summary of much of the received wisdom about songs written to be performed in music halls:

> The writers of songs had to take into account the mixed nature of the audiences, the need for escapism, a catchy tune and sentiment, for it was the audience who made songs and stars. So songwriters sought to dramatize general attitudes, and songs strongly reflected a set of regular themes: love (treated as romance), marriage (treated as a trap and disaster), work (and how to avoid it), city life, food and drink, clothes and holidays.[5]

Some additional features might be adduced here. The first is that the 'regular themes' of the songs should include topical political subjects and double entendre and sexual innuendo that were distinctly different from the themes of romantic love or unhappy marriage. Secondly, music-hall songs were structured to include audience participation. Their refrains or choruses were designed for communal singing by singer and audience together.

The most important addition to Richards's list is that music hall's greatest stars were the vocalists, notably Marie Lloyd, who drew admiration from a wide range of observers including George Bernard Shaw and T.S. Eliot, a figure not renowned for his devotion to popular culture. He wrote of Lloyd's 'capacity for expressing the soul of the people'.[6] He may not have been thinking of Lloyd's reputation for what a more recent scholar has called 'knowingness'[7] in such songs as 'She'd Never Had Her Ticket Punched Before'.[8]

---

[4]   Jeffrey Richards, *Imperialism and Music: Britain 1876–1953*, pp. 324–5.

[5]   Ibid., p. 325.

[6]   T.S. Eliot, *Selected Essays*, p. 457.

[7]   Bailey, *Popular Culture and Performance in the Victorian City*.

[8]   Midge Gillies, *Marie Lloyd: The One and Only*, p. 119.

Individual songs were indelibly linked with specific vocalists, for whom they were written by an industrious cohort of specialist songwriters. A typical and successful music-hall composer was George le Brunn, who died at 42 in 1905 having written over 1,000 published and performed songs, of which only 'Oh Mr Porter' (for Marie Lloyd) is likely to be familiar to anyone in twenty-first-century audiences. Le Brunn was claimed to be able to write melodies in three or four minutes and to compose up to thirty of these a week, something even Elton John in his heyday might have struggled to equal.

After a new song had been chosen by a star singer, its music publisher would attempt to enforce the performance 'ownership' of the song by naming and often portraying the relevant singer on sheet music, adding such minatory rubrics as 'this song may be sung anywhere without fee or licence with the exception of the various Music Halls where the [artist name] has the sole right'. Even if such a 'sole right' was not so strictly defined, the original artist could aggressively pursue other professional singers who performed a certain song.

The primary source of income for songwriters and publishers was sales of sheet music for the domestic piano market, and the link with star vocalists was a key marketing tool. Classical music pieces reduced for the piano and parlour ballads for the middle classes were sold through musical instrument shops for comparatively high prices. In contrast, printed copies of music-hall songs were sold at street markets for sixpence by popular music publishers like Francis, Day and Hunter, while from 1898 the working-class Sunday newspaper *News of the World* included the words and music of a current hit song each week. Publishers additionally brought out annual collections of some of the biggest-selling titles of the previous year.

As well as acquiring an exclusive repertoire, many of the most famous singers enacted characters or social types recognized by their mainly working-class audience. There was the upper-class 'swell' portrayed by such 'lion comique' singers as George Leybourne ('Champagne Charlie'), Charles Coburn ('The Man Who Broke the Bank at Monte Carlo') and the proletarian 'coster' with exaggerated Cockney accent created by Gus Elen ('If it Wasn't for the Houses in Between') and Albert Chevalier ('My Old Dutch').

Female singers were less 'actorly' in their personae, although many of the large number of cross-dressing male impersonators chose to simulate upper-class males rather than plebeian ones, notably Vesta Tilley (aka Algy the Piccadilly Johnny with the Little Glass Eye) who, possibly coincidentally, married into the aristocracy.[9] There were also some proletarian character types embodied, for instance, by Jenny Hill. She portrayed the Coffee Shop Gal, the Landlady, the Servant Girl and the Costerwoman.

All of these singers were London-based (where the first music hall opened for business in 1850) as was much of their repertoire, and histories of music hall have sometimes taken a metropolitan bias. But there were halls all over Great Britain

---

[9]   Sara Maitland, *Vesta Tilley*.

and Ireland and many regions and nations had their own distinctive features. The specifically local character of songs, performers and even trade magazines are described, for example, by Dave Haslam for Manchester,[10] Dave Harker for Tyneside[11] and Frank Bruce for Scotland.[12]

Scotland, in particular, was notable for its intensely local and national singers and songs. There the key figure was Harry (later Sir Harry) Lauder. He was the acme of the 'Scotch comedian', 'speaking English with a Scots accent'[13] to reach international audiences, and presenting a caricature Scot on stage with kilt and tam o'shanter and mixing comic numbers ('Stop Your Ticklin' Jock!') with sentimental love songs ('Roamin' in the Gloamin'') and, at the time of the First World War patriotic ballads ('Keep Right on to the End of the Road').

Lauder belonged to the nineteenth-century construction of Scottish identity known as 'tartanry', and while there may be superficial resemblances to later comedians who presented as Scottish, the style of Lauder's act brought criticisms that he was a self-hating Scot. Bruce quotes the view of a 'middle-class patron' on the Lauder era that 'it was then, I suppose, a sort of convention that Scottish comedians should present Scottish life at its lowest, and Scotland really owes something to its laughter-makers of a later day, who had the genius and courage to smash the convention'.[14] This comment is a rare example in recent times of a clear rejection of music-hall conventions and a celebration of the fact that that these no longer haunt the work of Scottish identity-formation through popular culture carried out by such late twentieth-century figures as Stanley Baxter, Chic Murray and Billy Connolly. It should equally be noted, though, that there were a considerable number of twentieth-century inheritors of tartanry in popular music and dance, who included a number of Lauder's songs in their repertoire and performed regularly (and, it seemed, interminably) in the 1960s and 1970s on the BBC television show *The White Heather Club*.

The Politics of Music Hall

It is notable, but not often noticed, that music hall thrived in an era of political quietism for the British working class, following the upsurge of Chartism in the 1840s and preceding the outbreak of strikes at the end of the century by unskilled workers and the formation of the Labour Representation Committee, the immediate forerunner of the Labour Party. It was during the interim period that part of the leisure time of plebeian elements in society – sections of the working class and

---

[10]   Dave Haslam, *Manchester, England*, pp. 42–53.

[11]   Dave Harker, 'The Making of the Tyneside Concert Hall'.

[12]   Frank Bruce, *Scottish Showbusiness: Music Hall, Variety and Pantomime*, pp. 13–40.

[13]   Ibid., p. 36.

[14]   Ibid., p. 38.

the artisan class – became commercialized, just as middle-class leisure had been commercialized differently in the eighteenth century.

The role of music hall as an institution in relation to the 'disciplining' of the Victorian working class has been a preoccupation of social and political scholars of the late twentieth century.[15] Music hall provoked fierce opposition from the proponents of 'rational recreation' for the working classes, as well as from evangelical moralists. Nevertheless, music hall thrived, reaching its peak in the last decades of the nineteenth century and the first decade of the twentieth century.

Scholars of music hall have also commented on the political implications of the songs in terms of working-class ideologies in the latter part of the nineteenth century. Writing only about the metropolis, Gareth Stedman-Jones paradoxically concluded that 'music hall appealed to the London working class because it was both escapist and yet strongly rooted in the realities of working class life'.[16]

The views expressed in the lyrics of individual songs show a mixed and sometimes conflictual political consciousness. Much emphasis has been placed on certain pieces that put forward strongly pro-imperialist views, in particular the Great MacDermott's highly popular version of 'Jingo', a song of 1877 whose chorus began 'We don't want to fight but by jingo if we do, / We've got the ships, we've got the men, we've got the money too'. On the other hand, while there were no pacifist hits in the music-hall repertoire, there were several topical pieces in support of, or in sympathy with, the working-class heroes of strikes and victims of industrial accidents.

This broad political background is also relevant to the non-commercialized dimension of popular music in this period, including the brass band movement and amateur choirs. In an implicit rebuke to the emphasis placed on the glamour and bawdiness of music hall by other historians, Dave Russell devoted over 100 pages of his standard history to such 'community' music but only 70 pages to what he called the music of 'capitalism', i.e. the music halls.[17]

Decline and Fall

The music hall maintained its importance for plebeian audiences into the first quarter of the twentieth century, when some of its greatest performers flourished – for example, Marie Lloyd and Harry Lauder. However, it was gradually superseded as a leading popular entertainment form. There were three important developments that transformed the music sphere between about 1920 and 1940, both in Britain and elsewhere in northern and western Europe.

---

[15] Kift, *The Victorian Music Hall*; Bailey, *Popular Culture and Performance in the Victorian City*.

[16] Gareth Stedman-Jones, 'Working-Class Culture and Working-Class Politics in London 1870–1900', p. 108.

[17] Russell, *Popular Music in England, 1840–1914*.

The first of these was social dancing, centred on a new institution, the ballroom, dance hall or *palais de danse*. The first purpose-built dance hall in Britain was the Hammersmith Palais in London, opening in 1919. The business was rapidly commercialized by the owners of dance-hall chains such as Mecca, founded by Carl Heimann, a Danish immigrant. Almost 11,000 dance halls and night clubs were opened in Britain between 1918 and 1926.[18] In one working-class district of Manchester (Hulme) there were 12 dance halls.

The second development was the cinema. Originally, short films were shown as part of the entertainment mix in music halls or variety theatres, but by the end of the First World War the cinema had displaced music hall as the central form of plebeian entertainment. By then, films had become established as a separate cultural form and cultural industry with purpose-built venues. In 1919 the music-hall industry newspaper the *Era* warned of the 'Cinema Invasion', and by 1926 there were 3,000 cinemas in operation.[19] When a soundtrack was added at the end of the 1920s, the cinema was to become the second biggest major entertainment destination for the next 30 years, alongside the dance hall.

The third development was radio. Having been developed for military communication at the beginning of the century, radio became a mass medium – a one-way communication from a single broadcast source to many receivers – in the 1920s. Unlike dancing and films, it was a domestic entertainment form, bringing music and speech into the home, alongside the piano and the gramophone. In Britain, as in most European countries (with the notable exception of Spain), radio broadcasting was strictly controlled by the state, which set up the British Broadcasting Company, later Corporation, as a monopoly. There were only half a million licensed listeners in 1923, but five million in 1932.

Music was an important component of each of these three new entertainment forms. It was obviously essential for the dance halls and ballrooms, which provided thousands of jobs for members of dance bands or orchestras. There were many musicians employed in the early cinemas, since even if the films themselves were 'silent', they were always accompanied by music. In addition, many of the early sound films were 'musicals', although the only employment they provided was for orchestras at recording sessions in the film studios. And musical performances, sometimes relayed from ballrooms, were a major element in the BBC radio schedules.

The provenance of the majority of the music to be heard at dance halls, in the cinema and on the radio was American. Many of the popular dances were American in origin, from the Bunny Hug and Foxtrot to the Charleston and the Jitterbug of the 1940s, and the music of the dance bands was popularly known as 'jazz', although it bore little relation to what has since been canonized under that name.

---

[18]   James Nott, *Music for the People: Popular Music and Dance in Interwar Britain*, p. 151.

[19]   Ibid., p. 154.

The clash of cultures between the 'old school' music hall and the new American music was highlighted by an incident that occurred when the Original Dixieland Jazz Band made their famous visit to Britain in 1919. The ODJB's first London appearances took place between the matinee and evening performances of a show called *Joy Bells* at the Hippodrome. The veteran music-hall comedian George Robey was top of the bill and he was reported to have approached the promoter of the ODJB's tour in a seething rage with the ultimatum that either he or the jazz band would have to go. In this case, the band went, but only to play highly successfully for two weeks in a rival variety show at the London Palladium.[20]

Music-hall songwriters could not ignore ragtime and other examples of the American invasion. But attitudes were ambivalent: several compositions ridiculed ragtime, but others sought to ride the ragtime bandwagon. American music had, in any case, been a feature of British popular culture in the nineteenth century, both through the importation of songs and styles and through performances by United States-born artists. The most distinctive import was the blackface minstrel show, which was a prominent feature of popular entertainment.[21] A small number of US-born acts were among the leading music-hall performers. Among these were the blackface minstrel singer Eugene Stratton and the song and dance duo the Richmond Sisters.

Nevertheless, American music represented only a small minority of the repertoire performed and sold to British audiences until the First World War, with the professional minstrel shows, for example, fading away in the 1890s. Thereafter, the transatlantic repertoire easily outsold British-originated material. In his book *Music for the People*, James Nott provides a list of the most popular songs in 1919, 1925, 1930, 1935 and 1939. Of these 183 songs, 73 per cent or almost three-quarters were American in origin. As early as 1919, only five of the 19 songs listed by Nott were British, and the titles of two of these – 'I've Got the Sweetest Girl in Maryland' and 'Missouri Waltz' – showed that they were masquerading as being made in America. By the 1930s, about one-third of the hit songs were from American films.[22]

In this context of the rise of new media and the encroachment of American music, music hall itself went into decline, to be succeeded by 'variety', which was superficially similar but less broad in its range of acts (no animal acts and fewer novelties). According to some authors, variety embraced more respectable and cosmopolitan elements than music hall, although there is a considerable imprecision of terminology among historians and industry professionals when variety and music hall are mentioned. That is, the same performer or show or venue may be identified as music hall by one individual or as variety by another.

One crucial technical feature that distinguished variety from the Victorian music hall was the microphone. By the 1930s, variety shows provided vocalists

[20] Catherine Parsonage, *The Evolution of Jazz in Britain, 1880–1935*, p. 125.

[21] Michael Pickering, *Blackface Minstrelsy in Britain*.

[22] Nott, *Music for the People*, pp. 237–43.

with fixed microphones at the centre of the stage that not only enabled newer singers to emote in a more confidential style but limited their stage movements compared with the ability of music-hall singers to roam around the stage.[23]

Another feature was the weakening of the link between one song and its exclusive singer. The predominance of American songs meant that no individual British performer could lay claim to an imported composition, while the speed by which radio could disseminate a song nationally considerably shortened the period during which a star act could retain exclusivity. As Mander and Mitchenson write, 'gone were the days when a song especially written was the sole property of one artist. Now a new style of song presented in many ways was to be sung by all and sundry.'[24]

Partly through the vagaries of terminology, shows designated 'variety' during and after the 1930s could be anything from a near reincarnation of music hall to the post-Second World War 'road shows' that toured the country, often incorporating current pop or skiffle stars and having much in common with the package show tours of the pop music era.

Revival and Preservation

Despite the confusion over terminology, the classic music-hall performance apparatus survived beyond the 1920s only through deliberate attempts at preservation or revival of a cultural heritage, in a limited number of theatres and through individual plays, shows and television series.

The revival process began as early as 1929, when the residual status of the entertainment form was acknowledged in a show called *Veteran Stars of Variety*.[25] The variety format was revived in 1947 at the London Casino and in 1948 at the London Palladium theatre by the impresarios Bernard Delfont and Val Parnell, with many American acts such as Danny Kaye topping the bill.[26] At the other end of the venue spectrum, the shows presented by Queenie Watts at the Waterman's Arms in East London favoured torch singers and female impersonators with a taste for simple sexual innuendo.

The historically minded British Music Hall Society, with its journal *The Call Boy*, was founded in 1963. But for many years, the venue most dedicated to preservation of music hall was the Players' Theatre Club in London, whose historically precise Victorian music-hall shows were first given in 1937. In the late twentieth century the architectural preservation movement joined with music-hall aficionados in the restoration of Wilton's Music Hall in East London. Elsewhere, special shows were created to preserve and celebrate the memory of

---

[23]   Raymond Mander and Joe Mitchenson, *British Music Hall*, p. 171.

[24]   Ibid.

[25]   Ibid., p. 196.

[26]   Ian Bevan, *Top of the Bill: The Story of the London Palladium*.

individual stars. For example, the Geordie songwriter and performer Joe Wilson was celebrated in *Joe Lives!*, a show devised and written by the contemporary Tyneside songwriter Alex Glasgow in 1971. Glasgow wrote new melodies for many of Wilson's lyrics.

But the most influential element of the preservationist movement was BBC television's *The Good Old Days*. This was broadcast from the Leeds City Varieties and was criticized by purists for its 'fantastic hotch-potch of periods and styles' and lack of fidelity to the classic music-hall ethos,[27] although its chairman, Leonard Sachs, traced his pedigree to the Victorian music hall of the Players' Theatre. Its stars included Danny La Rue. *The Good Old Days* inspired similar shows performed at summer seaside venues and by amateur dramatic companies in the 1970s and later.

A more piecemeal form of preservation and revival was the incorporation of individual music-hall songs into other entertainment practices. This first occurred in variety and the concert parties that superseded it. More importantly, Nott's study of the popular music industry between the world wars claims that the personnel of music hall and what he believes to be its comic essence were preserved through incorporation into the new media and entertainment forms that had superseded music hall as a commercial industry. He writes that these new media 'offered a huge supply of music-hall based performances',[28] and points out that one (but the only one to be based on British repertoire) of the four light entertainment series introduced by the BBC in 1931–33 was called 'Music Hall'. He adds that dance bands 'owed more to music hall than the US'[29] and that the music-hall inheritance was responsible for the popularity of comic songs in the 1920s and 1930s.

Nott's view that what survived of the music-hall repertoire was limited to its comedy elements is partially supported by the case of the Crazy Gang. In 1932 the impresario George Black introduced this sextet of comedians and singers at the London Palladium and the Holborn Empire in shows that Mander and Mitchenson call 'Music Hall Revue'.[30] The Crazy Gang's primary appeal was comic, but, *pace* Nott, Crazy Gang shows also featured the close harmony sentimental songs of (Bud) Flanagan and (Chesney) Allen. This duo, who had been in touring revue since 1924, crooned sentimental songs such as 'Underneath the Arches', 'The Umbrella Man' and 'Run Rabbit Run', that brought both hit records and comparison with the music-hall repertoire of two or three decades earlier. Unlike most self-conscious inheritors of the music-hall practices, Flanagan and Allen generally favoured sentiment over comedy, as did their own 1970s acolytes Chas & Dave. It is significant that all these artists were London-based and their work contained resonances from the Cockney culture upon which many early music-hall artists had drawn.

---

[27]   Mander and Mitchenson, *British Music Hall*, p. 196.

[28]   Nott, *Music for the People*, p. 117.

[29]   Ibid., p. 201.

[30]   Mander and Mitchenson, *British Music Hall*, p. 172.

Two important non-Cockney figures in the popular song of the 1930s and 1940s that incorporated music-hall elements into their music were Gracie Fields and George Formby, both of whom had music-hall pedigrees. As a child, from Rochdale in Lancashire, Gracie Fields had made her music-hall debut in 1905, but made her name in revue in the early 1920s. Later, she was a major recording artist and film star. Although he was the son of a noted music-hall star, the ukulele player and comic songster George Formby was known through his radio and film appearances (he made 16 movies between 1932 and 1946). Formby's lyrics shared with some music-hall material an interest in salacious scenarios and double entendre, exemplified by his hits 'When I'm Cleaning Windows' and 'With My Little Stick of Blackpool Rock'. Both Fields and Formby also included more mainstream love songs, although these lacked the specificity of reference for which sentimental music-hall numbers were noted.

While there is a direct link between the Crazy Gang, Formby and Fields and music hall, even in their heyday, songs that originated in the music halls could cross to quite separate sectors of popular music activity. The journalist and critic of imperialism J.A. Hobson wrote of music hall at the beginning of the twentieth century that 'its words and melodies pass by quick magic from the Empire or the Alhambra over the length and breadth of the land, re-echoed in a thousand provincial halls, until the remotest village is familiar with air and sentiment'.[31]

One site of such incorporated music-hall song was the repertoire of amateur rural singers whose existence was publicized through the English folk music revival of the second half of the twentieth century. When folk-song collectors fanned out into the countryside, they frequently found that their (usually elderly) informants unconcernedly mixed music-hall items with more purely 'traditional' items in the repertoire they sang at family or pub gatherings. For instance, John Howson's collection *Songs Sung in Suffolk* includes a number of songs collected around 1980 from Tom Smith of the village of Thorpe Morieux. Tom was born in 1918 and had learned his songs (presumably in the 1930s or later) in the oral-tradition method from his father. While these included the well-known traditional song 'John Barleycorn', many were easily traceable as music-hall 'hits' from the 1890s.[32]

The younger singers of the English folk revival of the 1950s and 1960s, who performed songs learned from such 'source singers' in clubs and at festivals, invariably focused on properly traditional material. Nevertheless, music-hall song was also a small element in the revival through performers such as Derek Brimstone, and it also occasionally appeared among the blues and American folk songs of skiffle. The Vipers, for example, recorded the melodramatic ballad 'Sam Hall', first performed by W.G. Ross in the 1840s.

There were other isolated instances of recordings of individual music-hall songs by contemporary performers in the 1950s and after. In 1957 Peter Sellers

---

[31]   John Atkinson Hobson, *The Psychology of Jingoism*, p. 3.

[32]   John Howson, *Songs Sung in Suffolk*, pp. 93–102.

revived Harry Champion's 'Any Old Iron' as part of his sequence of novelty recordings with George Martin. In the beat group era, Herman's Hermits sold a million copies of their version of Champion's 'I'm Henery the Eighth I Am' in the American market in 1965. Below the radar of the recording studio, the teenage Reg Dwight (soon to be renamed Elton John) included Marie Lloyd's 'My Old Man Said Follow the Van' in his 1963–65 pub performances as part of an eclectic repertoire of songs associated with Al Jolson, Jerry Lee Lewis, Jim Reeves and others.[33]

A certain kind of incorporation had been a key element in the skill set of the pub pianist, a profession that was in severe decline when Dwight joined its ranks. Writing in the mid-1950s, Richard Hoggart described the process as one of playing new songs 'so that, though their main lines are kept, they are transmuted into the received idiom ... the new ... has been made part of the emotionally unified whole which contains songs from fifty years ago onwards'.[34]

The process described here has been carried over into post-rock'n'roll by the practices of such figures as James Last and certain symphony orchestras that take contemporary rock pieces into their customary performing styles, usually after extracting the sonic and emotional essence. In fact, the general effect of incorporating a cover version of a music-hall song since the 1950s has been to emphasize its otherness and archaic character. Reg Dwight was performing to a mainly middle-aged audience who certainly did not see 'Great Balls of Fire' as part of an 'emotionally unified whole' with 'My Old Man Said Follow the Van'.

Music hall had been 'recovered' in a different sense at the turn of the 1960s by the social commentator and novelist Colin MacInnes. He had already written his celebrated novel of teenage life in London *Absolute Beginners* (1959) and would go on to write a popular study of music hall itself (*Sweet Saturday Night*, 1969). By this time, the music-hall genre of song now meant only songs of good humour or mild social comment ('forgetting', for instance, the chauvinist or patriotic items popular with Victorian and Edwardian audiences), and MacInnes harnessed his praise of music hall to a search for authenticity in the face of the Americanization of British popular culture. In a much quoted article, 'Young England, Half English', he claimed that, 'until some forty years ago, the English song about English life resounded boisterously in the music halls. Since then, new American musical idioms ... have swamped our own ditties.'[35] In taking this position, MacInnes was articulating a current of feeling that had previously taken the form of a call by the Songwriters' Guild for the BBC to restrict the amount of American music in its broadcasts.[36]

---

[33] Dave Laing, 'Nine Lives in the Music Business: Reg Dwight and Elton John in the 1960s', p. 244.

[34] Richard Hoggart, *The Uses of Literacy*, p. 155.

[35] Colin MacInnes, 'Young England, Half English', p. 14.

[36] Cyril Ehrlich, *Harmonious Alliance: A History of the Performing Right Society*, pp. 114–19.

However, while the songwriters had made no distinction of genre in their campaign for music composed by Britons (which began in 1947 and lasted for a decade), MacInnes claimed that music hall in particular offered an example of a healthy expression of the experience of life in Britain in contrast to the sentimentality of US-influenced music. It was a touchstone for indigenous music resistant to American imports. MacInnes warned that 'if a people – like the English – sings about another people – the Americans – this may be a sign that it is ceasing to be a people in any real sense at all'.[37]

Music Hall and British Pop

MacInnes was the first of a succession of writers (and sometimes musicians themselves) to discover traces of music-hall-style authenticity in later twentieth-century British pop. MacInnes specifically singled out the skiffle and rock'n'roll singer Tommy Steele for comparison with Marie Lloyd et al. After praising the songwriting of Lionel Bart and Mike Pratt for having 'a certain English essence of sentiment and wit', he wrote: '[p]erhaps one day Tommy will sing songs as English as his speaking accent, or his grin. If this should happen, we will hear once again, for the first time since the decline of the Music Halls, songs that tell us of our own world.'[38]

This conditional aspect of MacInnes's approval of Steele was extended to skiffle in general. On the one hand, these performers were 'speaking American at the recording session and English in the pub round the corner afterwards'; on the other, MacInnes praised 'the eruption of amateur performers in the skiffle cellars, ungluing their ears from the juke-box to pick up and play themselves the washboard and guitar'.[39]

Steele never did perform 'songs that tell us of our own world', in the sense meant by MacInnes, but some of the successors to Colin MacInnes in the pop culture commentariat were to discern something of the music hall in such artists as the Beatles and the Kinks in the 1960s, the Sex Pistols and Ian Dury in the 1970s, Chas & Dave and Madness in the 1980s and Blur in the 1990s. Of these musicians, Suggs of Madness said of his band in retrospect, 'we wanted to be entertainers, for want of a better word, like a fairground attraction or like music hall performers',[40] and Damon Albarn of Blur was unique in making explicit an opposition to American music, at one point planning to call the band's second

---

[37]   MacInnes, 'Young England, Half English', p. 15.

[38]   Ibid.

[39]   Ibid., pp. 14, 15–16.

[40]   Quoted in Dave Laing, Afterword to 'Roll Over Lonnie (Tell George Formby the News)', p. 17.

album *England vs. America*.[41] Although that idea was rejected, Blur did record two music-hall songs in 1993. 'Daisy Bell' (first sung by Katie Lawrence in 1892 and better known by the final line of its refrain, 'a bicycle made for two') and Charles Whittle's 1910 hit 'Let's All Go Down the Strand' appeared on one of several formats of the hit single 'Sunday Sunday'.[42]

In the years before they made their first recordings, the Beatles had a repertoire in live performance (mainly in Liverpool and Hamburg) of almost 200 songs. Of these about 10 per cent were Lennon and McCartney compositions while all but one of the others was American. Most of these were rock'n'roll songs; others were from the African-American styles later classified as rhythm & blues and soul music.[43] And, as Richard Middleton has shown, there was a massive musicological difference between the discursive repetition at the level of the phrase of music-hall song and the musematic repetition of the riffs and call and response patterns of American-derived rock.[44]

Despite this overwhelming American influence on their music, the Beatles were claimed to be distinctly 'British'. Commentators and critics, then and now, have struggled to define this 'Britishness' – was there something formal to be discovered by musicological analysis or was it simply the accident of birth, signified by the Liverpudlian accents and humour? Some early writers – notably the jazz singer and cultural critic George Melly, the musicologist Wilfrid Mellers and a *Melody Maker* columnist in 1963 who wrote that the band 'have given pop music a gaiety and zest that vanished with the old music halls'[45] – saw or heard elements of the music-hall spirit in the music of the Beatles. Even as late as 1994, Ian MacDonald, the most astute of the song-by-song commentators, noted that 'When I'm Sixty-Four' looked 'back to the music-hall of George Formby and the seaside postcards of Donald McGill'.[46]

Writing of later bands, some authors have argued that, rather than looking back, they were creating contemporary equivalents to music-hall songs albeit by sometimes adopting what Laing[47], writing of the Kinks, called a 'music hall stance'. The same writer claimed that Ray Davies's songs of the mid-1960s such as 'Autumn Almanac' and 'Dead End Street' were 'the first post rock'n'roll songs to concern themselves with the details of English life without treating them purely

---

[41] John Harris, *The Last Party: Britpop, Blair and the Demise of English Rock*, p. 80.

[42] Unfortunately for Albarn's commitment to English authenticity, 'Daisy Bell' had been composed by the New York songwriter Harry Dacre.

[43] Dave Laing, 'Six Boys, Six Beatles: The Formative Years 1950–62'.

[44] Richard Middleton, *Studying Popular Music*, p. 270.

[45] Quoted in Keith Swanwick, *Popular Music and the Teacher*, p. 48.

[46] Ian MacDonald, *Revolution in the Head*, p. 176.

[47] Laing, 'Roll Over Lonnie (Tell George Formby the News)'.

comically', with Davies involved in 'a delicate balancing act between nostalgia and mockery'.[48]

Conclusion

It is now time to return to the question posed at the start of this chapter. How can we account for the presence of music hall in the field of late twentieth-century popular music?

A useful starting-point is the category of 'residual cultural forms' devised by Raymond Williams in the 'Reproduction' chapter of his 1981 work *Culture*. In his discussion of 'dynamic forms' Williams distinguishes between the residual, the dominant and the emergent. He defines the residual as 'work made in earlier and often different societies and times, yet still available and significant. ... Certainly the dominant can absorb or attempt to absorb [the residual]. But there is almost always older work kept available by certain groups as an extension of or alternative to dominant contemporary cultural production.'[49] By the middle of the twentieth century, music hall, or more precisely music-hall song, was such a residual form.

The principal ways in which a residual form can be 'kept available' are through its preservation as a minority art form or through its revival, often using newer media technologies. One extreme example of the obsessive preservation of a repertoire and a performance style from the era in which music hall was a dominant form is that taken by the D'Oyly Carte opera company with the operettas of Gilbert and Sullivan, which were first performed in the final quarter of the nineteenth century. While the works remained in copyright, the D'Oyly Carte company retained a monopoly on the performance of Gilbert and Sullivan, ensuring that the operettas were done in a historically 'authentic' style. Though the Players' Theatre, *The Good Old Days* and other revivalists attempted something similar with music hall, there was no continuous or influential tradition of re-creating the performance apparatus of the institution.

A third, less institutionalized mode in which the residual is made available to later generations is through its recurrence as a component of newer emergent or dominant forms, through the sporadic incorporation of individual music-hall songs into the repertoire of 'folk' singers, pub pianists and pop bands. However, the general impact of such incorporation was unimpressive, in that its principal affective content was nostalgia, a commodity with which English culture was already over-endowed. In 1972, Laing pronounced that 'the music-hall tradition, embedded as it is in only the more archaic aspects of British life, is incapable of providing the basis for any more far-reaching music'.[50] This view is supported by the fact that the occasional return of music-hall song was dependent on the

[48]   Ibid., p. 14.
[49]   Raymond Williams, *Culture*, p. 204.
[50]   Laing, 'Roll Over Lonnie (Tell George Formby the News)', p. 14.

survival into the 1950s and beyond of the national (Scottish) or regional (Cockney or Geordie) stereotypes that music hall helped to construct.

None of these three modes managed to resuscitate music hall as a vibrant part of the contemporary musical performance scene in the latter part of the twentieth century. Instead, the afterlife of music-hall song took the form of its transhistorical invocation as a genealogical predecessor, or unconscious inspiration, of very different musical practices in the twentieth century.

In his discussion of residual cultural forms, Raymond Williams pointed out that the residual 'is often a form of cultural alternative to the dominant in its most recent reproductive form'.[51] This is certainly how Colin MacInnes and later critics influenced by him saw 'music hall' (whatever they meant by it) in relation to what Iain Chambers, writing about the later 1950s, defined as 'the heart of British pop ... drawn from the more assimilable American developments'.[52] MacInnes et al. supplied an explicitly ideological interpretation of music hall, citing it as an exemplary mode of national popular music, available to inspire later musicians with similar ambitions to express or reflect a national identity. From the informed discussion of Colin MacInnes to the throwaway remark of Paul du Noyer, 'music hall' has been hailed as an innocent ancestor of contemporary pop music, an ancestor from an era before the Americanization (and for some the commercialization) of British popular culture in general and its music in particular.

Such assimilations of pop or rock to music hall necessarily involved an avoidance of music-hall song's character as a specific historically situated cultural formation and an elision of the significant differences between that genre and post-1950s music. The most important of these differences is the primary derivation of the latter from American vernacular musics, making it inevitable that, in terms of origins, any modern national music would be a hybrid genre: Damon Albarn's stark opposition of 'England vs. America' and even The Clash's 'I'm So Bored with the USA' could only be fully credible if 'the heart of British pop', the transatlantic roots of rock guitar and rhythms, were disregarded.[53]

Nevertheless, the increasingly abstract equation of 'music hall' with an authentic Englishness (or Britishness?) has remained as a feature (if only a minor one) of the discourse of British pop. It may be that the Sex Pistols will not be last to be hailed as 'the last great music-hall act'.

---

[51]   Williams, *Culture*, pp. 204–5.

[52]   Iain Chambers, *Urban Rhythms*: *Pop Music and Popular Culture*, p. 39.

[53]   In the twenty-first century, the increasing diversity of the population and growth of hyphenated identities – such as British Asian or British Caribbean – makes this version of national music seem even more archaic.

Chapter 2
Skiffle, Variety and Englishness

Jon Stratton

I want to examine the impact of American popular music on English popular music during the late 1950s and early 1960s. However, rather than the impact itself, which is well known, I want to think about the ways that American popular music was indigenized and incorporated into a continuity of English popular music that was focused on music hall and its mass media renovation as variety. In this chapter I shall be arguing that skiffle, although originally an American, indeed African-American, form, became, in its English reworking by artists such as Lonnie Donegan, a means of resistance to the impact of rock'n'roll. Many artists who started as skifflers went on to play important roles in the beat bands, helping to mould their distinctively English sound. As skiffle gave way to the beat groups so the English music-hall heritage resurfaced. This chapter ends with a brief overview of that music-hall influence on the early beat groups such as Herman's Hermits, supplementing some of the remarks made at the close of Dave Laing's chapter.

In the generally accepted narrative about popular music in England 1963, the year after the Beatles first made the singles chart with 'Love Me Do' and the year *Please Please Me* reached the top spot on the album chart, is identified as a watershed. On one side are crooners and English attempts to imitate American rock'n'roll artists, which come out of what are understood to be the retro preoccupations of the skiffle movement. And all this placed within the framework of a faded and rapidly disappearing music-hall heritage. On the other side are the beat bands, the heralds of a new, Americanized popular music connected somehow with affluence and the acceptance in England of consumerism as a way of life – twin developments that form the basis of an explosion in cultural production that, altogether, is described as the 'Swinging Sixties' or, more partially, 'Swinging London'.

In another version of this history, English groups, led by the Beatles and the Rolling Stones, appropriated African-American rhythm and blues, transformed it into beat music by simplifying the rhythm and placing a new emphasis on melody, and in this way made it understandable and desirable to white American teenagers. Michael Hicks quotes an American critic writing, probably, in the late 1970s: 'English critics like to speak of American rock since 1964 as a lame attempt to respond to the innovations of the Beatles and the English groups that have come since'.[1] While English narratives tend to distinguish between the pop bands like the Beatles, Herman's Hermits and Freddie & the Dreamers, and the rhythm and blues groups like the Rolling Stones, the Yardbirds, the Kinks and the Animals, American versions of this narrative tend to lump all these bands together under the single descriptor of the 'British Invasion'.

I want to generate an alternative reading of English popular music through the 1960s. At the core of my argument is a claim about the fundamental continuity of the English musical tradition through the 1960s, a continuity that includes the assimilation and transformation of American elements. Underlying this tradition was music hall, transformed after the Second World War into what came to be called variety, and the repertoire of styles, and indeed of songs, that was associated with music hall. Variety was basically a cleaned-up, and generally more middle-class, transformation of working-class music hall. Generally speaking, it was less sexually explicit and had a humour that was less class-related in the sense of taking the mickey out of middle- and upper-class practices. It nevertheless retained the same kind of mix of entertainers as music hall, including acrobats, jugglers, comics, singers and dancers. Acts performed for a maximum of twenty minutes.

Variety developed in the post-Second World War period partly in relation to the impact of the mass media, radio in the first instance and then television. These media delivered a larger and more varied audience than had attended live music hall. Of course, I do not want to imply here that English music hall had been without American influence. There had been a constant exchange of artists between music hall and American vaudeville through the second half of the nineteenth century and American influence on music hall was increasingly important from around the turn of the twentieth century. To take one example, as Dave Russell notes, 'from the early twentieth century the halls saw the steady increase of syncopation, culminating in the full-scale arrival of ragtime from 1912'.[2] Moreover, American minstrel songs like Stephen Foster's 'Camptown Races' and Tin Pan Alley songs such as 'Daisy Bell' became incorporated into the genre of English music-hall songs. Nevertheless, music hall, in its new guise of variety, was generally considered to be a quintessential element of English popular culture. What was new was the amount of commercial American culture, including consumer goods, that impacted on English culture in the 1950s and 1960s.

England, Cultural Imperialism, Consumerism

One useful way of thinking about this is in the theoretical terms of cultural imperialism. Now, since John Tomlinson's deconstruction of the idea in his 1991 book *Cultural Imperialism*, and the roughly concomitant rise in theories

---

[1] Michael Hicks, *Sixties Rock: Garage, Psychedelic, and Other Satisfactions*, p. 111.

[2] Dave Russell, *Popular Music in England, 1840–1914: A Social History*, p. 108.

of globalization, cultural imperialism as a way of describing the impact of an economically more dominant society on economically weaker ones has become unfashionable. However, it remains a good way of describing the relationship between the United States and other Western countries in the decades following the Second World War. Following Herbert Schiller's classic work on cultural imperialism Livingston White writes that: '[c]ultural imperialism proposes that a society is brought into the modern world system when its dominating stratum is attracted, pressured, forced, and sometimes bribed into shaping its social institutions to correspond to, or even promote, the values and structures of the dominating center of the system'.[3] In my use of the term I do not want to suggest anything quite so dramatic, and, of course, it goes without saying that England was already a part of the modern world system – indeed, England had been the most important creator of that world system through the eighteenth and nineteenth centuries. However, after the Second World War, the increasing relative weakness of the British economy contrasted with an expansionary United States whose economy needed to find new markets for its consumer goods. Peter Mandler describes how, during this time,

> There was a concern that affluence and the decay of traditional working class culture – and the apparent failure of education and uplift to transmit 'high' culture downwards – had left a vacuum into which commercialized American culture had rushed, a concern most eloquently and honestly expressed in Richard Hoggart's 1957 book, *The Uses of Literacy*. Working class people were putting their faith in televisions, Coca-Cola, cheap comic-books, and rock-'n'-roll singers (though in truth these were but the latest versions of older products – radio, beer, sixpenny novels, and Tin Pan Alley crooners – that were just as commercial and only somewhat less American).[4]

Mandler is right to emphasize the continuity. However, what is lacking is a recognition of the qualitative shift in economic power between Britain and the United States that had been occurring since the beginning of the twentieth century but that had altered radically because of the financial burden on Britain of conducting the Second World War.

Moreover, while Britain, in common with other Western countries and Japan, increased economic growth during the period of the long boom, which ran from around 1950 to 1973, relatively Britain's growth was significantly lower than other countries except for the United States, which already required a globalization of consumer markets in order to sustain its economic expansion. Indeed, we need to remember that one important influence on the rapid economic growth in Europe was the Marshall Plan, which saw large amounts of American financial aid used to reconstruct the European economies, including West Germany's and Italy's,

---

[3] Livingston A. White, 'Reconsidering Cultural Imperialism Theory'.
[4] Peter Mandler, 'Two Cultures—One—Or Many?', pp. 135–6.

shattered during the Second World War. This was not entirely altruistic. Renovating the economies of Europe produced countries able to pay for American consumer goods.

In the United States, incomes had already increased greatly: 'Between 1939 and 1950, managers saw their income rise 45 percent, supervisors, 83 percent, and production workers, 106 percent. By the late 1940s, the average family could afford to acquire some middle-class comforts'.[5] During the period of the long boom, in gross domestic product per head of population, France increased by 4.8 per cent, West Germany by 4.9 per cent, Japan by 8.0 per cent and the United Kingdom by only 2.5 per cent.[6] Correspondingly, as B. Alford puts it, 'there was a sharp rise in the degree of import penetration of manufactured goods'.[7] By 1961 imports constituted 10 per cent of domestic sales and by the end of the decade this had increased to 15 per cent.[8] What all this meant was that Britain was being transformed into a consumer society, as the United States had become prior to the Second World War, and that an increasing amount of the goods consumed came from the United States.

As Dominick Sandbrook writes: '[t]hroughout the fifties and sixties ... British families bought cars and television sets, fridges and washing machines, new houses and foreign holidays, telephones and paperbacks and records and clothes, all the paraphernalia of a society becoming increasingly focused on consumerism as an activity and a source of self-definition'.[9] However, as Sandbrook also tells us, 'many of the most recognizable products were provided by American manufacturers like Hoover, Heinz, Colgate or Gillette, and sold by American advertising executives'.[10] In other words, in Britain the acceptance during the 1950s and 1960s of consumerism as a way of life was deeply imbricated with the increased availability of American commercial culture and American consumer goods.

Cultural Transmission and Popular Music in England

One element in this process of cultural imperialism was American popular music. One way of thinking about the impact of American popular music on the production of popular music in England is in terms of cultural transmission. As I have already suggested, it is often argued that English groups appropriated African-American music for their own purposes. However, there is a larger point

---

[5]   Grace Palladino, *Teenagers: An American History*, p. 101.

[6]   Alan Booth (ed.), *British Economic Development since 1945*, p. 1.

[7]   B.W.E. Alford, *Britain in the World Economy since 1880*, p. 251.

[8]   Ibid., p. 252.

[9]   Dominick Sandbrook, *Never Had It So Good: A History of Britain from Suez to the Beatles*, p. 517.

[10]   Ibid., p. 114.

to be made: that this appropriation took place in the context of the greater impact of American popular music on the English popular music tradition. In this broader context it was the English who were the subordinate group. Now, from the point of view of the subordinate group, cultural transmission, as Bruce Ziff and Pratima V. Rao explain, 'can connote an *assimilative* practice – a process whereby cultural minorities often are encouraged, if not obliged, to adapt or assimilate the cultural forms and practices of the dominant group'.[11] This is the process that took place in England during the 1950s and, especially, the 1960s. From this point of view, as we shall see, there was a constant process of assimilation and adaptation of American musical forms.

Within particular bands this process tended to involve a development that would start with the group's covering American songs, proceed through the group's adapting American songs in some way to the English popular music tradition and, finally, coming to write their own material that, at times, would include elements from England's own popular music tradition, in some cases folk music but more often music hall. While this was a process through which many artists moved from Lonnie Donegan onwards, it is also a way of characterizing the general process of assimilation and adaptation that ran right through the 1960s.

From this point of view, the apparent watershed that I mentioned at the beginning of this chapter, which is usually identified with the Beatles' chart success in 1963, can be better understood as the moment when the rhythmic form of American rhythm and blues and early rock'n'roll had been indigenized in a way that made it meaningful in its own right to English audiences. We can contrast this with the early English rock'n'rollers such as Cliff Richard and Tommy Steele who rapidly dropped rock'n'roll and became all-round, variety, entertainers. Essentially, as we shall see, this indigenization involved a process of making the music 'whiter', that is, simplifying the African-American originated rhythm and making the melody more prominent. As it happens, this process of adaptation to English ears also made the music more understandable to white American teenagers, resulting in what the Americans call, as I have already mentioned, the British Invasion.

Once we begin to understand the English musical developments in the 1960s from this point of view we can also identify a second important moment that spans 1967 and 1968. The year 1967 saw the release of the Beatles' *Sgt. Pepper's Lonely Hearts Club Band* and the Who's *The Who Sell Out* albums and also Cream's *Disraeli Gears*, which includes, at the end of the second side, the traditional urban song 'Mother's Lament' also known as 'My Baby's Gone down the Plughole', sung in music-hall style. *The Kinks Are the Village Green Preservation Society* and the Small Faces' *Ogden's Nut Gone Flake* were released the following year. All these albums, and works by other artists around this time, show a strong music-hall stylistic influence. This is often discussed as an exemplification of English nostalgia for an earlier time, a time when Britain had an empire and was

---

[11]   Bruce Ziff and Pratima V. Rao, 'Introduction to Cultural Appropriation: A Framework for Analysis', pp. 5–7 (emphasis in original).

stronger economically. As Jim Melly reminds us, this predilection for the Victorian era was not confined to music: '[t]he fashion through 1966/67 was for Victorian paisley patterns and dress, from cod-Victorian names (the hip clothes shop "Granny Takes A Trip" and even *Sgt. Pepper's* itself) to the wearing of Victorian British army red tunics'.[12] From this point of view the post-Second World War era in Britain was a period of quite precipitous decline. India and Pakistan achieved their independence in 1947 and by the end of the 1960s so had Britain's African colonies. In 1956 the failed attempt to take control of the Suez Canal signalled that Britain was no longer a world power and, more, could be easily brought to heel by the financial dominance of the United States: a lesson reinforced by the forced devaluation of sterling in 1967. Yet, I want to argue, it was not just nostalgia that was the cause of the presence of music-hall styles and references in the albums I have mentioned above. This presence was also a consequence of the resurfacing of an English traditional music, fundamentally urban and working class, that had not died out but that, in the arena of popular music, had been smothered for a while as English musicians assimilated, and then incorporated, American musical styles into the English tradition. From this point of view we can understand 1966/67 as a key moment in the assimilation of American cultural influences in English popular music and the reassertion of a transformed English popular music tradition in which music-hall stylings are a central aspect.

The Englishness of Skiffle

In order to understand the Englishness of the beat bands of the latter half of the 1960s we need to start with a discussion of skiffle. This is because skiffle was a direct influence on the beat bands not only because the members of those bands grew up listening to skiffle but also because so many members of beat groups, including Paul McCartney and John Lennon of the Beatles, Jimmy Page of the Yardbirds and later Led Zeppelin, Freddie Garrity of Freddie & the Dreamers, Mick Jagger of the Rolling Stones, Dave Dee of Dave Dee, Dozy, Beaky, Mick and Tich, and, of course, artists from just before the beat boom such as Joe Brown, Marty Wilde and Tommy Steele, all of whom we shall meet again during this chapter, began by playing in skiffle groups.

The origins of skiffle lie with Lonnie Donegan and his work with, and outside of, Chris Barber's Jazz Band. 'Rock Island Line', along with 'John Henry', the single's B-side, and three other songs were all recorded for, and released on, a Chris Barber album titled *New Orleans Joys*. Skiffle was originally an African-American musical form played at rent parties in African-American ghettos in the 1920s and 1930s. Donegan reinvented the form, whitening its musical reference points.

---

[12]   Jim Melly, *Last Orders Please: Rod Stewart, the 'Faces' and the Britain We Forgot*, p. 71.

Most of all, what connected the skiffle Donegan pioneered with the earlier African-American form was the idea of informality, and of a music anybody could play. Like the original skiffle, the skiffle that developed in England can be thought of as a do-it-yourself kind of music. As Iain Chambers notes, skiffle 'offered a major democratisation of music-making. With little money and limited musical skill it became possible to be directly involved in a popular music.'[13] At a time in England when popular music was dominated by professionals such as Dickie Valentine, Petula Clark and Frankie Vaughan, and controlled by the music industry that looked to adults for sales, and when there was a perceived divide between the making of music and its consumption, skiffle, with its cheap and often homemade instruments, such as the washboard, and easily learnt American folk songs, enabled a reconnection, for urban English working-class youth especially, with a tradition of informal music-making. Russell, for example, discussing what he calls 'informal music' in the latter part of the nineteenth century, writes about the 'deep levels of genuine musical sensibility amongst the working class population' and suggests that '[t]he purchase of a piano was often simply another manifestation of the contemporary appetite for music, and an attempt to satisfy it'.[14]

Skiffle's basic instrumentation remained one of its characteristics when Donegan reworked it in England. Spencer Leigh quotes Wally Whyton, who played with the Vipers: 'It had to be acoustic. The flavouring was essentially three guitars, an acoustic bass and if you could slap the bass even better, and a washboard that was played with thimbles. Some people used banjos and mandolins instead of guitars'.[15] The relative cheapness of the instruments and the accessible nature of the folk, rather than jazz, songs that Donegan and other skifflers played, enabled skiffle to become a music form played by large numbers of mainly working-class young people. Alan Clayson comments that:

> ... like punk after it, anyone who'd mastered basic techniques could have a go at skiffle – and the more do-it-yourself the sound, the better. No one howled with derision at tea-chest bass, a washboard tapped with thimbles, rasping comb-and-paper, dustbin lid cymbals, biscuit tin snare drum and other instruments fashioned from household implements.[16]

The comparison with punk is well made. In both musical movements an important element in their Englishness was the basic instrumentation and improvised nature. These have their English foundation in working-class singalongs at music halls, in pubs and in the family home. In this sense, then, skiffle, like punk, returned music to the English working class and allowed elements of its American form to be

13 Iain Chambers, *Urban Rhythms: Pop Music and Popular Culture*, p. 46.
14 Russell, *Popular Music in England, 1840–1914*, p. 181.
15 Spencer Leigh, *Puttin' on the Style: The Lonnie Donegan Story*, p. 57.
16 Alan Clayson, *The Beat Merchants: The Origins, History, Impact and Rock Legacy of the 1960s British Pop Groups*, p. 31.

integrated into the English popular music tradition. It is, therefore, no surprise that Donegan, while born in Glasgow, was brought up in the working-class London East End suburb of East Ham, where he would have become familiar with the working-class musical tradition.

Iain Chambers remarks that:

> In Britain, the adoption of the guitar was more striking. Lacking the American precedents, the guitar was considered a rather exotic instrument, largely confined to the rhythm section of dance bands. It was rock'n'roll and the subsequent popularity of skiffle that established it in British pop.[17]

Chambers makes a good point about the positioning of the guitar in English popular music. However, I would question his implication that skiffle came after, and was in some sense a consequence of, rock'n'roll. In 'Alternative Rock Cultures: Lonnie Donegan and the Birth of British Rock', Iain Ellis makes the point that 'Rock Island Line' was recorded just one week after Elvis Presley recorded his Sun session that included 'That's All Right Mama'.[18] It was skiffle that indigenized the guitar as a popular music instrument in England, making it available to those who wanted to play rock'n'roll but, more importantly, making it the instrument of choice for the beat bands that evolved out of the skiffle groups.

However, we also need to remember Whyton's comment that some skifflers played the banjo. Like the guitar, the banjo was originally an African-American instrument. It seems to have been introduced to England in the closing decades of the nineteenth century. Thomas Riis tells us that 'Horace Weston, billed as the "Black Bonanza", created a sensation in London in 1878 with his virtuoso banjo playing in a production of *Uncle Tom's Cabin*'.[19] Riis goes on to quote from an English obituary of James Douglas Bohee, one of the Bohee Brothers, published in 1897:

> As banjo players they did more to popularise their instrument than any other American entertainer who has visited these shores, either before their arrival or since; and they were the favoured instructors of Royalty. They soon came to the [music] halls where their popularity was very great.[20]

The final acceptance of the banjo in English music hall came in the 1920s when George Formby, who in the 1930s, became England's most popular entertainer, started using a banjo and ukulele hybrid known as a banjolele. Formby called what

---

[17] Chambers, *Urban Rhythms*, pp. 22–3.

[18] Iain Ellis, 'Alternative Rock Cultures: Lonnie Donegan and the Birth of British Rock'.

[19] Thomas L. Riis, 'The Experience and Impact of Black Entertainers in England, 1895–1920', p. 51.

[20] Ibid.

he played a ukulele and, in 1933, recorded 'With My Little Ukulele in My Hand', a song full of characteristically music-hall double entendre. Banjos were also used in early jazz bands such as King Oliver's Creole Jazz Band, and when Chris Barber asked Donegan to join his band he asked Donegan to play the banjo.

Crudely, if jazz was associated with the banjo, the blues were associated with the guitar, and Donegan's liking for the blues seems to be linked to his shift from banjo to guitar when playing skiffle. However, the banjo had been indigenized through English music hall and so it is not surprising that Whyton should mention it as a possible skiffle instrument. In the 1950s Terry Walsh, who went on to play in the Frantic Five skiffle group and later worked as a session guitarist, 'started on banjo but swapped to guitar when a relative observed, "They're not using banjos any more."'[21] More, in the 1963 film, *What a Crazy World*, which starred the early English rock'n'rollers Joe Brown and Marty Wilde, when Brown, playing the East End working-class lad Alf Hitchens, sits in his bedroom strumming a melody, he is playing a banjo. That same year Joe Brown & the Bruvvers released a version of Formby's 'Little Ukulele' as a single only to have it banned from airplay by the BBC because of its questionable content. Illustrating the shift away from the banjo and the indigenization of the guitar, Brown plays a guitar on the recording of this by-now classic music-hall song. In fact, Brown was a more than competent rock'n'roll guitarist and backed Gene Vincent and Eddie Cochran when they toured England in 1960.

'Rock Island Line' and 'John Hardy' were both American folk songs that had been collected and recorded by Leadbelly in the 1930s. Donegan's primary interest was in this kind of pre- and proto-blues music and folk music by artists like Woody Guthrie, the Weavers and Pete Seeger, who had previously performed with the Weavers. Following on from his jazz roots, Donegan's influences were American. However, as Leigh remarks in his biography of Donegan, 'right from the start, he added elements of British music hall'.[22] The skiffle boom lasted only about three or four years. In 1958 Donegan released the medley 'Lonnie's Skiffle Party' as a single. Leigh describes it as 'an ill-advised and unsuccessful attempt to regenerate life into skiffle, which with "Knees Up Mother Brown" and the occasional gay joke is more like music hall'.[23] Donegan starts with 'Li'l Liza Jane', a song first recorded in 1918 and thought to be a take-off of the songs of the blackface minstrel genre that included 'Camptown Races'. It actually uses the tune of 'Camptown Races' into which Donegan segues and which, as I have mentioned, had been indigenized as a music-hall song alongside the English 'Knees Up Mother Brown' with which the single finishes. The track, which also includes a section of Donegan's hit remake of Vernon Dalhart's 1926 country song 'Putting on the Style', melds together American folk song and English music hall.

---

[21]   Mo Foster, *Play Like Elvis: How British Musicians Bought the American Dream*, p. 57.

[22]   Leigh, *Puttin' on the Style*, p. 9.

[23]   Ibid., p. 52.

In the 1963 film *What a Crazy World*, which I have already mentioned, Joe Brown and Marty Wilde, Alf and Herbie, go to a dance held by the British Legion. The group playing is the beat band Freddie & the Dreamers, here thinly disguised as Frantic Freddie and the Dreamers. They play a version of 'Let's Twist Again' that includes verses and the melody of 'Camptown Races'. They also perform a version of the Royal Teens 1958 novelty rock'n'roll hit 'Short Shorts', which is about the wearing of short shorts. During this, Freddie takes off his trousers and daks the members of the band, revealing their boxer-shorts underpants. Here, again, we find the indigenization of American music through its association with the kind of off-colour, scatological humour typical of English music hall.

The Continuity of Music Hall and Variety

It was not just music-hall songs that retained their vibrancy, especially in the East End of London where Donegan, Brown and Tommy Steele, a rock'n'roller who went on to become an all-round, variety entertainer, were all brought up. Marty Wilde, born Reg Smith, the son of an army sergeant, grew up in Greenwich on the south side of the Thames opposite the East End. Music hall, now renamed variety, continued to be the most important form of entertainment in England. Leigh notes that 'Vaudeville had faded out in the US by 1950 and the US country star, Slim Whitman [on tour in England], was surprised to find that he was on a show with comedians and acrobats because he was only working with other country performers in the States.'[24] Until the end of the 1950s and well into the 1960s, holiday resorts and large towns across England had theatres devoted to variety.

By the end of the 1950s many of these theatres were closing down because of the successful competition from television. However, this was by no means the end of variety. Rather, variety became the entertainment mainstay of the new mass medium. Indeed, the shift from music halls and theatres to radio and then television was one reason for the movement from the aesthetics of music hall to variety. One of the defining differences between the two linked forms was the relative lack of sexual innuendo in variety, which was a consequence of the reach of radio and television into the middle class and because middle-class families were now going to see variety at the seaside resorts where they stayed on their holidays. *The Black and White Minstrel Show*, firmly located in the heritage of the American blackface, minstrel tradition, was televised by the BBC from 1958 to 1978 and, Sarita Malik writes, 'could almost always guarantee an audience of at least 16 million, but frequently managed to top 18 million viewers'.[25] As Laing has noted, the BBC also broadcast *The Good Old Days*, a show that overtly celebrated

---

24   Ibid., p. 30.

25   Sarita Malik, 'The Black and White Minstrel Show'.

Victorian and Edwardian music hall, including making the audience dress up in period costume. Each show ended with a rendition of Florrie Forde's 'Down at the Old Bull and Bush'. The show ran for thirty years, from 1953 to 1983 with the height of its popularity in the 1970s. *Sunday Night at the London Palladium* first went to air on ITV, the commercial channel, in September 1955 with the music-hall legend Gracie Fields as one of the guests. The Beatles performed on the show in October 1963 and January 1964. The Rolling Stones performed in January 1967 and notoriously refused to join the other acts on the revolving stage at the end of the show to wave goodbye. That same year the show finally finished. At its peak, around 28 million viewers watched each week.

In the late 1950s, Leigh writes, '[t]he first American rock'n'roll stars to visit the UK including Buddy Holly and Charlie Gracie, had to perform in variety shows'.[26] Holly, to whom we shall return later, toured in 1958. By 1960 rock'n'roll artists were touring together rather than being packaged into variety shows. As we have seen, they were, though, still appearing on television variety shows and also radio shows. Indeed, as one commentary on the web remarks, distinguishing between the pop, beat bands and the rhythm and blues bands, 'the chirpy style of Merseybeat had fitted well into variety programs like The Billy Cotton Band Show, long haired R&B and psychedelic were a different matter entirely'.[27] *The Billy Cotton Band Show* was a popular radio show compered by the long-time dance-band leader Billy Cotton. It functioned as variety with Cotton introducing each show with the cry of 'Wakey wakey!' The programme's run ended in 1968.

The Popularity of Music-Hall Songs through the 1960s

Artists continued to record, and often have hits, with music-hall songs right through the 1960s. In 1960 Tommy Steele recorded and released 'What a Mouth', a song originally performed by the music-hall artist Harry Champion in 1905. It remained in the charts for seven weeks, getting as high as number 5. There is a story that Steele recorded 'What a Mouth' to prove to his father that he could sing what his East End working-class father regarded as 'real' music. Donegan's final chart appearance was in 1962 with another song collected and recorded by Leadbelly, 'Pick a Bale of Cotton'. However, his last number 1, which stayed there for four weeks, was 'My Old Man's a Dustman', a Liverpudlian urban folk song. According to Donegan himself the song probably started life in the nineteenth century as 'My old man's a fireman on the Elder Dempster Line'. The Elder Dempster Line was a Liverpool shipping company.[28] Donegan's version, in which the humour comes from the various things the dustman finds in the bins, has a typically working-class, music-hall quality to it. Joe Brown recorded the 1924 Australian

---

[26]   Leigh, *Puttin' on the Style*, p. 66.
[27]   Nostalgia Central, 'Variety, News and Sport'.
[28]   Leigh, *Puttin' on the Style*, p. 71.

music-hall song 'Turned Up,' which in England was sung by Florrie Forde, and put out a remarkable rock'n'roll version of Shelton Brookes's minstrel song, 'Darktown Strutters' Ball', as his third single in 1960. His second single was a music-hall-style song written by the then-unknown Lionel Bart called 'Jellied Eels', which had on the B-side a rocked-up version of the 1920s Tin Pan Alley song 'Dinah'.[29] In this string of singles we can read Brown's attempt to find an English voice amidst the impact of American rock rhythms, something that his audience might find familiar enough to provide the sales that would give Brown a hit.

Brown was also recording songs by the American Brill Building composing couple Doc Pomus and Mort Shuman, including 'People Gotta Talk', his first single. The soft, melodic ballad-style songs of the Brill Building composers were as popular with the pre-beat boom English singers as they were later with the Beatles and other beat bands. Around this same time that Brown was recording Pomus and Shuman compositions, in 1960, Donegan went to New York at the invitation of Atlantic Records boss Ahmet Ertegun to work with Brill Building composers Jerry Leiber and Mike Stoller, but with no great success.

I have already mentioned that Joe Brown released a version of Formby's 'Little Ukulele' in 1963. In 1961 he released an up-tempo rock'n'roll version of the music-hall song 'Henerey the Eighth' sung by Harry Champion in 1910. Brown's version had a complex, rockabilly rhythm and was not a hit. It was, nevertheless, his arrangement that was recorded by the Manchester group Herman's Hermits on their 1965 *Herman's Hermits on Tour* album. Herman's Hermits, though, slowed the tempo and used the simplified beat that characterized the beat bands' music. This will be discussed in the next chapter. Released as a single in the United States, 'I'm Henery the VIII I Am' reached number 1 on the singles chart, following up the success earlier the same year of 'Mrs. Brown You've Got a Lovely Daughter'.

We should pause here to consider Herman's Hermits. A post-beat boom band, coming as I have mentioned, like Freddie & the Dreamers, from Manchester, it is said that, during the mid-1960s, the only English group to outsell Herman's Hermits in the United States was the Beatles.[30] The group achieved this by capitalizing on an image of Englishness located in music-hall songs. 'Mrs. Brown You've Got a Lovely Daughter', a new composition, was written by Trevor Peacock in the style

---

[29]   Like Brown and the others I have already mentioned, Lionel Bart was brought up in London's East End, in Stepney. He wrote a number of hits for Cliff Richard ('Livin' Doll' in 1959) and Tommy Steele ('Rock with the Cavemen' in 1956 and 'Little White Bull' in 1959) but is more famous for his work on musicals such as *Fings Ain't Wot They Used T'Be* (1959) and *Oliver!* (1960).

[30]   Even more, in an article on Herman's Hermits, 'Herman's Hermits: British Pop Band of the Sixties Who Enjoyed Enormous Stateside Success', Nigel Smithers writes that, '[i]n the six years of their chart career, they scored twenty British hits and seventeen American hits (including four Top 5 smashes in as many months), and they were at one stage second only to the Beatles in terms of worldwide record sales'.

of a traditional music-hall song for his 1963 television play, *The Lads*. Appearing on the group's eponymously titled first album, which came out in 1965, like 'Henry the VIII' it was never released as a single in Britain. The group's first single in the United States, it was a number 1 hit. Around this time Herman's Hermits also released a version of George Formby's 'Leaning on a Lamppost' in the US, which climbed to number 7 on the Billboard chart.

Herman's Hermits were the friendly, nostalgic face of England during the British Invasion. Lead singer Peter Noone had been a child actor appearing on *Coronation Street*, the long-running soap opera about working-class life in a northern town, playing Len Fairclough's son, Stanley. His facility with accents enabled him to sound like a cockney to the American audience. In England, Herman's Hermits tried to portray themselves as a melodic pop band with what, by this time, was the ubiquitous rhythm of a beat band. However, the music-hall influence was pervasive in their style. Recording music-hall songs was, from this point of view, simply making obvious what was otherwise, for English audiences, implicit. Given this, it is no wonder that they included 'Mrs. Brown You've Got a Lovely Daughter' on their first album even if, as has more recently been claimed in what may well be a rewriting of history, it was meant as a joke.[31]

Herman's Hermits' first release was a cover of Gerry Goffin and Carole King's Brill Building song 'I'm Into Something Good'. Originally recorded by Earl-Jean of the girl group the Cookies, the song then had a bluesy, soul feel to the melodic vocal. Herman's Hermits transform the song into a bouncy, catchy singalong song; in other words, a song with music-hall stylings. In their hands it reached the top of the British chart and made it to number 13 in the United States. This jaunty singalong quality, with the addition of the beat-band beat, typified the group's British hits including 'Can't You Hear My Heart Beat' (1965), 'Silhouettes' (1965), 'No Milk Today' (1966) and also the more balladic 'There's a Kind of Hush' (1967), which was the group's last significant hit in the United States, where it reached number 4. The group's penultimate hit in the United States, not released in England, which suggests it was considered to be too obviously music hall in style for the group's mainstream teenage audience, was the Ray Davies composition 'Dandy', which had been released by the Kinks on their *Face to Face* album in 1966. As Stewart Mason writes about the Kinks' version, '[m]usically, the tune harks back to the music hall tradition of George Formby; Dave Davies' guitar is so trebly and clear that it sounds like a ukulele … and the gently swinging tune sounds like it could have been an old vaudeville hit'.[32]

While, in the wake of the beat boom, it might have embarrassed Herman's Hermits to seem to English audiences like they were drawing too obviously

---

[31]   In his biography of Herman's Hermits on allmusic.com Bruce Eder writes that '[t]he song was done almost as a joke by the group, its guitar/banjo sound and Noone's vocal performance – cockney accented and laced with a vulnerable wide-eyed innocence – deliberately reminiscent of George Formby'.

[32]   Stewart Mason, Review of 'Dandy' on allmusic.com.

on music hall for their material, the same concern did not affect the Fourmost, another Merseybeat band managed, like the Beatles, by Brian Epstein and whose first two singles had been Lennon and McCartney compositions. In 1966 they released 'Auntie Maggie's Remedy', a song recorded by Formby in 1941. Lonnie Donegan released the song at the same time (he plays banjo on it) and, although the Fourmost's version got quite a lot of airplay, neither gained the individual sales to make a chart entry. In 1968, however, it was a different story for the Scaffold's version of the nineteenth-century drinking singalong song, 'Lily the Pink', which was about the patent medicine first manufactured by the American entrepreneur Lydia Estes Pinkham. The Scaffold included Paul McCartney's brother, who took the stage name of Mike McGear. Demonstrating the English audience's continued liking for music-hall-style songs, 'Lily the Pink' topped the chart for four weeks.

In this chapter I have shown how skiffle formed the basis for an accommodation of American popular music, most specifically rock'n'roll. This accommodation and incorporation of American influences led to the development of the beat sound. At the same time, the nativization of the rock'n'roll sound by means of the indigenization of the skiffle form provided a space for the reassertion of music-hall songs that was not simply nostalgia but, rather, the reassertion of an English popular music.

Chapter 3
Englishing Popular Music in the 1960s

Jon Stratton

My purpose in this chapter is to focus on the ways that the rock'n'roll rhythm was reworked, providing the basis for the characteristic beat of the beat groups. I shall then go on to discuss how, in the so-called Swinging Sixties, music hall returned not directly in the songs of the early twentieth century but in the stylings of many songs of groups such as the Who and the Rolling Stones who are often thought of as marking a break with that earlier period and accepting and reworking American traditions. This reassertion of English tradition is nowhere more obvious than in the songs of the Kinks, the compositions of Ray Davies.

The Indigenization of the Beat

Chapter 2 identified the underlying continuation of the music-hall tradition during the period of the impact of American popular music, most especially rock'n'roll and rockabilly, in the late 1950s and early 1960s. Within this continuity of music-hall songs there was a crucial transformation. This involved the indigenization of the rock'n'roll rhythm. In the first place this involved a rhythmic shift from 12/8 to 8/8. This shift did not start with the beat bands. Alexander Stewart describes how boogie-woogie rhythms are often in 8/8 and goes on to write about this influence on Little Richard:

> Little Richard Penniman's string of rock'n'roll hits, from 'Tutti Frutti' (1955), 'Long Tall Sally' (1956), 'Lucille' and 'Keep A Knockin'' (1957) to 'Good Golly Miss Molly' (1958), mostly featured straight eighths. He and other early rock'n'roll pianists such as Jerry Lee Lewis did not have jazz or swing backgrounds – their blues-based rock'n'roll has more in common with the non-swinging style of boogie-woogie.[1]

Stewart also writes about the importance of bluegrass and country-blues styles on Chuck Berry's tendency to play in 8/8 metre. Stewart sums up this part of his argument by writing:

---

[1]   Alexander Stewart, '"Funky Drummer"': New Orleans, James Brown and the Rhythmic Transformation of American Popular Music', p. 295.

What seems clear is that, though early rock'n'roll often maintained the 12/8 metre along with other things it borrowed from R&B, by the early 1960s an even-ing of the basic subdivision of the beat linked to new styles of dance movement had become emblematic of modern youth, while jazz, swing and shuffle were largely relegated to the previous generation.[2]

However, in England, while Little Richard and Chuck Berry were influential, there was a different history. As we have seen, Lonnie Donegan's playing background was in jazz. When he started increasing the tempo of his music, skiffle began moving towards a straighter 8/8 beat. At the same time, English audiences preferred the 'whiter', more melodic music of Buddy Holly, Gene Vincent and Eddie Cochran to the harder, more beat-driven rhythms of the African-American artists. As one website remarks, 'Buddy Holly and the Crickets were very popular in America but in England they were even bigger, their impact serious [*sic*] rivalling that of Elvis and, in some ways, even exceeding it.'[3] While this could be put down to Holly touring England, at its most fundamental the preference for Holly and the others in England had more to do with a lack of familiarity with African-American musical forms and the concomitant preference for melody over expression. The consequence is that early rock'n'roll in England as played by, say, Joe Brown & the Bruvvers and Billy Fury, sounds more like rockabilly than the kind of rock'n'roll played by Little Richard and Chuck Berry. And this rockabilly tended to be played in 12/8.

Moreover, by the late 1950s, with ballads dominating the charts, as both Dave Laing and Dick Bradley have individually remarked, '... young audiences seeking live dance music turn away from the charts, just as some American teenagers did in the early 1950s. A live dance music style which becomes known as "the big beat", and later as "Beat", develops'.[4] Central to this development was that this beat was in 8/8 rather than 12/8, making it much easier to dance to for an English public familiar with syncopation but much less at ease with African-American rhythmic patterns.

The development of this rhythm, and the drumming style that underpinned it, took place in Germany's Hamburg rather than England. As Alan Clayson has well documented in *Hamburg: The Cradle of British Rock*, a large percentage of the so-called Merseybeat bands, and many bands from elsewhere in the country, including Freddie & the Dreamers, played lengthy sessions night after night in the clubs of St Pauli, Hamburg's red-light district, during the late 1950s and the first half of the 1960s. Clayson writes:

[2]   Ibid., p. 296.
[3]   Bruce Eder, 'Buddy Holly'.
[4]   Dick Bradley, *Understanding Rock'n'Roll: Popular Music in Britain 1955–1964*, p. 13.

In the light of new and rediscovered information about the scene from the late 1950s compared to what is left of it today, the deeds and personalities of some of the more obscure acts turned out to be just as much the embodiment or prototype of some facet of British pop in Germany as those of the Beatles, Searchers *et al* who became popular on a global scale.[5]

He goes on to comment that, for example, at that time Dave Dee & the Bostons, later known as Dave Dee, Dozy, Beaky, Mick and Tich, were more popular in Hamburg, and across Germany, than the Beatles.

Clayson describes the rhythm that developed in the St Pauli clubs as a 'changeless four-four offbeat on the snare drum'.[6] In *The Beat Merchants*, he amplifies on this in describing the audience participation 4/4 clap and stomp, which became known as *mach schau*:

> [A song] such as 'Whole Lotta Shakin'' could last a full hour during which all but the drummer might abandon instruments to appeal to dancers to clap along to what they recognised as the *mach schau* – later, corrupted to 'let's go' – beat: pounding hi-hat, snare and bass drum in the same lone four-in-a-bar rhythm for chorus after chorus amid yells of encouragement until the levelling guitars surged back in again and the snare reverted to its usual off-beat, and the hi-hat to eight quavers a bar while the bass drum continued to clump fours rather than the standard rock'n'roll on-beat.[7]

Clayson goes on to comment, '[t]he most celebrated exponents of *mach schau* – a backbeat that a half-wit couldn't lose – were Dave Dee and the Bostons. Years later it would underpin 'Hold Tight', 'Hideaway', 'Touch Me, Touch Me' and other hits.'[8] It was, we can hypothesize, the very simplicity and insistence of Dave Dee and co.'s emphasis on the beat for a white audience unused to rhythmic complexity that made the group so popular in Germany and later in England. 'Hold Tight' reached number 4 on the British chart in 1966 and 'Hideaway' reached number 10 later that same year.

This beat evolved in circumstances where the groups needed to be able to play anything and everything. This was in part because of the pressures in the St Pauli clubs to keep finding new material and partly because audiences both in Germany and in Britain could request a very large variety of songs. Here is Clayson again on the Hamburg experience:

---

[5]   Alan Clayson, *Hamburg: The Cradle of British Rock*, p. 15.

[6]   Ibid., p. 154.

[7]   Alan Clayson, *The Beat Merchants: The Origins, History, Impact and Rock Legacy of the 1960s British Pop Groups*, p. 78.

[8]   Ibid.

The monotony of dragging out a British palais repertoire was sufficient impetus to rehearse strenuously the most obscure material that could be dug up from the common unconscious. Anything went: calypso, barrack-room ballads, Boy Scout campfire ditties, oompah band drinking songs, songs-with-actions, music hall, the Hokey-Cokey, even rocked-up cracks at all the detested trad stand-bys. The hairiest old chestnuts were tried though preferment was often given to those granted stage and vinyl blessing by rated US artists.[9]

The point here is that this new version of the 8/8 beat was thoroughly flexible. It could be used to give a rhythmic propulsion, and therefore a simple dance beat, to anything – including music-hall songs. Comparing the style of playing to that of Little Richard and Buddy Holly, Dave Laing has explained that,

> … in the Liverpool beat style, the chord-playing of the rhythm guitar was broken up into a series of separate strokes, often one to the bar, with the regular plodding of the bass guitar and crisp drumming behind it. This gave a very different effect from the monolithic character of rock, in that the beat was given not by the duplication of one instrument in the rhythm section by another, but by an interplay between all three. This flexibility also meant that beat music could cope with a greater range of time-signatures and song shapes than rock&roll had been able to.[10]

Here, we can remember, from Chapter 2, Freddie & the Dreamers in *What a Crazy World* merging the melodies of 'Camptown Races' and 'Let's Twist Again' into a single song sequence sewn together by the drummer's 8/8 beat. This beat is also the crucial difference between Joe Brown's version of 'Henery the Eighth' and Herman's Hermits' version four years later.[11]

Serving the need for dance music and background music, beat bands played everywhere from the St Pauli clubs to English palais dances, to variety shows to Butlins holiday camps where, Clayson tells us, '[a]mong a group's duties was accompanying the competitors in the camp's "pop singing" and jiving contests …

---

[9]   Clayson, *Hamburg*, pp. 154–5.

[10]   Dave Laing, *The Sound of Our Time*, pp. 115–16.

[11]   In *Sixties Rock: Garage, Psychedelic, and Other Satisfactions*, Michael Hicks gives a different version of the English groups' influence on the development of the rock beat. Hicks's primary focus is on the distinction between a backbeat, found in rhythm and blues, and an offbeat, found in country music. Within this context, he argues that 'British groups concentrated less on the accentuation of the beat than on the speed of the beat' and that English rhythm and blues groups like the Rolling Stones and the Yardbirds speeded the beat up from the African-American versions of songs. Hicks argues that '[o]ne emphasizes force, the other action' (p. 30) and that it was this faster beat that travelled back to the United States and was picked up by the garage bands.

as well as delivering the music night after night'.[12] Moreover, as Bradley writes from the vantage point of 1992,

> ... [t]o this day, hundreds of Beat groups, often now wearing evening dress and calling themselves 'Cabaret', but Beat groups in musical terms none the less, provide cheap live dance music at parties, dance halls, Christmas 'dinner dances', British Legions, working men's clubs, etc., all over Britain, performing rock and Beat and soul-pop standards mixed perhaps with crooner-type ballads, Country songs and a smattering of whatever is in the pop charts this year.[13]

This, then, is how the rock'n'roll beat was indigenized to English needs and then was exported back to the United States to white teenagers there in the British Invasion where the style became incorporated into the suburban garage band explosion of the mid-1960s.[14]

As the quotation above from Laing suggests, compared to the African-American rock'n'roll of Little Richard and Chuck Berry, and the white American groups influenced by the African-American sound, the way the rhythm and the beat were organized in beat groups and, indeed, also the English rhythm and blues groups to a significant extent, enabled the melody to be greatly foregrounded. This was another key element in the whitening of the musical form to make it meaningful for English, and subsequently white American, teenagers. It was the Beatles who developed this innovation most successfully. Iain Chambers remarks that the Beatles '... did not dramatically tear up Tin Pan Alley and previous popular music. Their music was described as "fresh" and "exciting", not "alien" and "offensive"';[15] and in the same vein Peter Mandler has more recently commented that '[t]he Beatles had a peculiar genius which allowed them to blend the harder black American styles with traditional British musics – music hall, Tin Pan Alley melodies and lyrics – and appeal across classes and generations'.[16] Those 'harder black American styles' were primarily those of Chuck Berry and Little Richard, for the reason already discussed, of whose songs quite a few – three of Berry's – can be found on the notorious *The Beatles Live at the Star Club, 1962* album. At the same time the rockabilly of Buddy Holly was a mainstay for the group. For example, Lennon and McCartney's skiffle group, the Quarrymen, used to play

---

[12] Clayson, *The Beat Merchants*, p. 86.

[13] Bradley, *Understanding Rock'n'Roll*, p. 73.

[14] Philip H. Ennis, in *The Seventh Stream: The Emergence of Rocknroll in American Popular Music*, reminds us that '[i]t is essential to understand ... that the Beatles, Stones and so on did not create the mature small rock band. The mould had been made in the U.S.; from 1946 onwards ... The Beatles, nevertheless, provided a powerful and constraining model that thousands of young American garage bands found exactly to their liking' (p. 332).

[15] Iain Chambers, *Urban Rhythms: Pop Music and Popular Culture*, p. 63.

[16] Peter Mandler, 'Two Cultures—One—Or Many?', p. 141.

'That'll Be the Day' while the Beatles played 'Crying, Waiting, Hoping' at their audition for Decca in 1962, and put 'Words of Love' on their *Beatles for Sale* album in 1964.

The ballads from the Brill Building composers, of which there were three that had been previously recorded by African-American girl groups on *Please Please Me*, exercised at least as strong an influence.[17] In his book on these composers, Ken Emerson argues that, '... [t]he Beatles and the British groups whose invasion they spearheaded admired and exploited the songcraft of the Brill Building and 1650 Broadway. John Lennon and Paul McCartney proclaimed King and Goffin their favorite songwriters'.[18] The Beatles took this melodic ballad tradition, wrote their own songs, and set them into the English beat-group structure, placing the beat behind the melody. Herman's Hermits followed their lead.

The Reintroduction of Music-Hall Stylings

By 1967, when the Beatles were looking for a way forward, their choice was to return to the still-living English music hall and variety tradition:

> Already trapped, in their early twenties, the Beatles had to find a way out. *Sgt. Pepper's Lonely Hearts Club Band* was born. 'Pepper was probably the only Beatle album I can say was my idea', McCartney says. 'It was my idea to say to the guys, "Hey, how about disguising ourselves and getting an alter-ego, because we're the Beatles and we're fed up".'[19]

The basic conceit of the album was of the Beatles playing as a variety band. Thus, Ringo is introduced as 'the one and only Billy Shears' for his performance of 'With a Little Help from My Friends', while 'Being for the Benefit of Mr Kite!' and 'When I'm Sixty-Four' are composed in the music-hall singalong genre. Indeed, 'When I'm Sixty-Four' works in the same terms of age and long-term partnership and is coded in sentimentality in the same ways as Albert Chevalier's 'My Old Dutch', a well-known music-hall song from 1892. 'When I'm Sixty-Four' was one of Paul McCartney's first compositions, written when he was 16, so the music-hall influence would not be surprising. Herman's Hermits covered 'My Old Dutch' on their *Both Sides of Herman's Hermits* album released in 1966. It would be wrong

---

[17]   For a more detailed discussion of the impact of the Brill Building composers on the Beatles, see Ian Inglis, '"Some Kind Of Wonderful": The Creative Legacy of the Brill Building', especially pp. 220–23, 'The British Invasion', and, especially, Timothy E. Scheurer, 'The Beatles, the Brill Building, and the Persistence of Tin Pan Alley in the Age of Rock', pp. 89–102.

[18]   Ken Emerson, *Always Magic in the Air: The Bomp and Brilliance of the Brill Building Era*, p. 195.

[19]   From Stephen Thomas Erlewine, 'Sgt. Pepper's Lonely Hearts Club Band'.

to see this simply as an exercise in nostalgia. It is, rather, an example of cultural transmission, of assimilation, incorporation and transformation of English culture. Stephen Thomas Erlewine argues that, in *Sgt. Pepper's*, 'the Beatles consciously synthesized such disparate influences as psychedelia, art-song, classical music, rock&roll, and music hall, often in one song'. He goes on to write that 'the genius of the record is how the vaudevillian "When I'm 64" seems like a logical extension of "Within You, Without You"'.[20] In this album the Beatles were able to meld together the indigenized rock beat with American Brill Building song stylings and early twentieth-century English music hall within a concept based in the idea of variety, which together is now thought of as quintessentially English.[21]

Nowhere was this synthesis in the context of a reaffirmation of the English tradition better expressed than in the Pop Art cover of *Sgt. Pepper's* designed by Peter Blake, which had wax models of the Beatles in faux-Victorian military uniforms at the centre of a large number of predominantly English and American well-known figures. Blake and his artist wife Jann Haworth called the collage 'People We Like'. As a unity it suggests the Beatles' Englishness and acknowledges the many diverse influences, especially American, out of which that Englishness is now composed, including the English music-hall artists Issy Bonn and Max Miller. Miller was the acknowledged master of the comic, salacious double entendre.

Released the same year as *Sgt. Pepper's*, the Who's *The Who Sell Out* was 'envisioned [by Pete Townshend] as a celebration of the zeitgeist, a joyous reaffirmation of the discrete cultural elements that had defined British post-war popular culture'.[22] Central to this was the acknowledgement of the acceptance of consumerism as a way of life exemplified on the album by the faux-advertisements scattered between the tracks and the celebrated Pop Art cover, with photographs by David Montgomery, that has each of the four members of the group seemingly advertising a product. What is missed in discussions of the album as a Pop Art concept piece is the role of music-hall humour in centring the album in the English tradition. The cover, which includes Townshend holding a giant container of Odorono roll-on deodorant under his scrawny left armpit and Roger Daltrey sitting in a bath full of baked beans while holding a giant Heinz baked-bean can, smacks of a humour that undermines the seriousness with which most mass advertising functioned in the new, British consumption society. This same music-hall humour that deflates the self-important and pompous also runs through the advertisements on the album itself. Similarly, the lyrics of one of the album's catchiest tracks, 'Mary Anne with the Shaky Hand', depend for their meaning on music-hall 'nudge nudge, wink wink' humour. We never find out what Mary Anne's shaky hand does for her man but it is clearly – nudge, wink – an amazing experience for him! And more, in light of this recognition of pervasive music-hall influence on this

---

[20] Ibid.

[21] There were further music-hall-style influenced songs on the Beatles' album known as the White Album, released in 1968, including 'Honey Pie' and 'Martha My Dear'.

[22] John Dougan, *The Who Sell Out*, p. 90.

album, we can also consider the possible influence of the American vaudeville song from 1918, 'K-K-K-Katy', also known informally as the stuttering song, on Roger Daltrey's stuttering in 'My Generation' – Townshend, though, claims as his influence John Lee Hooker's 'Stuttering Blues', while an urban myth suggests that Daltrey's stuttering was supposed to suggest somebody on speed, the drug of choice for English mods. In any case, the reception of the song would have been influenced by the familiar 'K-K-K-Katy', which had become assimilated into English music-hall repertoire.

The Who had started out as a rhythm and blues band, covering two James Brown tracks on their first album released in 1965. However, showing the lack of distinction Americans made between bands in the British Invasion, on their first visit to the United States in 1967 the group supported Herman's Hermits. By this same year, though, the Who, like the Beatles, were synthesizing a rock sensibility that originated in the United States with the English popular music tradition embedded in music hall.

As, indeed, were the Rolling Stones, who released 'Something Happened to Me Yesterday' on their *Between the Buttons* album in 1967. The song uses a music-hall-style bouncy beat and a singalong chorus to disguise its drug references. It ends with a spoken outro that is, in part, reminiscent of the homiletic ending to each episode of the early BBC television police series *Dixon of Dock Green*, and concludes with Jack Warner's welcome to each episode of that show: 'Evening all'. While not music hall itself, it is an iconically English way to end a rock song soaked in music-hall reference. At the end of the following year the Stones organized and filmed *The Rolling Stones Rock and Roll Circus*, which, in addition to performances by Jethro Tull, Marianne Faithfull, Taj Mahal, the Who and the Stones themselves, also included clowns, acrobats, a classical pianist and trapeze artist. Mick Jagger compered the show, introducing it as music hall: 'You've heard of Oxford Circus, you've heard of Piccadilly Circus, and this is the Rolling Stones' Rock and Roll Circus. And we've got sights and sounds and marvels to delight your eyes and ears … '[23] Thus, although the Stones' conceit was that this was a circus, and indeed the performers came from the Robert Fossett Circus, the impression was more of a variety show held in a circus tent. As with *Sgt. Pepper's*, then, music hall became a framing device for the rock performances, reintroducing variety, which remained the most popular form of entertainment in England, to rock'n'roll as a means of contextualizing and adding value to it.

Also in 1968 the Small Faces, whose points of departure had been American Stax and Tamla Motown soul, released *Ogden's Nut Gone Flake*, one side of which had songs linked together by the invented English of South African expatriate variety comedian Stanley Unwin. Like Donegan, Brown and Steele, Steve Marriott, the group's lead singer, and most of the other members of the group were brought up in London's East End. Marriott's father often played piano in the local pubs. At 13,

---

[23]   Mick Jagger, at The Internet Movie Database, 'Memorable Quotes for The Rolling Stones Rock and Roll Circus'.

Marriott played the Artful Dodger in Lionel Bart's musical adaptation of *Oliver*. All this experience was suppressed in favour of rhythm and blues for the first two years of the Small Faces' recording career. On *Ogden's*, however, Marriott and the band's heritage in East End music-hall songs surfaces in 'Rene' and, especially, 'Lazy Sunday', a song about the experience of living in a terrace house where the noise travels through the walls. It has a rock beat and a singalong, music-hall-style chorus. 'Lazy Sunday' is another example of the assimilation of African-American music and its incorporation in a new music-hall song that transforms the genre. In its subject matter and sonics, 'Lazy Sunday' is similar to the songs that Ray Davies was writing for the Kinks during this period, which is not surprising given that both groups were primarily composed of working-class Londoners who had started out playing rhythm and blues before turning back to their music-hall song heritage.

In the liner notes for the 2007 collection of Joe Brown's recordings in the early 1960s for Pye and Piccadilly, David Wells writes that Brown's 'trademark combination of cheeky East End humour and Rock-meets-Music-Hall approach was borrowed wholesale by the likes of former child actor Steve Marriott for the Small Faces'. Rather than wholesale borrowing, with the imputation that Marriott was putting on a performance, we can understand here a continuity of tradition where in each case across the period of a decade there was an attempt to assimilate the American rock, and rhythm and blues, music and then incorporate it into, and in the process transform, the English popular music tradition located in music hall and variety.

The band that most epitomized the resurfacing of music-hall styles as rock'n'roll, now with an indigenized beat, in the English popular music tradition was the Kinks. Much has now been written about the Englishness of the Kinks' music, focusing especially on Ray Davies's compositions, so I will not belabour the point here.[24] Indeed, Patricia Gordon Sullivan has devoted an entire article to Ray Davies and group's relationship to music hall, in which she argues that

> ... [t]he Kinks parallel the music-hall tradition in several ways: they establish stage personas ... their musical presentation makes use of traditionally non-rock instruments like tubas and kazoos; they appropriate various musical structures such as ragtime and honky tonk to create different layers of music; they employ witty sly plays on words –[25]

and so on. In short, Sullivan's argument is that every facet of the Kinks' work shows the influence of music hall. However, Sullivan writes as if the Kinks were

---

[24] See, for example, Nick Baxter-Moore's extensive discussion in '"This is Where I Belong": Identity, Social Class and the Nostalgic Englishness of Ray Davies and the Kinks'.

[25] Patricia Gordon Sullivan, '"Let's Have a Go at It": The British Music Hall and the Kinks', p. 96.

resurrecting a bygone form of entertainment. As should be clear from my argument throughout this chapter and the previous one, music hall, reconfigured as variety, had never died. Ray Davies and the other Kinks were drawing on a living, and very popular, tradition.

Like the Who and the Small Faces, and indeed the Rolling Stones and to an extent the Beatles, the Kinks started out playing American rhythm and blues. The band's eponymously titled first album contained Chuck Berry and Bo Diddley compositions as well as a version of Lightnin' Hopkins's 'Bald Headed Woman', a song that was also recorded by the Who. Davies's early compositions, such as the Kinks' breakthrough hit 'You Really Got Me', released in July 1964, was in this style.

By 1966 Davies was beginning to write the songs of social observation and commentary for which he would become renowned. In February, 'Dedicated Follower of Fashion' was released as a single. While the lyrics can be read as a criticism of those London swingers obsessed above all else with the latest fashions, the music has a jaunty, bouncy rhythm drawn from music hall including a chorus, 'Oh, yes he is', that functions in the same way as the call-and-response set-up used by music hall and pantomime entertainers with their audience, in this case between Davies as lead singer and the rest of the band. Within this structure, and Davies's occasional putting-on of a posh accent, the social understanding of the song's meaning is founded in a shared knowledge of the genre of working-class music-hall song that takes the mickey out of the pretensions of the upper class. From this perspective, 'Dedicated Follower' is in direct lineage with the music-hall song made famous at the turn of the twentieth century by Vesta Tilley, 'Burlington Bertie' – not to be confused with the now better-known parody 'Burlington Bertie from Bow', which was first performed in 1915. 'Dedicated Follower' reached number 4 on the British singles chart. Later in 1966 the Kinks released *Face To Face*, which contains the music-hall-styled 'Dandy' that was covered for an American audience by Herman's Hermits and that was discussed in the previous chapter. Also on *Face To Face* is 'Sunny Afternoon'. Lyrically another ironic commentary on upper-class life, the melody is much less music hall-related and, consequently, the song was heard more as a celebration of 'lazing on a sunny afternoon / In the summertime'. It made number 1 on the charts.

Perhaps not coincidentally, at this time when Davies and the Kinks began to meld the indigenized rock beat with music-hall stylings the Kinks had been banned from performing in the United States – or, to put this the other way round, in this period the Kinks were forced to present their music to a predominantly British, but really English, audience.[26] Davies knew he was now writing for an audience well-versed in music hall and variety. As we have seen, there was also a more general,

---

26   The Kinks were banned from entering the United States through the influence of the American Federation of Musicians union at the end of the group's 1965 tour. It seems that, after much provocation, Ray Davies got into a fight with a representative of the television company making the *Dick Clark Show* on which they were appearing (a version of this

cultural shift taking place around this time that was founded on the assimilation of American musical styles and the renovation of the music-hall genre. Reflecting this shift, in the United States 'Dedicated Follower' only got to number 36 on the Billboard chart and on the Cash Box and Record World charts did not even make the Top 50. 'Sunny Afternoon', which, as we have seen, was less obviously influenced by English music hall, did much better, reaching number 11.

One of the reasons Davies was able to work so successfully with music-hall stylings is that, like the East Enders already discussed, Lonnie Donegan, Joe Brown, Tommy Steele, and most of the Small Faces, the Davies brothers came from a working-class family steeped in vernacular English popular song. The family lived in a terrace house in what was then the working-class north London suburb of Muswell Hill. Fred and his wife Annie supported eight children on a slaughterman's wages. In their biography of the band, Neville Marten and Jeff Hudson write that '[i]n the Davies house everyone would return from the pub a little worse for wear and set to it – "Mum used to sing when she'd had a few drinks and my dad used to dance", recalled Dave'.[27] And Miller in his book *The Kinks Are the Village Green Preservation Society* makes explicit the connection between these singalongs and Davies's later compositions:

> Ray Davies acknowledges his family's influence on the way he wrote and presented his work. 'Growing up in that family, it had a strong musical basis. They were not great musicians, but music was very much part of the family, and we always had to sing songs at the piano. That really undoubtedly rubbed off on me. Things that my father saw, the family knew. I never went to the music hall, or any of that stuff. He went to see musical shows and used to go dancing, so I picked up a lot of it from my family.'[28]

We should note that, while Davies could have gone to variety shows like his father, though he didn't, he still came to know the music. The point here is the importance of tradition. Throughout this chapter I have emphasized the centrality of music hall in the English tradition of popular music. However, this is a tradition that is not only a function of such direct institutional influence. As I have already signalled in my discussion of skiffle, there is in England a long urban tradition of informal working-class involvement in popular music. Like Marriott's father playing piano in the local pub, the Davies brothers' family sing-songs are just one more exemplification of this.

As I have already explained, variety shows, where music-hall routines and songs were performed, continued to exist in England through the 1950s

---

story can be found in Neville Marten and Jeff Hudson, *The Kinks: Well Respected Men*, pp. 63–4). The group was not allowed back until 1969.

[27] Marten and Hudson, *The Kinks*, p. 17.

[28] Andy Miller, *The Kinks Are the Village Green Preservation Society*, p. 18.

and 1960s and later. The working-class family singalong pervaded Davies's way of composing. Here is Miller again:

> ... through the 1960s, The Kinks – who Davies wryly calls 'another family to me, however dysfunctional that family can be sometimes' – would rehearse in the manner of the Davies clan, gathered round the piano in Ray's front room while he led them through his latest composition.[29]

As Miller comments, it is no wonder that so many of the Kinks' songs from this period have a singalong quality to them. Perhaps, though, Davies's finest music-hall-styled song was released in 1970, 'Lola'. It, too, has a bouncy, singalong quality, as well as a nudge nudge, wink wink element to its lyrical interest in transvestitism and a first-person narrative style, all of which are typical of classic English music hall. At the same time the song does not have the feel of something deliberately constructed in an archaic form – which could be said of Lionel Bart's confection for Joe Brown, 'Jellied Eels', released, as was mentioned in Chapter 2, in 1960. 'Lola' reached number 2 on the British chart and continues to be an English singalong favourite.

It is wrong, then, to see the reappearance of music-hall stylings simply as an expression of nostalgia. In this first instance it is a consequence of the incorporation of American musical forms and the consequent transformation of tradition. While the artists of the early 1960s like Donegan, Brown and Steele were tending to rework traditional songs in ways influenced by American musical styles, those like the Beatles, the Small Faces and the Kinks in the later 1960s were writing new songs in traditional styles with an indigenized beat that helped songs in the English tradition continue to sound familiar – remember here the crucial difference in the rhythm between Joe Brown's and Herman's Hermits' versions of the music-hall classic 'Henery the Eighth'.

In Chapter 2 there is a discussion of the application of the idea of cultural imperialism to the post-Second World War relationship between the United States and Britain. While the flooding of Britain with American popular music was not deliberate, it functioned as one element in a transformation of British society into the consumption-based culture described at the beginning of the previous chapter. Popular music became an element in the new youth culture centred in that novel category, the teenager. At the same time, the English popular music tradition was strong enough to weather the impact of American popular music, transform it, and incorporate it into that tradition – the process that was theorized at the outset of the previous chapter in the terms of assimilation and adaptation. This can be found in what I have called the indigenization of the beat, and the resurfacing of music-hall musical stylings, many of which themselves have a history outside of music hall in urban working-class family and everyday life.

---

[29] Ibid., p. 19.

This does not mean that in the resurfacing of music hall in English popular music there was not also a certain nostalgia for a time before Britain's loss of military and financial power, and the complex impact of Americanization and the consumerism that went along with it. All this underlies *The Kinks Are the Village Green Preservation Society*. The village green is an iconically English, pastoral, indeed pre-industrial, image. Its invocation suggests an idyllic English past. Davies sings in 'The Village Green Preservation Society' that we – an inclusive term that could be read as being the Kinks but also those who listen to the song and, indeed, the English, or perhaps British, more generally – are the Village Green Preservation Society, and also the Desperate Dan Appreciation Society. The singer asks God to save Donald Duck, vaudeville, variety, strawberry jam, and all the different varieties of jam. Referencing vaudeville, the American version of music hall, suggests a cultural commingling. Variety was, as we saw in the previous chapter, music hall transformed for television and a middle-class audience. Donald Duck was an American, Disney cartoon character but, having been popular in Britain since before the Second World War, could be thought of in nostalgic terms. Desperate Dan, a character in the British comic *The Dandy*, was American, living in the Wild West. The comic strip, started before the Second World War, was itself a kind of British comedic indigenization of Americana. The hugely strong Dan lived in Cactusville, shaved with a blow torch and ate cow pie. Jam is, simply, another iconically English reference. A cheap staple for the working class, for the middle class it invokes summer afternoon teas overlooking that village green. The English psychedelic band, Pink Floyd, in their 1969 song 'Grantchester Meadows', on the double album *Ummagumma*, invoke a similar English pastoral nostalgia, which, in referencing Grantchester, a place with which two members of the group were closely associated, also echoes the homesickness expressed in Rupert Brooke's 'The Old Vicarage, Grantchester', written while Brooke was visiting Berlin just before the Second World War, where, at the end, rather than jam, the poet asks, 'And is there honey still for tea?'

Davies goes on to sing that the Village Green and Desperate Dan appreciation societies preserve 'the old ways from being abused' and protect 'the new ways for me and for you'. We can read this as recognizing that tradition is always a work in progress. In his lyrics, Davies seems to be acknowledging the incorporation of American elements into English culture and their naturalization into a transformed tradition that, nevertheless, remains English. What is perhaps most remarkable about *The Kinks Are the Village Green Preservation Society* is that it is a commentary on the very transformations that underlie the existence of that album itself.

In this chapter, and the previous one, what I have wanted to show is the persistence of a tradition of English popular music located in music hall that transforms and survives in spite of the impact of American cultural imperialism. It is coloured by a nostalgia for a lost, British imperial past, but it is first and foremost the expression of a local, working-class culture – a culture in which, complicating matters, nostalgia and sentimentality are integral elements. This tradition of English popular music, with its music-hall heritage, continues in, for example, Pato Banton's 1994 popular reworking of Eddy Grant's Equals' hit 'Baby Come Back' with its self-deprecating humour, its bouncy beat and singalong, anthemic chorus, and in artists such as Robbie Williams.[30] As both Dave Laing and Derek Scott indicate in other chapters in this collection, the music-hall tradition was a resource for Britpop. In English popular music of the later 1960s we find the resurfacing of a musical tradition that had been submerged but had never disappeared.

---

[30]   See, for example, Neil McCormick's article in *The Telegraph*, 30 June 2003, 'A little bit music hall, a little bit rock'n'roll', where he writes: 'Spectacle-wise, it must be ranked a disappointment. There are nubile dancing girls in go-go costumes, just about saucy enough for an old seaside special. It is like an end of the pier show staged in a stadium. Small wonder he is having problems in America: he seems such a quintessentially British entertainer, a little bit music hall, a little bit rock'n'roll. His cheeky chappie persona already seems quaintly old fashioned, a leftover from the boozy lad culture of the Nineties, lock, stock and roll out the barrel.'

Chapter 4

Trainspotting: The Gendered History of Britpop[1]

Sheila Whiteley

It is no great revelation to find that the guitar-led bands of 1990s Britpop are predominantly male – how many English women lead guitarists can *you* name? Nor is it surprising to hear the influence of such iconic bands as the Beatles, the Kinks, and Small Faces or, indeed, David Bowie, the Sex Pistols, the Smiths and Happy Mondays. If, as the argument goes, Britpop was a deliberate attempt to oust grunge and reinstate 'Britishness' into rock,[2] then such reference points are significant in establishing a recognizable musical identity. Obvious influences from the Beatles (Oasis, 'Whatever'; the Beatles, 'I am the Walrus) and other 60s pop groups (Oasis, 'Don't Look Back in Anger'; Manfred Mann, 'Pretty Flamingo'[3]) suggested both pastiche and homage (a light-hearted cultural nostalgia for groups whose music inflected social commentary in an upbeat rock style) and a 'pop cultural revivalism – the imagery of modern culture as a data base and dressing up box'.[4] With songs as diverse as Pulp's 'Common People' and their controversial 'Sorted for E's and Wizz', Oasis' '(What's the Story) Morning Glory?', and Supergrass's pop slogan 'We are young! We are free!', this sense of nostalgic reverence was important in giving Britpop a musical DNA that transcended often disparate musical styles. As John Covach writes,

> … listeners organize new musical experiences in terms of previous ones: any new song is heard in terms of other songs the listener knows or has at least heard. In the simplest cases, a new song that shares many musical characteristics with a number of other already known songs is easily assimilated … Sometimes characteristics are held in common among a large number of works … Such

---

[1]   For my granddaughters, Luisa and Bella.

[2]   Britpop has been described, not unfairly, as a 'defiantly nationalistic anti-grunge movement … firmly centred in snotty arrogance and aspirations to stardom' – 'The Empire Gobs Back', *Rolling Stone, Yearbook 1995*, pp. 32–40.

[3]   For further discussion, see Derek B. Scott, '(What's the Copy?) The Beatles and Oasis', pp. 201–11.

[4]   Michael Bracewell, *The Nineties: When Surface Was Depth*, p. 56.

commonly held characteristics are traditionally regarded as central to the identification of musical styles.[5]

It would seem, then, that Britpop's reference to its musical heritage provides a key defining characteristic. To simply describe it as guitar-based rock/pop with catchy tunes and the promise of a good time does little to capture its musical essence. Rather, it is the sense of déjà vu that is important, momentarily moving the listener back in time, while demonstrating how 'musically accomplished and lyrically clever' the groups were in composing 'serious and sincere pop songs which used archaic formats and styling to pass comment on society as they found it'.[6]

It is also suggested that journalistic reporting of Britpop bands as 'lad' culture revived notions of gender and sexuality that simplified the complexities of sexual politics and impacted upon the reception of its female bands. As Amy Raphael observed, Britpop 'didn't challenge ... it didn't threaten blokes',[7] and as if to nurture the current anti-feminist backlash[8] women were once again relegated to the status of dolly-birds, babes and sex objects. 'Girls and Boys' from Blur's 1994 album *Parklife*, for example, is considered instrumental in giving the lads-mag market (*Q*, *Loaded* and *Viz*) sufficient ammunition to associate Britpop with a loutish masculinity that was bolstered by ITV's comedy series 'Men Behaving Badly' and a resurgence in football hooliganism. With 'Geri Halliwell's snappily saucy micro-dress and Noel Gallagher's guitar sporting the Union Jack', it seemed that Britpop 'combined an infantile nostalgia for the popular culture of its practitioners' adolescence ... the born again maleness of laddism nouveau'[9] and a 'pan-media return to gender stereotyping'.[10]

As such, it is curious that the narrative surrounding Britpop should begin with Suede,[11] a sexually ambiguous band from Haywards Heath, Sussex, whose unlikely blend of fey petulance and somewhat depressing council-house-kitchen-sink lyrics owed as much to the influence of Bowie as it did to the scrutiny of northern life penned and performed by Morrissey.[12] Featured in the April 1993

---

[5]   John Covach, 'Pangs of History in Late 1970s New-Wave Rock', p. 170.

[6]   Bracewell, *The Nineties*, p. 17.

[7]   Amy Raphael, *Never Mind the Bollocks: Women Rewrite Rock*, p. xxv.

[8]   During the early 1990s feminism generally had been getting somewhat of a bad press, blamed for every problem then besetting women, from bad mothering to depression to spotty complexions, from meagre savings accounts to teenage suicides to anorexia, from drug addiction to teenage pregnancies.

[9]   Bracewell, *The Nineties*, p. 15.

[10]   Ibid., p. 21.

[11]   Suede and Blur are both acknowledged as kick-starting Britpop, although some critics suggest it originated with the Stone Roses.

[12]   Suede was co-founded by Justine Frischmann (rhythm guitar), who subsequently fronted Elastica (albeit that she is usually described as Brett Anderson's girlfriend, and was speedily ejected for not attending rehearsals).

edition of *Select* magazine, with lead singer Brett Anderson on the cover, backed by a Union Jack and the phrase 'Yanks Go Home', and championed by *Melody Maker* as 'the best new band in Britain', their debut single 'The Drowners' launched a renewed interest in British guitar-led pop/rock. Headlined as Britain's answer to US grunge, their debut album *Suede* (1993) achieved notable success in the UK, Canada and Asia, but despite being hailed as 'very, very British'[13] by pop journalist John Harris, their glam/indie sound and often dark lyrics failed to compete with the mainstream success of Oasis, Pulp and Blur. Maybe sexual ambiguity didn't quite fit with the tabloid's construction of Britpop's musical heritage, and the hype surrounding the super-lad persona of its super-star groups. For those versed in the wiles of the media, there was added speculation about the emphasis on national optimism, pride in Britishness and the kudos of being part of a 'Cool Britannia' under New Labour. As Michael Bracewell writes, 'one answer might have been that this sudden targeted mediation of Imperial Nineties London saw a kind of affectionately ironic Retro Cool in the Union Jack as a primary emblem of Imperial Sixties London – of pop Art, sourcing from Elton Entwistle's [*sic*] Union Jacket or the original Union Jack sunglasses from Gear boutique'.[14] It is also possible that, by selectively invoking the sound and sensibility of *English* popular culture[15] of earlier eras, Britpop managed to erase the troubling reminder that Britain is a multiethnic society. As Paul Gilroy pithily observed, *There Ain't No Black in the Union Jack*, an observation that seemed particularly apt for Britpop's imperialistic nostalgia[16] and the erasure of memory of the ska hits of the late '60s within the Britpop canon.

---

[13]   John Harris, *The Last Party: Britpop, Blair and the Demise of English Rock*, p. 57.

[14]   Bracewell, *The Nineties*, p. 225.

[15]   Although the majority of Britpop bands were English, there were exceptions: Ash came from Northern Ireland; the Supernaturals were Scottish; Manic Street Preachers, Super Furry Animals, Stereophonics and Catatonia were Welsh, and were dubbed 'Cool Cymru' (a pun on 'Cool Britannia') by their local media.

[16]   The 'Union Jack as a primary emblem of Imperial Sixties London' also reveals more fascistic overtones. 'Imperial Sixties London', with its connotations of Empire, was now home to a growing number of immigrants. 'In 1961, 66,000 arrived from the West Indies, 23,750 from India, and over 25,000 from Pakistan … By 1968 the total number of immigrants for the year was 66,700. Of these fewer than 5,000 were from the West Indies, 15,000 from Pakistan and 28,000 from India', the majority settling in London and its suburbs, the West Midlands, Manchester, Bradford, Sheffield, Cardiff and Glasgow. With ethnic concentration came problems – poor working conditions, substandard housing, high unemployment, criminal exploitation, and colour prejudice. Not least, racial discrimination was inflamed by the strain of economic recession and strikes, with the blame conveniently placed on immigrant communities who were marginalized to the edge of the law. Problems were further exacerbated by the rhetoric of Conservative Member of Parliament Enoch Powell's 'Rivers of Blood' speech (20 April 1968), which had stressed that, unless immigrants were repatriated, the streets would overflow with blood like the River Tiber

It is not insignificant that the challenge to white, super-lad supremacy was first confronted by singer-songwriter Sonya Aurora Madan, founder and frontwoman of Echobelly, 'a Deborah Harry sing-alike, a female Morrissey, our first Asian pop star … who has been known to wear a Union Jack T-shirt with "My Country Too" scrawled across it'. Nor is it insignificant that she was labelled 'a babe to die for',[17] a female pin-up of the Britpop era, so undermining the feminist agenda of much of her lyrics. It was a fate shared by Justine Frischmann (Elastica) and Louise Wener (Sleeper).[18] Wener, in particular, was placed high in the *Melody Maker* and *New Musical Express* 'Sexiest Woman' polls, arguably reducing her standing as one of Britpop's strongest lyricists and melody writers. In a cultural climate that 'revived archaic notions of gender and sexuality'[19] it seemed that one of Britpop's problems was how to accommodate its female groups, not least when they refused the dubious accolade of 'babes'. As such, the question arises as to whether Echobelly, Elastica and Sleeper offered an alternative version of Englishness that ran contrary to the media's construction of Britpop/Britculture, and whether their music enables us to place ourselves in a less hyped cultural narrative of national identity.

With punk and new wave as the major musical/cultural reference points for all three bands, it is, perhaps, inevitable that the rose-tinted nostalgia surrounding 1960s London would be ousted by shock politics and a more complex relationship with the social differences surrounding class, region, age, gender, sexuality and ethnicity.[20] As Lucy O'Brien writes,

---

of Ancient Rome. By the mid-1970s, it seemed to many that the national flag had become synonymous with a racist ideology, that its association with the National Front had given it an exclusivity that mitigated against the concept of a multicultural nation state. The use of 'stop and search' powers by the police escalated, with raids on black clubs, frequent passport and immigration checks; the treatment of carnival and other cultural events as threats to public order culminated in the inner city riots, which originated in the Toxteth district of Liverpool and the Brixton district of London.

For a more detailed discussion see Gilroy, *There Ain't No Black in the Union Jack*. The statistics in the paragraph above come from Paul Oliver, 'Introduction to Part Two: From the 1950s to the Present', pp. 83–4.

[17]   Raphael, *Never Mind the Bollocks*, p. 34.

[18]   Jon Stratton, in his *Jews, Race and Popular Music*, makes the point that Jews were marked by Thatcher as a model minority. As such, it is interesting to note that, of the three key women in Britpop, Frischmann and Wener were Jewish and, like Madan, were excluded, albeit in different degrees, from normative definitions of Englishness and hence provide telling examples of the hegemonic 'whiteness' and maleness of Britpop.

[19]   Bracewell, *The Nineties*, p. 15.

[20]   For a more detailed discussion of these issues see Roger Sabin (ed.), *Punk Rock: So What?: The Cultural Legacy of Punk*. It is also interesting, as George McKay notes, that despite the stylistic distinctions (both musical and visual) between the 'swinging' sixties and punk there were commonalities that informed Britpop's nostalgic nationalism – all three movements focused on the importance of the UK scene: 'there was something of

'We were trying to find a new vocabulary' (personal communication 1977), says Linda Sterling, or Linder, art terrorist and former lead singer with avant-garde punk Manchester group Ludus, who once sang at the Hacienda covered in pig's entrails and wearing a large black dildo. 'We just wanted to take the whole thing to its logical extreme' (personal communication 1990) with Siouxsie Sioux, who screamed of a suburban relapse and went into a Bromley wine bar in fetish gear with her friend Berlin on a leash and all fours. There were the Slits, defiantly naked and daubed in mud, on the cover of their debut album, *Cut*. And other girl groups like the Raincoats, the Mo-Dettes, and my own, the Catholic Girls, knots of resistance surrounded by incomprehension and hostility.[21]

With the 'sex wars' and battle for territory on stage highlighted by bondage fetish wear, Doc Martens, a 'fuck off you wanker' attitude and a fierce sense of individuality, female punk bands created aggressive statements of femininity that openly challenged the music industry's marketing of women as 'disco dollies or raunchy rock chicks'.[22] Not least, Germaine Greer's guest-edited special, *Cuntpower*, for the 1970 edition of the underground magazine *Oz*, influenced punk feminism by fronting the politics of female sexuality and included her polemic on the power of 'cunt' confrontation later adopted by, for example, punk artists Linder Sterling, the Slits and the Raincoats,[23] resurfacing in the 1990s with riot grrrls punk rock feminism, and the Britpop bands Elastica, Sleeper and Echobelly's witty critique of 'laddism' and gender stereotyping.

It is interesting, here, to briefly foreground the distinctive legacy of 'cunt' power and the 'pneumatic pretty punk' of Debbie Harry, identified by O'Brien as alternative defining features of both punk and Britpop, while acknowledging the commonality that situates both streams as 'other', i.e. outside the construction of guitar-led rock as both masculine and heteronormative. While a full discussion of politically grounded female music-making would include womyns' music, by the late 1980s and early 1990s the prescriptive nature of second-wave feminism had been rejected in favour of a more 'confrontational cultural activism which relied less on exposing gender differences than on deconstructing them'.[24] Taking their inspiration from earlier female punk musicians the Slits, the Raincoats and Poly Styrene from X-Ray Spex, the emergence of riot grrrls, in particular, saw

---

an antagonistic relation between Britain and the United States in the punk side of popular culture, as seen in the song "I'm So Bored with the USA" by the Clash' – 'I'm So Bored with the USA', in *Punk Rock: So What?*, p. 58.

[21] Lucy O'Brien, 'The Woman Punk Made Me', p. 186.

[22] Ibid., p. 194.

[23] For a more detailed discussion of the counter-culture's failure to confront sexual equality see Sheila Whiteley, *Women and Popular Music: Sexuality, Identity and Subjectivity*, pp. 22–31.

[24] Mary Celeste Kearney, 'The Missing Links. Riot Grrrl–Feminism–Lesbian Culture', p. 224.

a reaction against the gender orthodoxy of such popular cultural forms as rock and punk, which they used both as a means of self-expression and as a way of mobilizing their cause.[25] It is also important to note that riot grrrls were not gender separatist. 'Many of the iconic riot grrrl bands such as Bikini Kill and Bratmobile have had male band members',[26] and 'flexible forms of identification meant the movement's participants were free to embrace a range of femininities',[27] so providing a precedent for female Britpop, be it Frischmann's raunchy humour, Madan's playful girlishness or Wener's ultra-glam sophistication.

As a generic family tree, the combination of cunt-power, punk-confrontation, flexible forms of identification and bands that were no longer gender separatist provided a useful blueprint for Britpop's female bands. Elastica was founded by Justine Frischmann (ex-Suede), with Justin Welch (formerly of garage rock band, Spitfire, on drums and, like Frischmann, in an early incarnation of Suede), Annie Holland (bass) and Donna Matthews (guitar). While they first attracted media attention for playing twenty-minute sets performing two-minute songs, and for three recorded sessions on John Peel's BBC Radio 1 show,[28] 'Stutter' remains, perhaps, their best known track. Released on four different recordings in August 1994 (an original 7-inch, 1,500 copy run; the Sub-pop Singles Club release, also a 7-inch; the *US Geffen Stutter* release; the European/Australian Stutter release, which also included Pussycat, Blue and Spastica), their live performance was reviewed by Johnny Dee as 'Spiky, spunky and tighter than Brett Anderson's kinky vests; a sheer rush of frivolity and a sense of cool abandonment that only a band supremely confident of their impending celebrity could pull off.'[29]

Never one to accept a review without returning to source material, I found it useful to be able to access director David Mould's video of 'Stutter'[30] from their self-titled debut album *Elastica*. Underpinned by a brisk four-beat kick-snare-kick-snare, Frischmann's two-minute, two-verse, two-chorus rant about a boyfriend's sexual inadequacy is fuelled by fast fills on the drums, a chugging guitar and bass in the verse, and power chords in the chorus, with a short snare drum fill to weld the two together. As she explains in the FAQ, 'If you're watching a band you're not familiar with you wanna hear the verse, you wanna hear the chorus, you wanna hear the next song ... The whole thing of playing two middle eights and triple

---

[25] For a more detailed discussion see ibid., pp. 207–27; Marion Leonard, 'Rebel Girl, You Are the Queen of My World', pp. 230–55; and Jodie Taylor, 'Playing it Queer: Understanding Queer Gender, Sexual and Musical Praxis in a "New" Musicological Context', unpublished thesis.

[26] Taylor 'Playing It Queer', p. 159.

[27] Ibid.

[28] On 12 August 1993; 19 June 1994; 6 December 1994.

[29] Johnny Dee, *NME* review of 'Stutter'.

[30] Available at http://www.youtube.com/watch?v=mwNfiB4zBQo, accessed 19 April 2010.

choruses isn't music, it's brainwashing.'[31] Listening to Frischmann's sometimes conniving, sometimes in-yer-face delivery, there is little doubt that the framework suits the lyrics. She says what has to be said with no elaboration other than the momentary pause before a vocal lift on the final word of the verse ('Tell me you're mine, love / and I will not wait for other bedtime … treats'), so effecting a taunting put-down that, on the video, is enhanced by an 'I'm in charge' shot as she looks directly into the eye of the camera.

The overall mood is one of control, evident not only in the tightness of the arrangement but also in the band's backing vocals, which support Frischmann's put-down 'You've had too much wine to stumble up my street' with ooohs and aaahs against 'Well it isn't a problem'. It is, however, the seething and instantly memorable chorus that characterizes the song as a power-pop rant. Like the verse, much of its energy comes from the effectiveness of its punchy rhyming couplets with their harsh final consonants ('Is there something you lack / When I'm flat on my back?') against the somewhat laidback link line 'Is there something that I can do for you?'

Despite the underlying feeling that Frischmann's taunts are capable of undermining any surviving masculinity ('Is it just that I'm much too much for you?') there is an underlying raunchiness in the outro to the second, and final chorus, that resonates with the song's review as embodying 'cool abandonment'. Sandwiched between the 'Oh, oh, oh, ouah, oh ah' of the support vocals, the 'I really want you to' is provocative, anticipating the Spice Girls bantering 'zig-a-zig-a' ('Wannabe', December 1996) by well over three years. Is this a sexual come-on; is it more a tacit acceptance of drink-induced impotence as suggested by Frischmann's final dismissive hand-gesture; or is it addressed to the critics? As noted earlier, Dee's somewhat snide comment that 'only a band supremely confident of their impending celebrity could pull [this] off' draws into association the age-old problem surrounding 'who you know' and women's access to the popular music scene. In particular, it raises the question of whether Elastica's initial success was due, at least in part, to Frischmann's earlier relationship with Brett Anderson (Suede), and then-current boyfriend Damon Albarn (Blur) – the mystery keyboard player on the *Elastica* album, Dan Abnormal (anagram) – or whether her self-assured stage presence and the undoubted energy of the band would be sufficient to trigger national attention.

In retrospect, it seems it was the band's habit of lifting music from new wave classics that gave them notoriety. At its most evident in 'Connection' with its obvious comparison with Wire's 'Three Girl Rhumba', not least in the almost note-for-note introduction (an issue that was settled out of court), there was also evidence of the Stranglers' 'No More Heroes' in 'Waking Up', and Blondie's 'Sunday Girl' in 'Vaseline', to name but three. Given the weight of Britpop's musical heritage, there is, it seems, a fine line to be drawn between acknowledging

---

[31]   Available at http://www.stutter.demon.co.uk/elastica/faq.html#who#who, accessed 19 April 2010.

influences and ripping them off. As Derek Scott observes, '[t]he issue, in a nutshell, is whether Britpop works by way of simply copying earlier styles,[32] or whether there is an attempt to make creative use of those aspects of songs that might now, in the twenty-first century, be regarded as exemplifying the musical vocabulary of a British pop language.'[33] So what is important is the way in which ideas are developed. Despite having a distinctly '90s sound, and a provocative vocalist whose two-minute songs often reveal a dark, knowing humour, the obvious similarity between riffs and melodies from Wire and other new wave bands fed the accusation that Elastica were plagiarists.[34] Even so, the success of their debut album *Elastica*, which entered the charts at number 1 in March 1995 (director Mark Lamarq), their reception at the 1995 Glastonbury Festival, and the year of sell-out live gigs on the Lollapalooza Tour, suggest that plagiarism wasn't an issue for their fans; rather it was the catchiness of the songs, their instant memorability and wit that gave them the edge. Ranging from the bawdy, 'When you're stuck like glue, when you need some goo-ah' ('Vaseline'), to the provocative 'Tired of sitting here waiting, tired of debating, / Will you do me, will you do me now' ('All-Nighter'), and the more overt fantasies of the 'Car Song', 'Sometimes I just can't fun-ction, my heart's spaghetti junction / Every shining bonnet, makes me think of my back on it', the combination of sexual humour in an upbeat power-pop format was sufficient to maintain a loyal and enthusiastic following. As one fan tellingly wrote, 'Strangely enough, I get a similar vibe from all the songs that palpably rip off Wire (of which there are "more than a few", let's say) – I'd rather enjoy "Connection" than think about "Three Girl Rhumba", but that genie left the bottle a long time ago.'[35]

Praise for Elastica is not confined to fanzines, however. '2:1' (composed by guitarist, Donna Matthews) was hailed as 'properly detached/tight/sensual/threatening' on Guy Peters's music review of the soundtrack to *Trainspotting*,[36] a song that resonated with the film's narrative of drug addiction and often desperate

---

[32]   '1960s Britpopisms were characterized by variants of British regional diction, especially as heard in sung vowels, diphthongs, consonants, or finals such as "o", "a", "ai", "au", "r", or "er"; unembellished principal melodies; pervasive monorhythm; strictly accented strongbeats; limited use of vibrato; and lyrics and performance style that were often subtly humorous or ironic' – Annie J. Randall, *Dusty! Queen of the Postmods*, p. 47.

[33]   See Derek B. Scott, 'The Britpop Sound', Chapter 7, this volume.

[34]   As Jon Stratton thoughtfully pointed out in an earlier draft of this chapter, 'there may be a gendered issue in play here, given that the songs of Oasis, for example, have been discussed as being heavily indebted to various Beatles' tracks. The issue is whether the more vicious attack on Elastica, who were constantly being accused of, and indeed taken to court for, musical plagiarism has to do with their being outside of the Britpop coterie because they had two, and sometimes more, female members. It is possible that in the laddish world of Britpop, Oasis's appropriations were more acceptable to the mainstream press because they were "boys", and very laddish boys at that.'

[35]   At James, 'Famous Tales of the Formerly Young and Presently Stupid'.

[36]   Guy Peters, 'Trainspotting: Music from the Motion Picture (1996)'.

friendships. The 16-bar introduction, and the clock-like precision with which drums, bass and guitar are layered in a 4+4+6 bar stepped progression, establishes an edgy feel that continues throughout the song. Opening with a four-bar kick-snare motif with ticking sixteenths on closed hi-hat deep in the mix, the feeling of tension is precipitated by the repeated 'finger-nail-down-the-blackboard' fret slide of the G sharp–C sharp bass motif, and heightened by the clock-like stereo motion of the guitars, where a repetitive two-bar descending chord sequence (right speaker) adds tension to a bouncing staccato guitar motif (left speaker) before three unison quavers in bars 7 and 8 herald the opening lines of the vocal ('keeping a brave face'). Appropriately for a song that taps into the fear induced by withdrawal ('dark reflections, in my head, in my bed again') and need ('Don't ask for more'), the instrumental foundation continues throughout the 14-bar verse, creating an uneasy feeling of queasy perpetual motion before three crotchet triplets move the listener into the middle-eight where the rhythm shifts to an enticing tango-feel, evocative of the promised sensual release offered by 'the Sandman', before sinking back into the edgy mood of the second verse and a final reprise of the tango.

Frischmann's narrow-ranged vocal line is effective. Words are detached, spread over the 14-bar instrumental phrase already established in the introduction ('Keeping a brave face / in circumstances / is impossible'), to effect a disjointed counterpoint that locks into the emotions of the addict, waiting for the next fix. In context, the provocative rhythm of the tango-like middle eight that links the two verses suggests a musical metaphor of enticement: the allure of heroin to counter the cramps of withdrawal as suggested in the implied dialogue between conscience ('It's tragic / laid down on your side / too easy / you know that you know …') and addictive need ('Sandman comes / two to one / in the dark / dark reflections') that emerges in the double-tracked voices of the second verse.

Elastica were not the only female Britpop band to feature on *Trainspotting*. Sleeper, fronted by Louise Wener (vocals, guitar), recorded a 'sound-alike' cover version of 'Atomic' after Debbie Harry had refused permission for the original to be used on the soundtrack. While it is tempting to suggest that Wener's Blondie-like delivery made her an obvious choice, it is also interesting that Sleeper had supported Blur as opening band on their promotional tour for *Parklife* (1994) and, like Elastica, had established a useful association with Damon Albarn and the emerging Britpop fraternity.[37]

Jon Stewart (guitar) and Louise Wener had first met in a political philosophy lecture while undergraduates at Manchester University. They had moved to London after graduation, advertised for a bass player and drummer in *Melody Maker* – positions filled (respectively) by Diid Osman and Andy McClure – and signed to BMG/RCA in 1993. Although stating their influences as the Pixies (an indie band from Boston, Massachusetts, fronted by Kim Deal) and *The Partridge Family* (a humorous American soap about a family of musicians,

---

[37] The *Trainspotting* soundtrack features Blur's six-minute track 'Sing', Damon Albarn's 'Closet Romantic' and Pulp's 'Mile End'.

starring Shirley Jones and David Cassidy,[38] who released numerous successful
singles and albums, including the 1970 US chart topper 'I Think I Love You'), it
is also relevant to note the continuing importance of Morrissey to the emerging
1990s indie scene. By 1987, the year when Stewart and Wener met, the Smiths
were breaking up, and their final studio album *Strangeways, Here We Come* was
notable for its melancholia and Marr's experimental arrangements. Nevertheless,
it is apparent that the band's more established style – the infectious grooves,
singalong format, dark humour, and Johnny Marr's textured, melodic guitar
remained relevant. Not least, Morrissey's focus on Manchester and the North-West
highlighted the continuing significance of observation, everyday life and ironic
wit to British pop, evident in Sleeper's breakthrough release 'Inbetweener'.

As a parody of the ITV game show *Supermarket Sweep*, the promo video[39]
took full advantage of Dale Winton, the programme's presenter, who is seen
trailing behind Wener, filling the trolley and occasionally beaming at the camera
through the supermarket shelves. Supported by a trio of girly supermarket
shelf-stackers, and with narrative cuts to the laundrette and outside street, the
focus (like the eye of the camera) is predominantly on Wener. Close-ups ('she's
shopping for kicks, got the weekend to get through …') and tracking shots open out
her excursion around the supermarket, with neat cuts to the band, who are suitably
positioned in a supporting role. Harmonically simple – with an introduction based
on two alternating chords, F–F7, a 4/4 feel based largely on straight eights, layered
strummed guitars and a melodic line based on repetition and alternating in the
verse between two basic harmonies, F and B flat, the song's appeal is largely
due to Wener's deadpan vocal and witty rhyming couplets that deftly situate the
tedium of an everyday relationship ('He reads Harold Robbins, he flirts with
his neighbour / Ignores her at breakfast, he's reading his paper') and the cut to a
siren-like guitar interval in the middle-eight, which picks up on the 'he dreams of a
Roller, she dreams of a fast getaway' in the final line of the verse. As the song title
suggests, he 'is just the inbetweener', 'she'll leave him on Monday'.

It's not difficult to hear why 'Inbetweener' sits convincingly within the Britpop
genre. As the opening track to their 1995 studio album *Smart*, its witty lyrics and
riff-driven guitars attracted significant media interest, including a front-cover of
Wener on *New Musical Express* (14 January 1995). It was one of the first Britpop
albums to hit the charts and won the band a BPI gold disc for sales over 100,000.
The It Girl followed in May 1996. Produced by Stephen Street, who had earlier
worked with The Smiths, Morrissey and Blur, the album included 'Lie Detector',
'Statuesque', 'What Do I Do Now' (which had been released earlier as two single
versions in September 1995) and 'Sale of the Century' (released in April 1996).

The immediate impact of *The It Girl* lies in its catchy melodies, witty guitar
lines, and lyrics that come across as mini life-narratives. From the onset it is

---

[38]   See Sheila Whiteley, *Too Much Too Young: Popular Music, Age, and Gender*,
pp. 165–7.

[39]   At http://uk.youtube.com/watch?v=3MelvqUwCFs, accessed 6 January 2009.

apparent that Wener is the central 'character', telling the story, offering comments, personalizing the experience of the songs. 'Lie Detector', the opening track on the UK album,[40] for example, has no intro. Rather, the song launches into a breathy description of a girl that nobody trusts, 'a movie star arrangement, got a touch of Bergman to her face'. The lyrics, with their gossipy feel, confer a dramatic energy to the narrative: the vocal line dominates, with the guitars providing a rhythmic backing deeper in the mix. 'She' is the focus of attention, 'she wears suits and buys him flowers, / Smokes his cigarettes and bakes him cakes'. The words are simple and direct, but the subtext, with its references to Dostoyevsky, Einstein and 'a man from Stepford', implies a darker interpretation. She is, it seems, like a Stepford Wife – docile, submissive, beautiful, but strange, 'not to be trusted'. 'Lie Detector' is effective in setting the mood of the album, where catchy hooks and changing moods chart the ups and downs of relationships. Appropriately, the tempo and idiom of the songs vary with the different characters, from the introspective ('what did I do wrong' of 'What Do I Do Now'), the viciousness that accompanies a broken relationship ('after you left me you said I was cheap', 'Sale of the Century'), to the jangly, upbeat jauntiness that accompanies the 'old, kind, rich (bloke) with a dicky heart' of 'Nice Guy Eddie'.

Sleeper's third and final album, *Pleased to Meet You* (1997), was notable for its more cynical mood. As Howard Johnson wrote in the November issue of *Q*, it's 'the traditional coming-of-ager' notable for 'the way in which Wener wraps her voice around a deceptively simple hook in "Miss You" ... the whiff of a torch song in "Breathe"', the 'confident ballad [of] "Nothing is Changing"', and the acerbic 'Don't write, don't call me, unless you're dying' of 'Traffic Accident'.[41] While it is possible that the move to more personalized lyrics resonated with the tensions that presaged the break-up of the band, it is also suggested that Wener's gift for characterization, the often aggressive intellectualism that underpinned her sex-in-the-suburbs lyrics and, significantly, her assertive personality highlighted the problem that both Britpop and the music press contained a deep-rooted conservatism that resented her ultra-glam, ball-munching sophistication and dispassionate vocal delivery. *NME*, in particular, repeatedly castigated the male members of the band as 'sleeperblokes', a jibe that highlighted the disparity between Wener's high profile and their perceived role as seemingly personality-free backing musicians. It would appear, once again, that the combination of glamour *and* intellect can be problematic. Despite her obvious songwriting skills, Wener's tussles with the media compromised her significance as Britpop's biggest-selling female artist. As Johnson tellingly observed, '[w]ho'd have thought Lady Muck had it in her ... she's a girl with greater depth than the cartoon gobshite

---

[40]   The US and UK releases of *The It Girl* have different track orders, the former opening with 'Feeling Peaky', the latter with 'Lie Detector'.

[41]   At http://vu.morrissey-solo.com/sleeper/2000/info/rev/pleased.htm, accessed 11 May 2010.

she's often been portrayed as',[42] a backhanded compliment that highlights the popular press's inability to deal with the contradictions inherent in being both sexy and intellectually challenging.

Similar problems confronted Sonya Aurora Madan. Less than a year after the release of Echobelly's debut EP 'Bellyache' (October 1993), the novelty of an Asian woman fronting a rock band became the focus of media attention. As Hyder reflects, 'the very fact of a musician's Asianness is often enough to draw such attention',[43] not least when it is linked to a predominantly white Britpop scene. The combination of lyrics that fronted issues surrounding alienation and rejection, tuneful melodies, and Madan's 'exotic Asian babe'[44] image, provided the media with a heady mix, which was compounded by guitarist Glen Johansson's earlier career as editor of *Eros* (a Swedish porn magazine) and the addition, in spring 1994, of former Curve guitarist, Debbie Smith. It is interesting to note, however, that while issues of race, gender and sexuality[45] played an initial role in establishing Echobelly's media profile, critical reviews moved increasingly to an assessment of the band's sound, associating it primarily with Britpop rather than any of the less prominent Asian scenes.[46]

Musically and lyrically, the 'throbbing tremolo guitars and pent-up angst' (Epic Records liner notes) that characterized Echobelly's debut album, *Everybody's Got One* (1994), created a powerful backdrop for Madan's provocative lyrics and vocal style, where a combination of rueful irony and cheerful bounce evoked comparison with both Morrissey and Blondie. Appropriately, the album's title is an acronym, resonating with Madan's self-perception as a strong woman, fronting a band, anticipating attention. Its eleven tracks are confrontational, inciting Asian women to take control ('Give Her a Gun'), taking issue with the patriarchal assumptions surrounding marriage ('Father Ruler King Computer', a title inspired by Germaine Greer's *The Female Eunuch*), and post-abortion denial ('Bellyache'). It included the single 'Insomniac', where a promo video takes full advantage of Madan's dramatic presence.[47]

It is difficult not to read 'Insomniac' as a tongue-in-cheek comment on Britpop politics. Opening with a close-up shot of Madan, her eyes masked by black stage make-up, before a brief cut to her Union Jack T-shirt overprinted by the words 'My Country Too', the four-bar introduction foregrounds transformation, as she prances

---

[42]   Howard Johnson, *Q* Review of Sleeper, *Pleased to Meet You.*

[43]   Rehan Hyder, *Brimful of Asia: Negotiating Ethnicity on the UK Music Scene*, p. 101.

[44]   Raphael, *Never Mind the Bollocks*, p. 35.

[45]   Debbie Smith was originally in a group called Mouth Almighty, who she called 'the drinking lesbian's band', before joining the Darlings and Curve. She says she has never experienced homophobia in the press, but found it strange to be a black dyke guitarist in what is generically a white, male indie pop music (ibid., p. 54).

[46]   Hyder, *Brimful of Asia*, p. 101.

[47]   At http://uk.youtube.com/watch?v=o-BY1YU8Z1I, accessed 19 April 2010.

before the camera in a blonde wig, red sequinned dress and black boa. The contrast between blonde bombshell and boyish masked commentator continues throughout the song, highlighting the concept of masquerade and the reading of gender as a performative construction. As Madan remarked, '[i]t was a prime example of judging women on what they look like ... Is that what it takes? A wig and a bit of lipstick?'[48] At the same time, the lyrics highlight the cocaine-driven 'sublime' of Britpop's party-like atmosphere, a possible dig at London's nightclub lifestyle ('whatever turned you on, you put it up your nose' ... 'no sleep at all, will you carry me home'). Musically, the song is based on a 4/4 alternating verse/chorus structure, the former dominated by a bass guitar riff, the latter by the fuller texture of guitars, drum and bass. The vocal line with its sliding melodicism is evocative of Morrissey, not least in the final lines of the verse, where Madan's 'I think we're running out of time', the swooping melisma on 'go', and the 'will you be long dear' of the chorus recalls the 'I wouldn't say no' of 'Reel around the Fountain', creating a subtext that hints at the desire for more time, while suggesting a musical homage to one of the band's defining influences.

Their second album *On* (October 1995) is also characterized by Madan's thoughtful lyrics and poised vocal delivery. The opening track, 'Car Fiction', sets the mood, its upbeat guitar intro providing pace and drama to songs that interrogate the ups and downs of relationships against a backdrop of city life, prostitution and homelessness. While the social commentary and riff-driven songs could be described as typical mid-'90s Britpop, there is nevertheless an underlying edginess in such songs as 'Dark Therapy' with its chilling 'If you let me close your eyes/then I will take you all the way', and 'Pantyhose and Roses', where a focus on stereotyped role play ('she leaves her brains at the door', 'he cleans his car once a week ... dreams of sex on the street') is heightened by the monochromatic bleakness of the vocal delivery and a reflective chorus, where Madan's play on optimism/pessimistic realism ('it could change, it will never') creates a mood of yearning that culminates in a Morrissey-like melisma of resignation.

While it is recognized that a selective analysis of tracks can provide only a snapshot of Echobelly's five albums or, indeed, those by Sleeper and Elastica, as Madan reflected in an interview with Amy Raphael, her lyrics (like those by Frischmann and Wener) are written from a woman's perspective, albeit that they evidence obvious influences from Morrissey and, in common with Britpop bands generally, privilege social commentary within an urban frame of reference. It is also apparent that all three bands front their lead vocalist – both in promo videos and in the mix – and that, while the instrumentalists make an important contribution to the feel of the songs, they are primarily in a supporting role. What is distinctive, as my discussion shows, are the ways in which their songs and projected image effectively challenged the gender-stereotyping of Britpop through an ironic masquerade that highlights its laddist agenda of beer, babes and devout anti-intellectualism.

---

[48]   Raphael, *Never Mind the Bollocks*, p. 42.

Madan, for example, was acutely aware that her Asian parentage and upbringing would attract attention and while dismissing it as 'unimportant', the 'I don't belong here' from the band's debut EP comes across as throwing down the gauntlet and confronting prejudice head-on. There is also a shrewd understanding of the sexist attitude of the music business ('Any offers, any pre-sales we're the Umm & R') and the tabloid press ('Sell your soul, to papers that cater for cock 'n' roll'), which emerges in the lyrics of 'Talent' and the masquerade of 'Insomniac' where Madan's attempted role play ('I got dressed up as a transvestite') evokes memories of Dusty Springfield's beehive and camp tactics[49] and Annie Lennox's play on gendered images (a glamorous, long-haired blonde, a leather-clad brunette dominatrix and, briefly, an androgynous figure in a suit) in the video for 'Love is a Stranger'. The metamorphosis from woman to man, as Lennox pulled off her wig to reveal her cropped hair,[50] resonates with Madan's subversive gaze at the camera as she, too, pulls off her blonde wig to reveal a more androgynous image.

Madan's aim to be recognized as a lyricist rather than a girly pin-up also accounts for her often controversial subject-matter. 'Give Her a Gun', for example, fronts the problems of young Asian women who are subjected to forced marriage and honour-based brutality ('blame the mother / sell the sister'),[51] while 'Centipede' explores the paradox of being abused ('you're the evil world of the nursery rhyme') and loving your abuser ('you're my only friend, don't be cruel to me'). Like Morrissey's songs that hint at paedophilia,[52] the use of 'I/me/you' within a fictionalized mini-narrative in which the author takes the leading role heightens its dramatic impact, but as Madan reflects, 'most of my songs are written in a voyeuristic sense'[53] – an abused woman is an abused woman regardless of her background and religion.

What, then, do Elastica, Sleeper and Echobelly have in common with Britpop and to what extent do they highlight and challenge the seemingly exclusive boys'

---

[49]   As Patricia Juliana Smith notes, 'Using the tactics of camp, she adopted more visible (and modish) marginalized identities by "becoming" a gay man in drag (or, conversely, a *female* female impersonator) visually ... so pushing accepted notions of femininity to absurd extremes' – Patricia Juliana Smith (ed.), *The Queer Sixties*, p. xviii.

[50]   For a more detailed discussion see Whiteley, *Women and Popular Music*, pp. 119–29.

[51]   This is a problem that has only recently been confronted in Lord Lester's Forced Marriage Bill (2007) and is the subject matter of Jasvinder Sanhera's memoir *Shame* and recent sequel *Daughters of Shame*, which tell the stories of some of the thousands of women she has met through Karma Nirvana, the organization she founded in 1994 to support victims of forced marriage and honour-based violence.

[52]   See Sheila Whiteley, '"A Boy in the Bush": Morrissey, Sexuality and Dialogical Meanings' (forthcoming), which investigates four songs with possible paedophiliac connotations: 'The Hand That Rocks the Cradle', 'Handsome Devil', 'This Charming Man' and 'Reel around the Fountain', as well as the more explicit association with the Moors Murders in 'Suffer Little Children'.

[53]   Raphael, *Never Mind the Bollocks*, p. 44.

club image constructed by the popular press? More tellingly, why is it that the histories of Britpop rely so heavily on the anecdotal biographies of its principal protagonists Oasis, Blur and Pulp, so perpetuating the myth that its female-led bands were simply there as eye-candy, if they are mentioned at all? While one answer might focus on the longevity of the bands, with the implied suggestion that the continuing presence of Oasis and the prominence of Jarvis Cocker and Damon Albarn gives them a 'classic' status, situating them within the continuing family tree of guitar-inflected pop-rock, the problems surrounding such a teleological argument parallel earlier assessments of the Beatles, implying a longevity that was not inevitable at the time.[54] It is also suggested that the prevailing attitude of the popular press towards Frischmann, Wener and Madan – the emphasis on image, novelty value and eclecticism – highlighted an inability to take on board their ironic deconstruction of gender. A 1994 cover of *Select*, for example, showed Frischmann dressed as a man with a cigar in her mouth; Madan was labelled a 'dyke' when she cropped her hair; while *Loaded* predictably bypassed Wener's witty lyrics, voting her instead 'the 63rd most shaggable girl on the planet' (January 1995). While it could be suggested that such examples simply evidence the emphasis on sensationalism characteristic of celebrity culture – reproducing the dominant culture's patriarchal, racial and heterosexual gaze – it is nevertheless evident that gender remained an important issue within Britpop. Echobelly, for example, had been asked to change the title of their debut album *Today, Tomorrow, Sometime, Never*, which had been taken from a suffragette's reply when asked when women would be given the vote. As Madan reflected at the time, 'I feel led by similar frustrations, politically and morally, encompassing feminism and gender'.[55]

So is Raphael's contention that Britpop 'didn't challenge ... it didn't threaten blokes' justified? My answer is a qualified 'yes'. There is no overt confrontation, no battle for ascendancy by its three female-led bands. Rather, their lyrics evidence an ability to be subversive, to highlight inequality, to poke fun at laddism's macho posturing, to sell records without selling out.[56] Even so, it is evident

---

[54] Blur's third album was released in 1994; 1995 saw the battle between Oasis and Blur, with Oasis's massive sales in the UK and the US suggesting a parallel between the 1960s British invasion of the US music market and attracting the moniker Britpop. By 1997 Blur was again looking to America for influences; the Spice Girls brought a new dimension to pop – so-called 'playful feminism'; and as John Harris reflects, the release of Oasis's third album *Be Here Now* marks the moment Britpop ended. John Harris, *Britpop! Cool Britannia and the Spectacular Demise of English Rock*, p. 202.

[55] Colin Larkin (ed.), *The Virgin Encyclopedia of Popular Music*, p. 420.

[56] Sleeper's three albums all entered the UK charts (*Smart*, February 1995, 5; *The It Girl*, May 1996, 5; *Pleased to Meet You*, October 1997, 7); Elastica's self-titled debut LP entered the charts at number 1 (March 1995) and was nominated for the Mercury Prize; Echobelly produced seven albums in total, with *Everybody's Got One* (1994) reaching 8 on the UK pop charts, and three singles from their second album *On* (1996) reaching the UK's

that the definitions of Englishness and national cultural identity foregrounded by mainstream Britpop bands – who is included/who is excluded – are both heightened and challenged. The media attention on Echobelly, for example, draws attention to Debbie Smith's sexuality, and to the band's multicultural heritage (Asian, Swedish, Afro-Caribbean), an observation also relevant to Sleeper's bass player Diid Osman, who was born in Somalia, Africa. It is also apparent that, while all three bands were situated within the London scene, and benefited from their association with such high-profile performers as Morrissey, Damon Albarn and Michael Stipe of REM, their musical perspective and challenging attitude is informed by such role models as Kim Deal and Debbie Harry, so broadening Britpop's emphasis on regional/national identity through an expansion of its musical and cultural reference points. Not least, while it could be argued that all three bands were of their time (as sales of their albums and singles suggest), it is important to balance their significance to Britpop by broadening the frame of reference to include such contemporary female singer-songwriters as Tori Amos, Björk and PJ Harvey,[57] whose image, controversial lyrics and challenging vocals were scathingly summed up by *Q*'s group cover photo and the headline 'Hips. Tits. Lips. Power' (May 1994), so demonstrating parallels with the sexual stereotyping of Frischmann, Madan and Wener. More recently, the mainstream success of, for example, Amy Winehouse, Lily Allen, Duffy, Adele, Estelle, Corinne Bailey Rae, KT Tunstall and Florence Welch has continued to demonstrate that women whose music communicates a sense of personal emotion, and who can write and perform great songs (whether in the field of 'blue-eyed' soul, neo-soul, pop, rock or the more established feminine terrain of the singer-songwriter), have become definitive representatives of their respective genres. What is depressing, however, is the continuing gossipy focus on image, lifestyle and attitude that all too often outweighs their very real achievement and presence as key players in British popular music. But then, as the story goes, isn't this always the case with strong, groovy women?[58]

Top 20. Debbie Smith (rhythm guitar) left the band before the release of *Lustra* and the album was not commercially successful; disillusioned, Madan and Johansson started their own indie label, Fryup Records. Wener has since published four novels.

[57]   It is interesting to note that P.J. Harvey refused to be included under the Britpop banner.

[58]   To paraphrase Country Joe's reflection on the death of Janis Joplin – which he tellingly attributed to sexism. For further discussion of the issues surrounding 'integration v. self-identity', see Whiteley, *Women and Popular Music*, pp. 65–9.

Chapter 5

Missing Links: Britpop Traces, 1970–1980

Andy Bennett

A period often referred to in the historical lineage of Britpop, yet not documented in detail, consists of the years between 1969, by which time the British invasion had lost momentum, through to the early 1980s and the emergence of groups such as the Smiths, the La's, Ride and the Stone Roses (typically regarded as forerunners of Britpop). This period was characterized by a succession of performers whose music was also informed by a heavily articulated sense of Englishness – sometimes quite subconsciously. In many cases, the influence of such artists can also arguably be heard in Britpop. During the early to mid-1970s, a key example was Slade (whom leading Britpop group Oasis went on to cite as a primary influence). During the mid-1970s, Steve Harley and Cockney Rebel purveyed a mockney accent and musical eclecticism that bridged the gap between the likes of the Small Faces and Blur while imprinting a local distinctiveness on English pop during a period when many British artists pursued a transatlantic sound and audience. In the late 1970s, post-punk and new wave artists like the Jam, XTC and the Buzzcocks imprinted their music with lyrical qualities that bespoke a provincial Englishness – which in XTC's case would later develop, as with the Beatles, into a studio-based musical and lyrical collage of self-consciously selected cultural referents bound up with 'little' England. During the late 1970s and early 1980s, bands such as Madness and Squeeze continued to engage with aspects of mundane, everyday English life in their songcraft.

On the basis of the definitions of Britpop offered by critics and musicians in the mid-1990s, each of the artists referred to above could be said to have possessed quintessentially 'English' characteristics but appeared too early to be directly associated with Britpop. Certainly, all of these artists covered similar territory, musically, lyrically and aesthetically, to later artists categorized under the Britpop banner. To put this more succinctly, each of these artists – through a combination of accent, lyric content and musical aesthetics – displayed particular traits that align them with the Britpop rhetoric. This chapter considers the relationship of such groups to the English music tradition and their bearing on the Britpop scene of the mid-1990s. It is important to state at the outset that, given the time period focused on in this chapter, it has been necessary to delimit the number of artists discussed. The purpose of the chapter is not to discuss the merits of 1970s artists as forerunners of Britpop in any holistic sense. Rather, the intention is to consider how a particular range of artists, chosen because of their prominence at particular moments in the rapidly changing English popular music landscape of the 1970s, serve as a critical link between the late 1960s and early 1980s as purveyors of an English aesthetic. Wherever possible the term English has been used to distinguish specifically English bands who achieved national and, in some cases, international prominence during the years in question. In other places, the term British has been used to denote the interface between English performers and national institutions such as radio, television and the music industry.

Off the Map: English Rock and Pop in the Early 1970s

With several notable exceptions,[1] the early 1970s are not generally recognized as a particularly innovative or politically significant era in the history of contemporary English popular music. The disengagement of English popular music with politics during the first half of the decade could be perhaps attributed to the bleak political landscape as evident cracks began to appear in the postwar consensus and political divisions became re-entrenched. In early 1974, the Conservative Government was forced to introduce a three-day working week in response to depleted coal supplies as a result of strike action called by the National Union of Mineworkers in 1972 and 1974. A change of government in 1974 did little to stem the economic crisis in Britain.

Per capita GDP growth averaged 2.5 per cent between 1976 and 1979, while unemployment rose to 5 per cent.[2] The general election of 1979 saw the landslide victory of the Conservative Party under the leadership of Margaret Thatcher, whose 12-year period in office would see the transformation of Britain from an industrial to post-industrial nation. Against this austere socio-political backdrop, English popular music of the early 1970s is typically represented as bland, effete and largely escapist. Wedged between the musically and politically charged counter-culture of the late 1960s and emergence of punk and new wave towards the end of the 1970s, the early 1970s are often depicted as dominated by glam rock and bubblegum, and latterly transatlantic pop and stadium rock. During the early 1970s themselves, the discourse around music was significantly more nuanced with considerable critical acclaim reserved for artists in the rock, folk and folk-rock fusion fields. Even then, with the exception of folk and folk-rock, which tended to have their own specialist audiences, critics were far less interested in charting traces of Englishness in English popular music than in identifying aspects of musical authenticity as these came through in conventions of performance and musicianship. English rock and pop-rock performers tended to receive attention not because of any perceived 'English' qualities in their music and lyrics, nor because of any commentary that such artists might make on the state of the English

---

[1] See, for example, David Buckley's (2000) work on David Bowie: *Strange Fascination – David Bowie: The Definitive Story*.

[2] Colin Leys, *Politics in Britain: An Introduction*.

– or British – nation, but rather because of their perceived credibility as musicians and/or songwriters overall.

That a rhetoric of Englishness was significantly divorced at this point from the way in which critics and taste-makers regarded English pop and rock output is only too evident in a recently issued *The Old Grey Whistle Test*[3] retrospective DVD box-set where a range of English pop, rock, and folk-rock artists, among them Roy Harper, Lindisfarne and Brinsley Schwarz, are introduced in performance with no reference at all made to their Englishness and/or commentary (political or otherwise) on English life.[4] Ironically, the one attempt to portray a sense of Englishness in relation to a performance included in the box-set involves long-time presenter Bob Harris offering a reading of one-time Small Faces singer/guitarist Steve Marriott's performance of 'Black Coffee' with post-Small Faces group Humble Pie. In describing Marriott's performance as an example of his typical 'Artful Dodger' style,[5] Harris appears to be harking back to the Marriott's days with the Small Faces rather than on his work with Humble Pie, a band that traded squarely on a transatlantic style of boogie blues.

To try to overturn the history of 1970s English rock and pop in any wholesale sense, to re-read an entire historical minutia in terms of its unacknowledged Englishness is not the purpose of this chapter – though the chapter will endeavour to address this issue with reference to specific examples of English artists. Before embarking on this task, however, it is worth noting that, even among some of those English rock and pop artists where attempting to make a direct Britpop connection would be something of a stretch, an aesthetic was clearly at work in their music that often functioned to place them in a peculiarly 'English' space. For example, artists such as Peter Skellern came to prominence through the performance of piano-based ballads stamped with a distinctly English aesthetic. First coming to prominence in 1972 with his top 3 single 'You're a Lady', Skellern sang with a clipped English accent that, among with other elements of his songcraft, located the historical lineage of his musical influences in the inter-war years. This quality in Skellern's music gave him a further, minor, hit in 1978 with 'Love is the Sweetest Thing' (featuring the Grimethorpe Colliery Band).

---

[3]   Apart from *Top of the Pops*, during the 1970s *The Old Grey Whistle Test* was the only other dedicated popular music programme on British television. Unlike *Top of the Pops*, however, which had an uninterrupted run since its launch in 1964 until its last show in 2006, including spawning a special archive edition, *TOTP 2*, in the mid-1990s, *The Old Grey Whistle Test* ran in seasons between 1971 and 1987. In its early years, *The Old Grey Whistle Test* catered specifically for album-orientated bands. Artists such as Elton John, Alice Cooper and Queen benefited from early exposure on the programme.

[4]   Ironically, the Roy Harper song chosen for inclusion in the DVD compilation is 'One of Those Days in England'.

[5]   A character from Charles Dickens's novel *Oliver Twist*, set in the East End of London in the nineteenth century. As a child, Marriott had played the Artful Dodger in a stage production of Oliver Twist based on Lionel Bart's musical adaptation of the novel.

The same era saw a string of other hits released by English rock and pop groups who, while not as distinctively 'English' in their style, were nevertheless apt to draw on English traits in highly distinctive ways. For example, in 1977, Queen released the song 'Good Old Fashioned Lover Boy', taken from their *A Day at the Races* album released the previous year. Written by the group's vocalist, the late Freddie Mercury, the song developed a mock 1920s and '30s, quasi-music hall style that the group had perfected on the album tracks 'Lazing on a Sunday Afternoon' and 'Seaside Rendezvous' from their previous album *A Night at the Opera*, released in 1975. In particular Mercury sang the song with a faux Oxbridge inflection designed to mimic the style of a stereotypical English gentleman portrayed by earlier performers such as Noël Coward. Guitarist Brian May supplemented the song's English aesthetic with a mock brass and woodwind ensemble created using his signature multiple-overdubbed guitar sound; this was accentuated using compression, envelope filters and other studio effects to dramatically alter the sonic properties of the electric guitar he had built as a schoolboy with help from his father. Again, in the context of the mid-1970s, such experimentation made for a sound that, despite its intended humour and mimicry, was very much a nostalgic statement of a traditional English identity in the face of an increasing trend towards transatlantic rock (a trend that Queen would themselves embrace with future albums such as *Jazz* and *The Game*).

'Take Me Back 'Ome'

The rise to prominence of groups such as Queen, and fellow English rock band Mott the Hoople, came towards the end of the glam era (with each of these groups adopting to some extent a glam aesthetic). A number of writers[6] have suggested that in its heyday glam was a peculiar brand of British and American influences, the androgynous image of transatlantic artists such as Lou Reed, David Bowie and Roxy Music saying much more about the shifting nature of gender politics than anything related to aspects of national and/or local identity.[7] Arguably, however, there were two distinct sides to the British glam scene. Whereas the more 'serious' glam rock of transatlantic-orientated English artists such as Bowie and Roxy Music commanded critical acclaim and a firm footing in the album charts, Britain also produced a second tier of glam artists, whose allegiance to glam was often highly opportunist and for whom commercial success was largely measured in terms of singles sales. Moreover, unlike their transatlantic peers who had gravitated to music through art school training,[8] many of the more quintessentially English 'glam-pop' artists had served a musical apprenticeship working on the

---

[6]   See, for example, M. van Cagle, *Reconstructing Pop/Subculture: Art, Rock and Andy Warhol*.

[7]   See also Dick Hebdige, *Subculture: The Meaning of Style*.

[8]   See Simon Frith and Howard Horne, *Art into Pop*.

British pub and club circuit, the latter bringing a distinctly working-class English aesthetic to their style and performance punctuated by thick, unashamed regional accents. A notable example of this is the popular early 1970s group Slade. Slade originated from the English Midlands, a region already considered as the English heartland of heavy rock due to the Birmingham origins of Black Sabbath and also Led Zeppelin vocalist Robert Plant. Although grounded in a rock style, Slade's early success saw them sporting a skinhead style, the latter encompassing its own discourse as a provincial English identity based around machismo and camaraderie, and strong associations with working-class identity.[9] Within a brief time, however, Slade abandoned this image and appropriated elements of the emergent glam style. However, a distinctly English flavour remained within the band, this being exemplified primarily through a vocal style, musical approach and aesthetic attitude to stardom that marked them as a provincial English band. At a time when many English pop and rock singers adopted a transatlantic accent, Slade vocalist Noddy Holder stood out due to the more characteristically English element in his vocal delivery. The regional flavour of this was accentuated through the attempt to reproduce phonetically a regional English accent in titles and lyrics of Slade songs, as seen for example with the 1973 hits 'Cum on Feel the Noize' and 'Take Me Back 'Ome'. Although ostensibly a tongue-in-cheek device – and something that resonated well with the equally unpretentious style of Slade's music – such mis-spelt words were a far more accurate representation of Holder's actual pronunciation and thus emphasized his deeply regional accent. Never an aspect of 1960s English popular music,[10] where 'Englishness' in vocal delivery was generally played out through the 'Cockney rock'[11] of groups such as the Small Faces, the provincial elements introduced by Slade would become more widely articulated in 1990s Britpop, notably with Manchester band Oasis and Sheffield-based Pulp. In particular, the style of Pulp vocalist Jarvis Cocker was instantly recognized partly due to his use of elongated vowel sounds characteristic of his native South Yorkshire dialect.

Musically, too, Slade's stylistic repertoire, although drawing on elements from US-inspired rhythm and blues, still very much a basis for guitar-driven pop-rock at this time, embraced a more gritty, unpolished aesthetic that in many ways resembled a proto-punk style.[12] Although it would be presumptuous to describe this style as quintessentially 'English', its more aggressive tone, something accentuated by Holder's vocal delivery, set it apart from the more transatlantic

---

[9]   See, for example, John Clarke, 'The Skinheads and the Magical Recovery of Community'.

[10]   With the obvious exception of novelty groups such as Adge Cutler & the Wurzels' who were, in fact, more commercially successful in the early 1970s.

[11]   Dave Laing, 'Cockney Rock'.

[12]   Andy Bennett, 'The Forgotten Decade: Rethinking the Popular Music of the 1970s'.

rock fare of the time and ensured Slade's reputation as a primarily 'British' band.[13] Compositionally and sonically, Slade's guitar-heavy sound – emphasized by the group's having both a rhythm and lead guitarist (common in the 1960s but far less common in the 1970s and something of a novelty among glam rock bands) – was a considerable influence on punk and also an integral aspect of 1990s Britpop. Notable in this case are Oasis who, in addition to citing Slade as a key musical influence, covered 'Cum on Feel the Noize', releasing this as a double A-side along with 'Don't Look Back in Anger' in 1995.

Slade's unequivocal attachment to place was also something that set them apart from other glam rockers and, for that matter, most of the 1970s rock and pop fraternity. When references to place were made in 1970s rock music, it usually came through song titles, such as Led Zeppelin's 'Black Country Woman' (a reference to Robert Plant's West-Midlands roots). For Slade, however, their connection with place was made far more immediate. For example, television footage shot at the very height of Slade's popularity in Britain during 1973 portrayed them very much as 'local lads'. Thus, in one sequence, lead guitarist Dave Hill is seen emerging from the driveway of a large house he had recently purchased in the Wolverhampton area to speak to local fans. In later years, following their departure from the band, Slade members Noddy Holder and Jim Lea spoke in a television retrospective about the group's continuing attachment to the Midlands even as their commercial success frequently took them further afield. Lea, for example, remembers the long night-time drives back home following gigs in London, a memory supported by Holder's sentiment '[y]ou can take the boy out of the Black Country, but you can't take the Black Country out of the boy'. The refusal on the part of Slade as a collective to relocate to London, then the unchallenged centre of the UK music industry, was rare at this point. During the Britpop years, the tendency of bands to remain in their home cities, even as their national – and often global – popularity grew, became more common. A pertinent example of this was the group Pulp, who remained based in Sheffield throughout their career.

Mockney Rebels

Following the demise of glam, British radio and music television shows such as *Top of the Pops* became increasingly dominated by American artists. Moreover, emergent English bands of the era, notably the Electric Light Orchestra and Supertramp (actually two-parts American), crafted a transatlantic pop sound

---

[13]   Indeed, Slade's adopted style made the group very difficult to market in the US. During the mid-1970s Slade adopted a new, more melodic musical direction partly in an attempt to secure a following there. The group also periodically relocated to the US but subsequently returned to the UK during the late 1970s, enjoying a renaissance with hits such as 'We'll Bring the House Down' and 'Run Runaway', both of which marked something of a return to the musical style that had originally brought Slade success.

designed to appeal to a crossover (that is, albums and singles) market. Even during this period, however, the transatlantic pop feel that dominated British pop was occasionally broken by the quirkiness of a group or artist exuding an altogether more English aesthetic. London-based group Steve Harley and Cockney Rebel (formerly Cockney Rebel) are a case in point. Between 1974 and 1976, the group enjoyed a string of hits including 'Judy Teen', 'Mr. Soft' and '(Come up and See Me) Make Me Smile'. Singer and songwriter Steve Harley was in many ways a proto-Britpopper on several accounts. Noted by the British music press for his arrogance, and something of an enigma in the British pop world due to an image that drew heavily on Stanley Kubrick's highly controversial film about English gang culture *A Clockwork Orange*, Harley was a highly distinctive artist, and musical force, in a singles chart dominated by the transatlantic pop of artists such as Rod Stewart and Chicago. The songs of Cockney Rebel were deeply accentuated by Harley's 'mockney' vocal style. In terms of its association with Britpop, many consider the 'mockney' style of artists such as Damon Albarn, lead vocalist with Blur, to have evolved directly from 1960s groups, notably the Small Faces. In the context of the English pop soundscape, however, it seems likely that, whether explicitly stated or not, Harley's own mockney-take may have also been influential on the 1990s Britpop scene. Modelled to some extent on the style of Steve Marriott, but arguably more exaggerated, and blended with a glam aesthetic, there are obvious parallels between Harley's vocal approach and that adopted by Albarn on Blur tracks such as 'Country House'. Perhaps most important in this respect was Harley's experimentation with the mockney vocal style within a broader, more diverse musical repertoire. If the Small Faces had done much of their mockney posturing within a faux music-hall tradition, Harley went well beyond this trope, embracing a range of orchestral instruments, early synthesizer voicing, slightly exotic time signatures, and multi-layered vocal harmonies. In many ways, the complex and multi-layered arrangements of Britpop groups such as Blur and Pulp would appear to draw on these and other more musically accomplished English rock groups, such as 10cc, whose well-crafted, studio-orientated singles were a mainstay of the pop-radio soundscape during the 1970s when a number of future Britpop artists were first becoming aware of and taking an interest in music.

The mockney verve continued into the punk and post-punk years. As Laing[14] has illustrated, integral to the emergence of punk was the London pub rock scene of the early 1970s. Created against a large extent as a backlash to progressive and stadium rock bands such as Yes, Genesis and Emerson Lake & Palmer, pub rock adopted a more straightforward musical aesthetic and emphasized the importance of connection between performer and audience, something felt to be more easily achieved in the pub venue. Although undoubtedly a key contributor to an English inflection in popular music during the early 1970s, pub rock remained a distinctly low-key scene. For the most part it was restricted primarily to the London pub, and to a lesser degree the national college circuits. Few pub rock bands released

---

[14]　Dave Laing, *One Chord Wonders: Power and Meaning in Punk Rock*.

singles and were thus seldom heard on the radio or seen on British chart show *Top of the Pops*, then the critical point of television exposure for bands in the UK. In many ways, then, the pub rock legacy and its contribution to English popular music was more readily observed at a national level with the emergence of punk, a style and scene that quickly garnered widespread public attention – and outrage – through the media attention directed at the Sex Pistols.[15] Many of those punk, and latterly new wave, artists that emerged from 1976 onwards had served an important apprenticeship as part of the pub rock scene. Indeed, as Friedlander points out, '[s]ome band members, such as Joe Strummer of the 101ers [subsequently guitarist and vocalist with the Clash], simply stepped over the line from pub to punk'.[16]

A distinctly mockney inflection of the pub rock style was seen in second-generation punk group Sham 69. Originating in the Surrey village of Hersham (from where the band drew its name), lead vocalist Jimmy Pursey presented himself as an organic intellectual and 'man of the people'. In songs such as 'Hurry Up Harry' and 'Hersham Boys' Pursey, singing with a highly exaggerated mockney accent, explored aspects of local identity, male camaraderie and bravado as these expressed themselves in the place where he had grown up. Equally embedded in Pursey's lyrics is a passion for and celebration of working-class leisure. 'Hurry Up Harry' is an interesting case in point, combining a melody and chorus lyric clearly inspired by the English pub song tradition with a punk-derived guitar riff and rhythm section – the pub song association being completed by a pub pianist-style piano solo (comically mimed by Pursey on *Top of the Pops* during the song's stint in the UK Top 10 in 1978).[17] Such references to mundane, working-class life were to become a mainstay of Britpop in the 1990s when accounts of drink and excess were again portrayed as an antidote to boredom and frustration, and also a driver for friendship and sexual associations, in working-class and lower middle-class neighbourhoods. Similarly, Sham 69's celebratory association with the working-class 'boot-boy' culture, summarily documented in 'If the Kids Are United' and 'Hersham Boys', could be seen as a critical link between the early skinhead – and laddish – image of Slade circa 1970–71 and the 'new laddism' of Oasis. What each of these groups had in common, despite their appearance in quite different eras of British popular music, was the production of anthemic songs that translated easily from record to concert hall to football terrace.

Ian Dury & the Blockheads were another act whose mockney inflection contributed to their distinctiveness in the British popular music of the late 1970s. Formerly Kilburn & the High Roads (named after Kilburn High Road in London), a favourite act of the London pub rock scene, Ian Dury & the Blockheads created

---

[15]   See ibid.

[16]   Paul Friedlander, *Rock and Roll: A Social History*.

[17]   The re-popularization of the pub song tradition was to be fully realized two years later with the success of London-based duo Chas & Dave who, together with drummer Mick Burt, drew directly on the pub song genre in a series of Top 20 hits including 'Rabbit', 'The Sideboard Song' and 'Gertcha'.

a style that combined a highly eclectic songcraft with Dury's roughshod vocal style. Via a string of hits including 'Sex & Drugs & Rock & Roll', 'What a Waste' and 'I Want to Be Straight', the Blockheads often explored the more seedy side of ordinary, everyday English life. In doing so they helped to broaden the palate of public anticipation when it came to lyrical treatments of 'Little England', a door that would be further opened some sixteen years later in Britpop songs such as Oasis's 'She's Electric', Pulp's 'Do You Remember the First Time?' and Blur's 'Park Life'. Dury's links with Britpop are further evident in his references to English commodities, such as the Ford Cortina, and English place names, for example, Billericay, in his lyrics. A novelty in English pop during the 1970s, this became a staple device through which Britpop artists married their musical output with a highly self-conscious English aesthetic during the mid-1990s. Moreover, as Ian Collinson observes (see Chapter 10), this trend has continued with post-Britpop English guitar bands such as the Kaiser Chiefs and the Arctic Monkeys.

England's Dreaming

The often mooted notion that punk and post-punk served to redefine British, or even 'English', popular music in any wholesale way during the late 1970s is arguably more myth than reality. Even at the height of punk's success in 1977, the UK singles charts still contained a high percentage of commercially orientated pop. English pop-progsters the Electric Light Orchestra's double album *Out of the Blue*, released in the UK in October 1977, remained in the UK Albums Chart for 113 consecutive weeks generating four hit singles (the first double album to do so). Similarly, progressive rock giants Yes and Emerson Lake & Palmer, neither of whom had been noted for their singles success, had Top 10 hits in 1977 with 'Wondrous Stories' and 'Fanfare for the Common Man'[18] respectively.

Perhaps more pertinent is the evident contrast during the late 1970s between more mainstream English popular music and the new musical territories that opened up as the repertoire of punk expanded and gave rise to post-punk and 'new wave' musical sensibilities. Within these a punk aesthetic often merged with a repertoire of sounds borrowed from different pop and rock genres but reworked into a style that quite self-consciously played off an English frame of reference. A group who led the way in this respect were the Jam. Formed in Woking in 1974 by Paul Weller, Bruce Foxton and Rick Buckler, the Jam's musical and stylistic identity owed far more to mod than punk, as was to become quickly evident following the group's initial chart success with the obviously punk-inspired 'In the City' (from the album of the same name). Subsequent hits drew more clearly on the group's mod influences, also reintroducing instrumental voicings from this

---

[18]   A rock reworking of the original symphonic piece composed in 1942 by American composer Aaron Copland as a tribute to Second World War servicemen.

era, such as the jangly Rickenbacker guitar sound (the latter becoming a mainstay of Britpop in the 1990s) and the 'Leslie' organ sound (produced by powering an electric organ, typically a Hammond, through a special cabinet, produced by the Leslie company, with a rotating speaker). In addition to a rapid succession of self-penned hits (largely written by vocalist-guitarist Weller) the group also paid tribute to the Kinks, a primary influence on their own style, with a cover of Ray Davies's 'David Watts', a song that assumed a new resonance when sung in a context of 1970s educational reform and the alleged equality of opportunity ushered in by the comprehensive school system.[19] Sung by Weller with a gritty conviction, 'David Watts' brought home the fact that equal opportunity within the school setting was still largely a rhetorical exercise, with educational achievement still being interwoven with class background and associated peer group status. Also significant in charting the Jam's role in the lineage of English popular music from the 1960s through to Britpop is their adoption of British symbolism and imagery. Prompted by another key influence, the Who, the Jam reintroduced the salient image of the Union Jack as a marker of national identity. This came at a time when such imagery, together with the rehearsals of national identity that went along with it, had, following a period of non-reference during the first half of the 1970s, been savagely critiqued by punk rock artists such as the Sex Pistols. In later years, Weller would claim that the Jam's pro-nationalist, pro-Thatcherite stance had been misrepresented by the British music press. At the time, however, this re-engagement with such a potent symbol of nationalism in British pop, together with the Jam's high level of commercial success as both a singles and album group, sparked a new interest in the potency of British popular music and its distinctiveness as distinct from the angry pessimism of punk and overarching presence of transatlantic pop.

For all their visual investment in British symbolism, however, the Jam's lyrical exploration of post-industrial England often painted a far more critical picture of a nation undoubtedly in crisis. The group's pointed and stripped-back musical arrangements provided a fitting backdrop for a new post-punk vocal approach that drew unashamedly on regional English accents and the evocation of an English vernacular. Songs such as 'The Eton Rifles' launched a satirical assault on the public school system and the upper-class sensibilities underpinning it. Considering the state of the English nation from a different perspective, the song 'That's Entertainment' along with 'A Town Called Malice', from the Jam's final album *The Gift*, discussed the ravages of post-industrialization on the socio-cultural fabric of the working-class provincial English town. Both tracks offered a critically bleak insight into the plight of the ordinary English citizen at the beginning of the 1980s

---

[19]   The comprehensive school was widely introduced in England and Wales during the early- to mid-1970s. Replacing the former 11+ system, which selected children for grammar and secondary school education according to tests in reading, writing and mathematics at the age of 11, the comprehensive system was considered to offer equality of educational opportunity to a greater number of children regardless of academic ability.

– jobless, impoverished, politically disenfranchised, vulnerable to acts of violence and disillusioned.

Little England

Against such a bleak rendering of a nation in crisis during the late 1970s and early 1980s, the more stoic, and often comical, renderings of Little England heard in the lyrics of 1960s artists such as Ray Davies and Steve Marriott again came through in English popular music. A particularly off-beat example of this, and one that remains relatively unique to this day, was Jilted John's 1978 eponymously titled hit. Not quite a novelty song, yet clearly intended as a parody, 'Jilted John' climbed to number 1 in the charts and saw John on *Top of the Pops* backed by a misfit band self-consciously riding the punk bandwagon. John himself presented as a typical, slightly ruffled and unkempt teenager (later to become a staple, and more precocious, image among Britpop bands), his semi-rant-style lyric building on a heritage of self-mockery and English anecdote that situated the song and artist in a distinctly localized idiom. That Jilted John (the song and the artist) chimed so effectively with the sensibilities of a local audience while failing to translate to international markets says much about their local specificity – John singing with a highly pronounced English accent, the song racking up a series of instantly recognizable local idioms such as 'watching *telly*', crying all the way to the 'chip shop' (rhymed comically with 'bus stop'). A second example of this Little England sensibility is seen with John Otway, who, together with Wild Willy Barrett, produced a number of pointed, post-punk ballads, most notably 'Really Free' and, to a lesser extent, 'Headbutts'. Again the tenor of Otway's songcraft was a comical rendering of mundane English life.

But Little Englandism as explored in the English popular music of the late 1970s was not purely a parochial affair. On the contrary, the era also saw the emergence of several artists for whom a distinctively English aesthetic became something of an international trademark, securing such artists critical acclaim and sometimes significant commercial success at an international level. Among this category of English bands was XTC. Formed in Swindon in 1976 by Andy Partridge and Colin Moulding, XTC first came to prominence as a post-punk band with songs such as 'Statue of Liberty'. As punk gave way to new wave, XTC's musical style began to develop, demonstrating as it did a much richer level of influences and diversity than had been suggested by their earlier punk-influenced material. Dwelling on the 'quiet desperation' expressed by Pink Floyd's Roger Waters some years earlier as a quintessentially English quality, XTC's songs often focused on the melodrama of mundane English life, as seen with songs such as 'Senses Working Overtime' and 'Making Plans for Nigel'. The latter song in particular touched an important nerve, lamenting the destructive effects of dominating parents on teenage hopes and aspirations (symbolized in the narrativized figure of 'Nigel', an apparently unassuming and underachieving son). Cast in a time of deindustrialization and rapidly disappearing skilled apprenticeships, the poignant reference to 'British Steel' is followed by the prophetic reference to a young man's future being 'as good as sealed'. If groups such as the Jam had been concerned with a critical commentary on the class inequalities of English life, XTC brought a new perspective to this – their songs suggestive of an English middle class who felt equally trapped and frustrated due to life chances that seemed equally steeped in tradition.

Another English singer-songwriter whose fixation, at least in his earlier work, lay in the idiosyncrasies of Little England was Joe Jackson. In an early television appearance, on *The Old Grey Whistle Test*, in 1978 Jackson included the song 'Sunday Papers' from his then recently released debut album *Look Sharp!* Offering a satirical critique on the British tabloid press and its alleged hold on the public imagination of its largely working-class readership, 'Sunday Papers' demonstrated a clear point of departure in English popular music, supplanting the oblique social criticism of punk with a new witticism blended with laconic humour. Such qualities were further explored by Jackson in songs such as 'Is She Really Going Out with Him?' and 'It's Different for Girls', pithy explorations of boy–girl romance with a clear nod to the new masculinities that would be further explored by Britpop artists such as Jarvis Cocker.

Little England English melodrama was also a staple topic of Squeeze. Formed in 1974 in Deptford, Squeeze was based around the songwriting partnership of Chris Difford and Glen Tilbrook (who would later be compared in the British music press to Lennon and McCartney). Squeeze's lyrical repertoire ran the full gamut of everyday mundane tragedy and triumph, checking as it did a range of popular cultural referents (for example *The Sweeney*[20]) and familiar locations (such as Clapham Common). Very much a pop musical rendition of 'kitchen sink', a British film genre of the late 1950s and early 1960s that depicted English working-class life with a blunt social realism, one of Squeeze's most popular songs 'Up the Junction' even took its name from one of the more celebrated films of the kitchen-sink genre (itself based on a 1963 novel by Nell Dunn). Delivered in first person by Tilbrook, whose Lennon-esque vocal style was a further ingredient in the professed Englishness of the Squeeze sound, 'Up the Junction' recounts the doomed love affair of a young English couple whose initial infatuation with each other is marred by the responsibilities of parenthood, their relationship becoming increasingly acrimonious due to the man's acquired drinking habit and resulting domestic abuse. In other songs, such as 'Slap and Tickle', Squeeze further explore the everyday frustrations of the little English couple, humorously working through lyrical scenarios[21] of drunkenness, chauvinistic posturing, public squabbling and 'morning-after' remorse typically associated with working-class life.

---

[20]   A highly successful London-based police drama from the mid-1970s starring John Thaw (later of *Inspector Morse* fame) noted for its gritty depiction of crime and corruption.

[21]   It is significant to note that Squeeze's early material was released in the pre-video age and thus relied primarily on the vivid descriptions contained in Difford and Tilbrook's

In the same era that Squeeze enjoyed their initial chart success, another English group who would build a highly successful career forging a characteristic mirth and wit with catchy radio-friendly songs emerged in the form of Madness. Originating from Camden Town in London and led by charismatic lead vocalist Suggs (Graham McPherson), Madness took their musical inspiration from ska (Britain at this point experiencing a ska revival). Their first single 'The Prince' paid tribute to the group's idol Prince Buster (born Cecil Bustamente Campbell), a leading ska and rocksteady artist from Kingston, Jamaica. Although ska remained a key musical element in Madness songs, lyric matter often took a more local stance, pooling the band's collective memories of growing up in Camden as part of primarily working-class families. 'Baggy Trousers', a Top 10 hit for Madness in 1980, is a comical recollection of the group members' secondary education in a local comprehensive school, the lyrics detailing a series of typical schoolboy pranks – for example, attacking each other with projectiles such as plastic cups and messing about in woodwork classes. Like the 'lads' in Willis's celebrated ethnographic study *Learning to Labour* (1977), 'Baggy Trousers' also explores the ways in which such classroom and schoolyard pranks functioned as an antidote to the rigour and boredom of the school environment for young working-class boys who regarded fun and laughter as more important in daily life than lessons and homework. In a subsequent single, 'Our House', Madness explore the significance of the English working-class household as a place of both random chaos and excitement, children running around and playing games apt to spill out into the street in a loud and disorderly fashion. Similarly, 'Our House' also depicts the working-class household as a site of matriarchal love and support for a growing family who will one day fly the nest. Unlike other proto-Britpop groups of this era, Madness also utilized to full effect the promotional video, the storylines of their songs being played out in comic fashion by members of the group. In particular, the promotional video for 'Our House' offers a rich stock of visual imagery associated with working-class domestic life that would resurface some fifteen years later in 'Britpop' videos such as Blur's 'Park Life' and Pulp's 'Common People'.

Although the imagery and allegory of Madness was based very much around traditional white working-class English life as informed by memories of growing up in the 1960s, their musical lineage critically connected with issues of race and ethnicity as these were emerging in postwar Britain. As Hebdige observes,[22] since the late 1940s migrant groups from the Caribbean had been infusing British popular culture with new musical styles and influences. British youth cultures of the 1960s such as mod and skinhead were very much a product of this, their style and music drawing on an African–Caribbean aesthetic. By the time of the mod and ska revival of the late 1970s, race relations in Britain had reached a breaking point and a new musicalized sensibility – two tone – rapidly emerged. In important ways, two tone was a progression of the racial tensions that had been building

---

lyrical depictions to project the often harsh social realism of Squeeze's songs.

[22]   Dick Hebdige, 'The Meaning of Mod' and *Subculture*.

in Britain since the 1960s, a decade that had witnessed the passing of the 1962 Immigration Act, the formation of the National Front (in 1967) and the Notting Hill riot of 1968. In its musical style, visual image and the composition of its bands and audience, two tone embraced a multiethnic sensibility that had been gathering momentum in the UK since the early 1950s. In the wake of inner-city riots across England during 1981, leading two tone group the Specials (formerly the Special A.K.A.) released a chilling commentary on the state of the nation in the form of 'Ghost Town', a song whose hypnotic rhythm, combining ska and reggae beats, was complemented by a faux horror-film ambience produced though minimal use of brass and the organ fills of keyboardist Jerry Dammers and combined with a highly effective wailing chorus of voices produced by the Special's trio of vocalists Terry Hall, Neville Staple and Lynval Golding (who later left the group to form Fun Boy Three) and backing singers (see also Zuberi's reference in Chapter 11 to the 2009 reworking of 'Ghost Town' by Kode9 and the SpaceApe). In many ways, the aesthetic and ideological discourse of the Specials and other groups associated with two tone was a portent to the backlash that erupted in the wake of Britpop as groups such as Asian Dub Foundation offered a very different commentary – and musical soundscape – regarding the state of the English nation in the mid-1990s.[23]

Britpop Traces

This chapter has endeavoured to illustrate, through selected examples, the continuity of a tradition between the late 1960s and early 1980s in which English popular music artists expressed a felt sense of association with space, place and national identity through a series of musical and rhetorical posturings. While the list of artists explored in this chapter has been by no means exhaustive, a key point to emerge has been that many of those artists and songs examined not only provide a link between the late 1960s and the early 1980s, but have also arguably contributed in highly palpable ways to the character and definition of Britpop as this came to be understood by artists, audiences, journalists and the like in the mid-1990s. The critical distinction between those 1970s artists discussed and their 1990s Britpop predecessors is an overarching discourse of Englishness. During the 1990s, such a discourse became crucial in providing an aesthetic justification among the English music press for distinguishing 'home-grown' music from other – primarily US – popular music styles. During the 1970s, English popular music existed in an altogether different space. Following the successes of various English popular music artists in the US during the 1960s, the focus of music critics and the like turned away from Englishness as both a descriptor and embodied element of authenticity. As such, the concept of national identity as displayed in and through English popular music receded from view for much of the decade,

---

[23]   See Sanjay Sharma, 'Noisy Asians or "Asian Noise"?'

only resurfacing towards the end of the decade. Even then, as attention refocused on Englishness, this was subject to a plethora of competing and highly fragmented discourses spearheaded by punk. The political climate in the UK during the 1970s also conspired against the type of cultural consensus that became emblematic of Britpop. Such was the level of political dislocation and public alienation, particularly in the latter half of the 1970s, that any attempt to rally support through such a populist rhetoric as New Labour's Cool Britannia, within which Britpop was firmly implicated, would have been wholly ineffectual.

SECTION 2
Britpop

Chapter 6

Labouring the Point?
The Politics of Britpop in 'New Britain'

Rupa Huq

In 2009, twelve years after first winning office, the thrice-victorious electoral force that was New Labour appeared to be in trouble. The resignation of the Cabinet's youngest minister, 39-year-old James Purnell, after the close of polls in the crucial spring local government elections was seen as a blow not just to Prime Minister Gordon Brown but to the entire New Labour project. When Purnell, dubbed the 'baby faced assassin',[1] was interviewed after the dust had settled, he told the *Guardian* newspaper, '[f]or me, it's a bit like Britpop – I feel nostalgic for it, it was absolutely right for its time but that time was 1994 … We need to open up New Labour, reinvent it and eventually move beyond it.'[2] The same summer Noel Gallagher announced that he was quitting Oasis as he was unable to work any longer with his brother Liam, the band's lead singer. At the time of writing we are then some fifteen years after the moment Purnell dates as the birth of New Labour. The advent of Britpop was not far behind. The time is then ripe to look at the intertwined fortunes of both.

This chapter considers Britpop politically (with a capital and small 'p') alongside the phenomenon of New Labour to look at the messages, meanings and broader socio-cultural shifts implicated by the two. The electoral event of New Labour's accession to power in 1997 with its emphasis on Britain as a 'young country' will be examined in order to assess how far the two movements fed off each other. The key question to be addressed is how far Britpop spelt a fundamental break from what had gone before (e.g. indie) or a continuation of previous pop with a new name.

The '60s Turned Upside Down: Contextualizing Britpop

In spring 1996, the official England football team anthem for the European Championships, 'Three Lions', was released by comedians David Baddiel and Frank Skinner with music provided by Britpop act the Lightning Seeds. The chorus invoked the coat of arms on the England football strip and alluded to

---

[1]   See James Kirkup, 'Profile: James Purnell – the baby faced assassin'.

[2]   Allegra Stratton, 'James Purnell: I Lost Faith in Gordon Brown Months Ago'.

the passage of time since England's fabled 1966 World Cup win. Its key line, 'Three Lions on a shirt, Jules Rimet still gleaming / Thirty years of hurt, never stopped me dreaming', concluded 'Football's coming home'. In his Labour Party conference speech that October Tony Blair shamelessly plagiarized this sentiment of dashed hopes, claiming: '[s]eventeen years of hurt. Never stopped us dreaming. Labour's coming home.'[3] At once it showed him to be a man of the moment, in touch with popular culture and nostalgic for a past of sporting triumphs and Labour governments. The words were uttered to play out much wider than an address to the Labour faithful in the auditorium. The media outside lapped up the sentiments of a, by then, Prime Minister-in-waiting. Blair also engaged in a bout of futurology. Three decades earlier Labour Prime Minister Harold Wilson had enthused about the 'white heat of technology', while for Blair this was substituted with Y2K: '[a]t the time of the election, there will just be 1,000 days to the new millennium – 1,000 days to prepare for 1,000 years, a moment of destiny for us'.[4] The deliberate replay of the past then poses the question to what extent either 'New Labour' or indeed Britpop really were in any sense new. The latter was a self-consciously derivate style of pop borrowing from punk and the '60s. The former was a knowing rebranding of the party that was originally a creature of the trade union movement into a leaner (in terms of socialist ideological baggage), meaner (in its acceptance of market forces), election-winning machine. It could be argued that both to some extent were a retread of the 1960s, a time of optimistic Labour government and a self-confident Britain boosted by the export potential of its music, alongside other products of the creative and cultural industries such as film.

Echoes of the 1960s were most plentiful in the advent of Cool Britannia. The Wilsonian 'buy British' campaign against the backdrop of the self-confident 'Swinging London' of the age was evoked in the notion of 'Cool Britannia', the wider project undertaken by the first Blair government to update backward-looking images of Britishness with a new inclusive multicultural vision with which Britpop became entangled. The once-taboo Union Jack was part of the associated imagery of both Britpop and Cool Britannia, which had been reclaimed away from being the symbolic territory of the far right by New Labour in their election campaign. However, Blair had done this before, claiming to be the party of law and order (traditionally Conservative territory) with the soundbite '[t]ough on crime, tough on the causes of crime'. Cool Britannia's significance in updating old stereotypes was in keeping with New Labour's fondness for the modernization of political institutions and beliefs, exemplified in devolving power to Scotland and Wales and the jettisoning of the party's historic commitment to the public ownership of national assets enshrined in clause 4 of the Labour Party's constitution. Chris Rojek writes:

---

[3]   At BBC, 'Blair: In His Own Words'.

[4]   Ibid.

The aim was to identify with figures in British youth culture that carried international and multi-ethnic prestige, in keeping with the domestic realties of transnationalism and multiculturalism, and the opportunities presented by globalisation. This was an exercise in political location and cultural recognition that sought to exploit trends in British pop culture, music, art, music, fashion and comedy and film and present them as evidence that Britannia was reinventing itself from the crabby dowager of the recent Conservative era.[5]

Moves towards this were begun in opposition. Tony Blair himself appeared at the awards ceremony of pop magazine *Q* in both 1994 and 1995 to present gongs to and be photographed with popstars. His speeches frequently included references to 'New Britain' as a 'young country'. Photos of Blair sharing a joke with Noel Gallagher at a Downing Street celebration after his election were the culmination of this youth offensive and at once evoked images of the Beatles posing with Harold Wilson on being decorated with the MBE (Member of the Order of the British Empire) award.

Parallels with the 1960s were drawn by those who were there, those not yet born then and those who, to use the cliché, embodied the idea that 'if you can remember the sixties, you weren't really there'. The magazine *Record Collector* spotted the celebrity potential of the personalities' private lives and remarked:

> With guitars and classic chord changes lending the music a reassuringly old-fashioned feel, it seems that everyone who's ever liked the Beatles can relate to what's going on. Add the fact that Blur's Damon Albarn and Elastica's Justine Frischman [*sic*] seem uncannily to fit the role of Britpop's very own Hugh Grant and Liz Hurley, and you're left with a media-friendly phenomenon with almost universal appeal.[6]

Perhaps this universalism is a result of the eroded boundaries between high and low culture, itself a by-product of social mobility. In the 1960s the art school was the cradle of pop creativity, with middle-class students who had largely attended grammar schools as the prime movers. For all of his 'working-class hero' posturing John Lennon was probably the most middle-class Beatle, spending much of his childhood in a comfortable 1930s semi in a desirable suburb of Liverpool. Politically, though, in the meritocratic 1960s boasting of privilege was not politically correct. Prime Minister Harold Wilson was photographed with a man-of-the-people pipe, although it was said he was actually more of a cigar man. By the 1990s, hiding middle-class roots was de rigueur among politicians and Britpop proponents. Tony Blair did not hail from the usual accepted background of the standard Labour politician. His training as a barrister exemplifies a profession well represented in Parliament, but he had none of the Labour attributes of

---

[5]   Chris Rojek, *Brit-Myth: Who Do the British Think They Are?*, pp. 23–4.
[6]   Pat Gilbert, 'Britpop Now!', pp. 24–5.

humble origins or even a history of crusading for the underprivileged (such as the pre-politics social work of middle-class 1945 Labour premier Clement Attlee in the east London slums). He had no trade-union or public-sector background. Instead he was the son of a card-carrying Conservative father and had attended a public school. Butler and Kavanagh[7] quote the *Independent*, which observed during the 1997 General Election that '[o]n Tony Blair's head the cloth cap of Keir Hardie is ... invisible'. None of this stopped Blair affecting an estuary English accent when appearing on the Des O'Connor chatshow. The pop writer Mark Simpson claims that there has been a fragmentation of former class loyalties:

> The bitter irony of the Nineties was that now that the working class had ceased to exist as a political force, as a class in itself and for itself, everyone was for it ... Everyone wanted to like football, or to least be seen to be liking it. Everyone wanted to buy the football terrace anthems of Oasis, the 'singing plumbers' (as they were dubbed by Brett Anderson) ... Everyone, not just posh Indie boy-band Parklife tourists Blur, wanted a 'sexy' downwardly mobile 'mocknee' accent ... everyone, not just the rich art school students of Pulp lyrics, wanted to sleep with common people.[8]

Here, Morrissey-worshipper Simpson attacks both Oasis for their artlessness and Blur for being too middle class and good looking. Pop musicians have often been more middle class than horny-handed sons of toil. Blur and Suede, rather than being the inner-city street urchins they projected themselves as in song, were respectively from the comfortable commuter towns of Colchester in Essex and Hayward's Heath in Sussex. Simpson is particularly contemptuous of the character he calls

> Oasis fan and ropy Margaret Thatcher impersonator Anthony Blair, the New Labour leader elected by a chart-busting landslide in May 1997 ... [who] invited the usual suspects of Britpop round to Number 10 for a drink and some mutual publicity ... So the new executives of the English political establishment and English pop met in a morbid celebrity embrace for the cameras and it was more difficult to tell them apart than it should have been.[9]

Blair's history as member of a band at university helped him with his projected image as youthful leader for a new era. Early news footage of the Blairs moving into Downing Street included the well-choreographed shots of a guitar being moved in, in an echo of Edward Heath's piano unceremoniously being moved out after the first General Election of 1974 in which he had actually received more votes than his winning Labour opponent Harold Wilson.

---

[7]   David Butler and Dennis Kavanagh, *The British General Election of 1997*, p. 99.

[8]   Mark Simpson, *Saint Morrissey*, pp. 158–9.

[9]   Ibid., p. 173.

The Politics of Britpop: A Contradiction in Terms?

Just as Blair's masterstroke was to reject the long-established 'Labour' banner for his revamped version 2 of it as 'New Labour', the bands commonly understood to be Britpop acts often rejected this identification. Tony Smith of the label Deceptive, to which Elastica were signed, commented that the groups that were put under the Britpop banner all functioned independently of each other. To state the obvious, the members didn't even know one another. Nevertheless, journalists wrote about Britpop as if all the groups they identified shared a common understanding.[10] If we take the definition of indie proposed by Bannister of 'small groups of white men playing guitars, influenced by punks and 1960s white pop/rock, within a broader discourse and practice of (degrees of) independence from mainstream musical values',[11] much of its content applies to Britpop. Paul McCartney, in an interview with *Q* magazine,[12] praised the way that craftsmanship in composition and musicianship were prevalent in the new stable of Britpop bands, seeing it as on a continuum with the Beatles tradition and claiming, '[w]hat I like about Oasis and some of the Seattle bands is that they're *doing it*, they're not Take That, they're not miming and dancing – which is exactly the bag we came from'. Early 1980s indie was not only, as Bannister notes, self-positioned away from mainstream music industry values, but often had an anti-government orientation seen, for example, in tracks like Elvis Costello's 'Shipbuilding' (1983), Crass's 'How Does it Feel to Be the Mother of a Thousand Dead?' (1983) and chart pop such as 'Stand Down Margaret' (1980) from one time Midlands independents the Beat. This oppositional element was largely missing from Britpop. Although some Britpop acts were on independent labels (for example, Oasis were signed to Creation), most were signed to mainstream labels, be they offshoots of majors (such as Blur on Food/EMI) or medium-sized companies (Pulp on Island). In some ways Britpop was indie's nemesis. It began as an offshoot of the independent British music scene but arguably ended up killing it, as a convergence took place between indie and mainstream, removing the distinctive 'protest' element of British-based independent music. New Labour too had a defined sense of purpose to achieve power and eschew its donkey-jacket radical past in doing so. Tony Blair's 1994 leadership campaign leaflet declared, '[w]e must transform Labour from a party of protest to a party of government',

However, there were also significant dissimilarities between Britpop and what went before. The indie of the 1980s was heterogeneous in character and flowered on multifarious record labels in different parts of the country. Britpop was seen as more of a cookie-cutter movement resulting in near-identical acts. In the 'Pleased to Meet You' feature in *Q* magazine of October 1996,[13] Elvis Costello

---

[10]   See, for example, Barney Hoskins, 'The Third Invasion: Britpop Strikes!'.

[11]   Matthew Bannister, *White Boys, White Noise: Masculinities and 1980s Indie Guitar Rock*, p. 8.

[12]   Andrew Collins, 'Cello, Cello'.

[13]   Stuart Maconie, 'Elvis Costello and Justine Frischmann: Pleased to Meet You'.

and Justine Frischmann discussed the formulaic character that Britpop had assumed: 'EC: And like everything successful the A & R fraternity will send out for another... . JF: That's how the industry works. There are an awful lot of Oasises about at the moment.' Groups such as Menswear, Marion and Embrace can be slotted into this 'also ran' category. In place of the regionalism of 1980s, for example the indie-spanning Factory records in Manchester, Zoo of Liverpool and Postcard of Scotland, Britpop appeared to be a metropolitan movement. Acts were signed to national labels so that the resulting scene was not just London-centric but concentrated in certain drinking establishments of the fashionable north London district of Camden. The Good Mixer pub in Camden Town assumed landmark status as the natural habitat of Britpop acts, a magnet for those associated with the scene. In his autobiography, Alex James of Blur describes the circus-type atmosphere therein: 'Graham [guitarist] had moved to Camden and sometimes I went to see him there in the Good Mixer public house … He had become the king of a strange people who all looked like him, and he held his court at the Mixer.'[14] Even if Britpop kings Oasis came from Manchester they actually hailed from the suburban surrounds of Burnage rather than the inner-city hell that they implied was their original habitat, and band members variously relocated to the more salubrious parts of London and/or its stockbroker belt in any case. Noel Gallagher, for example, was famed for throwing 'all back to mine' wild parties in the 1990s at his then townhouse in London's Belsize Park named 'Supernova Heights', but also maintained a country residence out in Buckinghamshire. This ostentatious rockstar excess is the opposite of the dressed-down and austere aesthetic of 1980s indie.

Aside from a brash optimism audible in bold power-chords, politically Britpop had very little in the way of an overt, unified political message. There was no organized campaign for Labour in the same way as, say, there was Red Wedge in the 1980s. Causes championed by bands to mobilize around seemed to appear after Britpop, such as the anti-debt Live 8 concerts of 2005. Britpop lyrics tended to sit between the pen-portrait vignettes of Pulp and Blur or the nonsense rhyming of Oasis. With no apparent irony, the decennial October 1996 edition of *Q* magazine in its feature '10 Years in a Nutshell' relates the happenings of 1995 as 'Clause 4 Tippexed out of Labour manifesto. Oasis/Blur battle makes the news'.[15] In order to be electable under Tony Blair's leadership Labour pragmatically dispensed with some of the elements of its credo that had proved unpopular with voters. Butler and Kavanagh elucidate: '[t]alk of socialism, redistributive taxation and nationalisation was downgraded as an electoral liability'.[16] The accusations of sell-out inevitably followed – the same accusations that always follow around acts who make the transition from indie to mainstream, which could alternatively be described as 'from unpopular to commercial success'. Interestingly, Butler and Kavanagh also define New Labour's mission thus: 'to marginalise the party's

---

[14]   Alex James, *Bit of a Blur: The Autobiography*, p. 119.

[15]   *Q*, October 1996, p. 86.

[16]   Butler and Kavanagh, *The British General Election of 1997*, p. 64.

left-wing, to reassure middle-of-the-road voters, and to convince finance and business that Labour was a competent party of government'.[17] As an adjective, 'middle-of-the-road' is somewhat pejorative when applied to music; in its shortened form 'MOR' along with 'AOR' (adult-oriented rock) are seen as symbolizing all that is lifeless and dull in pop. Another insult used by its detractors against Britpop was 'dadrock', used to imply that even your parents' generation would have no problem at all accepting Britpop home for tea. Those sheltering under the dadrock umbrella included born-again Birmingham early '90s baggy/dance outfit Ocean Colour Scene, now a guitar outfit. Even elder statesman Paul Weller enjoyed a comeback and was celebrated by the younger musicians as founding father of Britpop for his earlier incarnation of angry young man singer of 80s mod revivalists the Jam.

New Labour's Youth Connection

New Labour's coming to power in 1997 signalled a break from 18 years of Conservative rule – at least in terms of government image (Tony Blair was the youngest premier since Lord Liverpool's election in 1812) given that some of the fundamental tenets of Thatcherism remained. In tune with his vision of 'New' Britain as a 'young country', Blair declared: 'I am ... from the rock and roll generation, the Beatles, colour TV, all the rest of it, that's where I come from'.[18] The central philosophy behind the renamed 'New' Labour Party was the 'third way' of sociologist Anthony Giddens, which eschews traditional left/right divides for a pragmatic approach of light-touch economic regulation forged in response to deal with a rapidly changing mixed post-industrial global economy. For Butler and Kavanagh, 'new' is 'a Blair mantra'[19] uttered 37 times in his pre-election conference speech and 107 times in Labour's 'Road to the Manifesto' document, along with 'change' used 36 times in that early manifesto. Other taboos were breached: the Union Jack flag, for a long time co-opted as an emblem of the far right figured heavily throughout Labour's 1997 campaign as it was argued that this was being reclaimed by the centre left. As mentioned above, Blair identified very publicly with youth culture, being photographed with Noel Gallagher of Oasis, Bono, Bob Geldof and sometimes holding a guitar. The commentator Bristow[20] criticizes 'New Labour's infantile obsession with Young Britain' as being highly selective and only identifying with the glamorous young as opposed to those who are, to use the government's own language, 'socially excluded'. The Blair Government's selective use of youth culture and young people as a recurring motif occurred in several policy areas. The post-1997 'Cool Britannia' mission aimed

---

[17]   Ibid.

[18]   Maureen Dowd, 'Labor's Love Lost?'

[19]   Butler and Kavanagh, *The British General Election of 1997*, p. 64.

[20]   In Jennie Bristow, 'Blair's Other Babies'.

to rebrand the UK as less stuffy, more forward-looking and culturally diverse, prioritizing the knowledge economy and projecting a youthful multicultural national image[21] in sharp contrast to predecessor John Major's much maligned retrograde monocultural, narrow version of Englishness based on nostalgia for an imagined past.[22] Power was accordingly devolved from London/Westminster to Scottish and Welsh parliaments. Foreign Secretary Robin Cook went on to declare that chicken tikka masala (a variant on Indian curry) was the new national dish of Britain.

Was New Labour a shift to the right, as its left-critics had it, or was it alternatively a return to the political centre that it had occupied before its lurch to the left in the 1980s wilderness years with the old postwar consensus of Butskellism, which was under threat in 1983, back in business? Anderson and Mann contrast the Labour manifesto of 1983 with the New Labour credo:

> Whereas in 1983 ... Labour ... backed widespread nationalization, a big increase in public borrowing to boost the economy, a hike in spending on social security, health and education, a shift in 'the tax balance to those who can best afford to pay' and a role for the trade unions in economic management, the party today has forsaken nationalization, is no longer Keynesian in its approach to macroeconomic policy, has ditched its explicit commitment to a redistributive tax and benefits system and has abandoned even the vaguest hint of openness to corporatism.[23]

The headline New Labour policies of the 1997 General Election were reduced to a credit-card sized pledgecard of five measureable target-led promises that were all non-contentious issues, inoffensive to most regardless of political persuasion. These included reducing class sizes in schools, faster-track sentencing of offenders, youth training to reduce unemployment and cutting NHS waiting lists. With the large working majority that was eventually achieved, the party could have gone much further in forging a leftward direction but chose not to, despite the Tory scaremongering up to the General Election date suggesting that Blair was a front for a more sinister socialist plot. Driver and Martell make the argument that many on the left repeatedly have proposed, namely that 1997, as Labour's electoral zenith, represents something of a lost opportunity: '[w]hen New Labour did have a chance in 1997 to shape public attitudes on a new radical, progressive

---

[21]   Kate Oakley, 'Not So Cool Britannia: The Role of the Creative Industries in Economic Development'.

[22]   John Major's words 'Fifty years on from now, Britain will still be the country of long shadows on cricket grounds, warm beer, invincible green suburbs, dog lovers and pools fillers' uttered in 1995 had many critics (at http://www.number10.gov.uk/output/Page125. asp, accessed 12 May 2010).

[23]   Paul Anderson and Nyta Mann, *Safety First: The Making of New Labour*, p. 383.

agenda post-Thatcherism it put safety first'.[24] Convincing the finance sectors and the world of business that Labour could deliver economic competence was one of the key planks of its strategy for election.

The focus-group consultations that had been conducted in the run-up to the election to arrive at such an arguably timid set of promises included soundings taken from what Rojek calls 'selected icons of "young Britain" ... [including] Damon Albarn (lead singer of Blur and ambassador of Brit-pop par excellence)'.[25] If New Labour aimed not to scare the voters of Middle England, Britpop, with tunes that were hummable by the milkman (even though this calling in life was rendered more and more obsolete by the onward march of large supermarkets such as Tesco), was also inoffensive and consensual. Its construction was not exactly by focus group but made possible as a result of decades of pop history up for plunder. One of the most enduringly memorable images of the immediate post-election period was Blair photographed with Noel Gallagher and his then-wife Meg Matthews. The incident was later chronicled in Downing Street Press Secretary Alastair Campbell's diaries thus: 'TB [Tony Blair] was worried that Noel Gallagher was coming to the reception tomorrow. He said he had no idea he had been invited ... TB felt he was bound to do something crazy. I spoke to [Creation Records boss] Alan McGee and said can we be assured he would behave.' In the event, '[h]e said he thought Number 10 was "tops", said he couldn't believe that there was an ironing board in there'.[26]

New Labour was in some ways not as new in terms of its political credo, which was driven by electoral logic, as it was in its campaign techniques of direct mail with tailored messages to targeted sections of the electorate all run from a professional media centre at the Millbank Centre in London seen to symbolize the new accepted orthodoxy of such strategies as 'rapid rebuttal'. This change in structures echoes the way that Blair had been unafraid to overhaul Labour party machinery in opposition (ditching its constitutional commitment to public ownership) and keen to remodel the UK's constitutional apparatus after taking power (devolution, House of Lords reform, etc.). A specific youth video was created for first-time voters and mailshot to relevant individuals selected from the electoral roll. The same was done for ethnic minority voters of Asian origin, illustrating the party's experimentation with the technique of triangulation in constructing a broadbased tranche of the electorate ready to deliver it victory. Reviewing one of the party election broadcasts, Butler and Kavanagh observe that stylistically it amounted to 'Quentin Tarantino without the violence. This was more about conveying impressions of newness, change and youth to Generation X voters than communicating its formal content.'[27] This criticism amounts to the same thing as 'dumbing down', a criticism that has been applied frequently

---

[24]   Stephen Driver and Luke Martell, *New Labour: Politics after Thatcherism*, p. 21.
[25]   Rojek, *Brit-Myth*, p. 23.
[26]   *NME*, 'Tony Blair was Worried Oasis would Trash Downing Street'.
[27]   Butler and Kavanagh, *The British General Election of 1997*, p. 152.

throughout the New Labour years to everything from educational standards in GCSE and A-levels to reality television. On the campaign trail, the theme tune used was the anthemic electro disco hi-energy track 'Things Can Only Get Better' from Irish multi-instrumentalist Peter Cunnagh who operated using the title D:Ream. It was, however, the Spice Girls who seemed most visible as an issue. Butler and Kavanagh bemoan the fact that, despite the seriousness of unemployment and a food-poisoning outbreak in Scotland during the campaign, 'more attention was given to the voting intentions of pop music's Spice Girls and John Major won headlines on 15 April by his inability to give the names of the five singers'.[28] By the end of the campaign, with a bit of coaching, Blair was able to name all.

We can construct parallels with UK politics/electoral cycles and the accompanying soundtrack. The recessionary throes of the early 1980s proved the backdrop for a period of acute polarization in political programmes on offer to the public: untrammelled market forces advocated by the victorious Conservatives versus state socialism whose proponents were the continually vanquished Labour party. Indie thrived in such conditions. The issues of the day included the Cold War, with its attendant threat of nuclear attack from the East, and the protracted and painful miners' strike that offered the last act of resistance on the part of historic communities to the onward march of capitalism, where imports from China flooded consumer-driven desires. By the late 90s, New Labour had been lucky enough to inherit an economy in positive growth. Fiscal stability and flexible labour markets became the order of the day. In the 1980s there were defined camps of indie and pop, reflected in their separate charts on the pages of the music press. By the 1990s, there was a melding of pop and political tribes. Britpop signalled the accommodation of both indie and mainstream pop under one banner. Perhaps, rather than a return to business as usual (old consensus politics), the New Labour offer, by accepting the 1980s privatizations, a penchant for low taxes and limitations of trade union power, was an acceptance of the shift in political gravity effected in that decade. The choices on offer at the 1997 election amounted to some extent to 'whoever wins, Thatcher has won'. Labour had, after years of battling the internal market, accepted the central tenets of Thatcher in according a role to market forces in delivering solutions. In their General Election manifesto of 1997 Labour promised no increase in the basic or top rates of tax and pledged to stick to the Tories' spending commitments. The more radical 1983 measures of unilateral nuclear disarmament and EEC withdrawal now seem unimaginable in any New Labour programme. Although in 1997 the Conservatives tried to construct Labour as Europhiles who would sell Britain down the river, as seen in their slogan '24 hours to save the pound', in retrospect the Blair–Brown governments have been decidedly Atlanticist in outlook and the UK still remains stubbornly outside the Euro-zone of currencies.

Certainly the House of Commons following New Labour's election looked very different in character. It was a more feminized workplace boosted by the

---

28   Ibid., p. 111.

election of 101 Labour women, dubbed the 'Blair babes'. It was also younger in age profile. There were ten Labour MPs elected in their twenties, an unprecedented record. In some senses there was a convergence of academic social science and politics, tangible in the importance attached to the New Labour chief ideologue, sociologist Anthony Giddens, but present elsewhere too. The Government began to legislate in areas that British governments had traditionally left alone. The Crick enquiry of 1998 examined the teaching of citizenship in schools, chaired by the political scientist Professor Bernard Crick, and is illustrative of the government's fondness to set up deliberative Royal Commissions and enquiries to conduct feasibility studies of policies before enactment, thereby validating eventual proposals. Crick's was only one of a series of reports in this area that could claim the adjective 'groundbreaking' or 'landmark'. It was later joined by the Macpherson report into the enquiry following the murder of black south-London teenager Stephen Lawrence and 2003's Cantle report into the spate of urban disorder in northern England in which Asian youth were prominent. The white-faced male posturing of Britpop seemed increasingly out of step with the 'New Britain' times. Alternative soundtracks included drum'n'bass[29] and Asian underground.[30] Almost deemed to be less sociologically significant due to the academic silence on the subject were also the bestselling boy- and girl bands. As Simpson points out in his inimitable way, '[t]he bragging, materialistic self-importance of all this [Britpop self-aggrandizing] was somewhat punctured by the fact that by the late Nineties, the Spice Girls, the manufactured "girl power" band whose professed inspiration was Margaret Thatcher, and who seemed to be a feisty bollocked version of eunuch boy band Take That ... outsold the main boy bands [*sic*] Oasis, Blur and Suede put together'.[31] Among the visual devices employed by the Spice Girls was the Union Jack dress of Geri 'Ginger Spice', entirely in keeping with the Cool Britannia aesthetic that could also be seen on Noel Gallagher's Union Jack guitar.

The Parekh report of 1999, published by the influential think-tank the Runnymede Trust, although extra-governmental also tapped into the prevailing 'Cool Britannia' climate and contemporaneous theoretical work on 'New Ethnicities' with its wide-ranging conclusions about Britain's contemporary multicultural vibrancy and combating continuing racism. The report's passage on hyphenated identities – '[m]ore and more people have multiple identities – they are Welsh Europeans, Pakistani Yorkshirewomen, Glaswegian Muslims, English Jews and black British ... Britain's potential to become a community of communities is not something to shy away from – its people should celebrate it'[32] – has similarities with the much-quoted passage of cultural theorist Stuart Hall on what have been termed the 'new ethnicities': 'Identities are never

---

[29]   Benjamin Noys, 'Into the "Jungle"'.

[30]   Sanjay Sharma, John Hutnyk and Ashwani Sharma (eds), *Dis-Orienting Rhythms: The Politics of the New Asian Dance Music*.

[31]   Simpson, *Saint Morrissey*, p. 173.

[32]   Bikhu Parekh, *The Future of Multi-Ethnic Britain: The Parekh Report*, p. 10.

Chapter 7 – Multilayered identities

unified and, in late modern times, increasingly fragmented and fractured, never singular but multiply constructed across different often intersecting and antagonistic discourses, practices and possibilities'.[33] One can also trace links with post-subcultural studies,[34] which also frequently employs adjectives like 'fluidity' and 'hybridity'. Yet while such postcolonial social theory is cited by theorists of music such as bhangra and jungle – which are in their own ways 'Britpop' variants if we take this term literally, given that such musics are also produced by young urban and suburban youth residing in Britain – academic analyses of Britpop seem to equate the concept with 'whiteness'.

Perhaps, then, Britpop can be characterized as a post-ideological soundtrack to post-political times. New Labour abandoned many tenets of accepted Labour ideology, beginning with its brazen junking of the party's constitutional commitment to public ownership, clause 4. Its main defining feature was arguably pragmatism. Britpop's vacuity too can be seen as tame and anodyne compared with earlier youth-musical subcultural sloganeering such as punk's nihilistic prescription to shake society to its very foundations ('anarchy in the UK', 'no future') or hippie idealism ('be reasonable, demand the impossible', borrowed from the Situationists). In the early 1980s, indie, with its kitchen-sink songs, offered a social-realist solution to the austerity of the era. The mainstream pop of the time offered glamour and excitement (Culture Club, Wham!, Duran Duran) in an escapist vision of hedonism in hard times. The technologically savvy 'New Pop', as it became known, was a precursor to the cultures of electronic dance music that became acid house. Political pop as a mainstream force has arguably been in decline since; Red Wedge-instigator Billy Bragg soldiers on, albeit largely neutered of his earlier radicalism and preferring more straightforward love songs.

Concluding Discussion: The Demise of Britpop and the End of New Labour?

It is easy to overstate the importance of Britpop. It existed alongside several other styles, from Asian underground and jungle to more commercially focused boy- and girl bands. When Take That split in 1996, the counselling service the Samaritans set up a hotline for suicidal fans, just a year before New Labour took power. Throughout Britpop's reign the Spice Girls were probably the most quantifiably successful pop phenomenon of the era, even going as far as to make a slapstick-style film in a 1960s Beatles-type vein. Tracing the 'end' of Britpop is not straightforward. It was only a matter of time before the bands associated with the style took on the trappings of stadium rock, forever under attack from indie fans for being bloated and arrogant. Blur played the stadium at Mile End. The review of

---

33   Stuart Hall, 'Introduction: Who Needs Identity?', p. 4.

34   See Andy Bennett, 'Subcultures or Neo-Tribes?: Rethinking the Relationship between Youth, Style and Musical Taste'; Rupa Huq, *Beyond Subculture: Pop, You and Identity in a Postcolonial World*.

Oasis's Knebworth concert in *Q* magazine (October 1996) begins with the words, 'It's a long way from Burnage'. Again here, as with much of the reported coverage of Britpop, the rivalry between Oasis and Blur surfaced. It is described how Liam Gallagher took to the stage to sing in a raucous football-chant style the chorus of Blur's 'Parklife', only to replace the title with the words 'sad lives'.

If we are dating here the end of the sixties boom that Britpop has been compared to, perhaps it was England's exit from the soccer World Cup in 1970 that helped the party's shock defeat in the General Election of that year. New Labour's decline could be dated to various trigger events: for example, the British support for the US-led Iraq invasion of 2003 or the departure of Tony Blair as Prime Minister in 2007. Either way we can trace two phases of New Labour: the first term from 1997 to 2001 characterized by a sunny youthful optimism, and the later Blair years that gave way to Gordon Brown's period at the helm. One can discern a hardening in New Labour's attitude with the coming of New Labour MkII that began with the 9/11 attacks of 2001 and resulted in the Government's signing up to George Bush's 'war on terror'. Domestically too, the old 1980s samosas'n'steel bands brand of multiculturalism came under attack for being patronizing from ostensibly unexpected quarters, e.g. Trevor Philips, head of the Commission for Racial Equality. Cool Britannia became a distant memory. In late 2006 Blair declared that immigrants had a duty to conform to British values or they would not be welcome. This was in keeping with government rhetoric of 'tough choices'. The British values in question were implicitly seen as including 'fair play' and 'playing by the rules'; however, there is continual disagreement about what the rules of the game are. Post-1997 governments have had a mixed record on youth policy and citizenship matters. It is facile to label them as merely a disappointing continuation of the Conservatives who preceded them, as some have done,[35] when they have made great strides in equality legislation with tightened anti-discrimination measures including new legislation to protect religious minorities and to legalize same-sex partnerships. However, New Labour's managing of multi-ethnic Britain can appear unsatisfactory: in the idea of 'tolerance' there is a notion that minorities are an annoyance to be 'tolerated' or 'put up with' as they readily and gratefully dissolve into what passes for the 'norm'.

New Labour's 1997 victory can be situated within wider global shifts at the time. It followed the Democrat Bill Clinton's re-election to the White House in 1996 and preceded the Socialist Lionel Jospin's election as Prime Minister of France. By the time of the Malmö congress of European socialist parties one month after Blair's victory, the momentum was with the left, cemented by Gerhard Schroeder's win in Germany for the Christian Democrats the following year. However, how left these parties really are/were is a matter of further debate. Driver and Martell remark in rather foreboding terms, '[f]or good or ill, British politics and British society continue to bear the marks of eighteen years of radical Conservative government.

---

[35]   For example, Liza Schuster and John Solomos, 'Race, Immigration and Asylum: New Labour's Agenda and its Consequences'.

Thatcherism's legacy remains profound'.[36] This has happened in other Western nations, for example, the effect of Reaganomics on the Clinton governments or the room for manoeuvre afforded to Kevin Rudd in Australia following the rightward shift of the political ground by the Hawke/Keating and Howard years. Just as Blair would argue that New Labour recast principles for the modern age, Britpop, too, updated an old formula to keep in step with modern times. Its lack of political message can be seen as an injection of realism rather than a lack of idealism. To bemoan the depoliticized pop of the present is to assume that pop was radical to start with. Political pop was always the exception rather than the rule. In the same way as Daniel Bell declaring in 1960 that we were witnessing 'The End of Ideology' so, at the start of the last century's final decade, Francis Fukuyama announced the 'End of History'.[37] Such claims have traditionally been made by the right, yet in hindsight it could be argued that in many ways the fall of the Berlin Wall signalled the beginning of history or rather a post-Cold War world: both New Labour's pragmatic prescription and Britpop's retreat from past pop's left posturing were logical conclusions, completely understandable when located in temporal context.

---

[36]   Driver and Martell, *New Labour*, p. 194.
[37]   Francis Fukuyama, *End of History and the Last Man*.

Chapter 7

The Britpop Sound

Derek B. Scott

This chapter explores the musical links between 1990s Britpop and the rock music of the 1960s and 1970s. In doing so, it reveals the shifting meanings that result when apparently similar messages are articulated at differing historic junctures, and raises questions about Britishness and Englishness in popular music. The view that the Beatles have been shamelessly plagiarized by Oasis, or the Kinks by Blur, is challenged. The issue, in a nutshell, is whether Britpop works by way of simply copying earlier styles, or whether there is an attempt to make creative use of those aspects of songs that might now, in the twenty-first century, be regarded as exemplifying the musical vocabulary of a British pop language. However, it is also necessary to relate those British sounds to a pool of musical and discursive means of constructing and valorizing Britishness that has been in existence since the late nineteenth century.

It should not be forgotten that the Beatles, the Kinks, and others drew upon existing signifiers of Britishness and Englishness, and that many earlier lyrical and musical conventions they used were also available for reworking in the 1990s. For example, when Damon Albarn, born and raised in Essex, chose to project a Cockney character, it owed more to the older music-hall Cockney than the entertainment found at that time in working-men's clubs of London's East End. The new thing in the 1990s was, of course, that pop music was already able to reference a British sound, thanks to the success of earlier British groups in imprinting their musical styles on the minds of audiences around the world. Therefore, Beatles references in the music of Oasis are in themselves recognized as signifiers of Britishness, because the Beatles had helped to establish the sound and style of British beat.

Music and Englishness

Many have remarked that Britpop should really have been called Engpop because, with few exceptions – among them Ash (Northern Ireland),[1] Teenage Fanclub (Scotland) and Super Furry Animals (Wales) – the bands were English. Yet, if the place of birth of performers and the lyrics of songs are set aside, it is remarkable

---

[1]   Ash were not keen to be labelled 'Britpop'; emphasizing Britishness could be interpreted as sectarian in Northern Ireland. Ash took a political step when they joined the campaign for the Yes vote in the Good Friday Agreement (1998).

how few commentators have tried to identify exactly what it is that is English about the music. Englishness in music is not an easy quality to define; there are no equivalents of the Irish jig or Highland reel to act as convenient stereotypes of national musical character. In order to understand how Englishness in music has been constructed, it is necessary to delve back into the closing decades of the nineteenth century when an anxiety about what it meant to be English arose in consequence of the numbers of those acquiring British identity in the expanding Empire.

Three categories of music clashed in the effort to construct Englishness in music: these may be loosely defined as Classical, Folk, and what I call simply the Third Type. I do so in order to avoid the ambiguity and conflicted meanings of the word 'popular' in the nineteenth century, when in some countries 'popular' and 'folk' were more or less synonymous, but in others 'popular' might mean anything that was liked by a large number of people (thus, Handel's *Messiah* could qualify). By the Third Type, I refer to the new kind of commercial entertainment music that arose in European and North American metropolises. It became known in Europe by such terms as *Unterhaltungsmusik*, *variétés* and *musica leggera*, and quickly developed its own musical features and devices. In England and America, the term 'popular music' eventually came to mean this type. It is easy, now, to regard music hall as a signifier of Englishness, but we need to be aware that, at an earlier historical juncture, the idea of a music-hall song being characteristically English would have been strongly resisted. Many of those who participated in the English folksong revival at the close of the nineteenth and beginning of the twentieth centuries hoped, as did Cecil Sharp, that, once having heard traditional English airs, people who 'vulgarize themselves and others by singing coarse music-hall songs' would soon see the error of their ways.[2]

The outcome of the clashes of musical categories was that Englishness in the twentieth century could be represented by old church music, traditional rural songs and certain music-hall 'character songs'. Examples of each are Vaughan Williams's *Fantasia on a Theme of Thomas Tallis* (composed in 1910, based on a tune from a Psalter of 1567 for the first Anglican Archbishop of Canterbury), the folksong 'Searching for Lambs' (date and authorship unknown) and the music-hall song 'Wot Cher! Knocked 'em in the Old Kent Road' (Chevalier–Ingle, 1891). From now on, it was not just blue-blooded nobles, or stiff-upper-lipped gents that represented Englishness, but also village dwellers and those who lived in strongly marked working-class neighbourhoods in cities (such as Cockneys). Where rock music is concerned, an interest in Old England and folk-like material is not found solely in the repertoire of bands like Fairport Convention and Steeleye Span; one has only to think of 'Lady Jane' from the Rolling Stones' album *Aftermath* (1966), Pink Floyd's 'Grantchester Meadows' (1969), the Genesis album *Selling England by the Pound* (1973) and, coinciding with the emergence of Britpop, Sting's 'Fields of Gold' (1993). Kate Bush has also, at times, used devices in her songs to signify

2   Cecil J. Sharp, *English Folk-Song: Some Conclusions*, p. 137.

Englishness. 'Oh England, My Lionheart' (1978) is an example, with its pastoral mood, modal melodic inflections and 'old' instrumentation (including recorders and harpsichord). The modal melody and harmony often found in the songs of the Beatles is most likely to have come from folksong, given the lively folk scene in Liverpool at the time. In American music, the Aeolian mode was more likely to be used to give an exotic character to songs about Native Americans (for example, Hank Williams's 'Kaw-Liga') rather than for a love song like 'Things We Said Today'. The Dorian mode, used in 'Eleanor Rigby', is found in old English songs such as 'The Broomfield Hill' and 'Lovely Joan'.[3] In Blur's 'This is a Low', which takes its cue from the British shipping forecast, the flattened sevenths are not blues inflections but, rather, relate to the Mixolydian mode that is often found in folksong.[4] This mode is also heard in Beatles songs (for example, 'Norwegian Wood'). Stylistic context is everything in determining the provenance of flattened sevenths: for example, the flattened seventh is clearly a blue note in Chuck Berry's 'Memphis Tennessee', and not the seventh degree of the Mixolydian mode.

Englishness as Stylistic Hybrid

It needs to be recognized that there is no homogeneous English culture. Therefore, it is unwise, as David Hesmondhalgh has cautioned, 'to think that any one particular genre can crystallise the massive array of histories, artefacts, attitudes, and feelings that make up the many different forms of national identity available in contemporary Britain'.[5] The concept of Englishness has been formed from an ideological concoction of history, myth and the pseudo-science of race. Nevertheless, it clearly possesses substance as a social, if not biological, reality, and exists as a jumble of discourses from which people can select according to their lived experience and the social milieu in which they move. There was already hybridization of style in English music of the nineteenth century: taking music-hall Cockney songs alone, 'The Ticket of Leave Man' (Vance–Hobson, 1864) shows Jewish melodic characteristics, and 'The Marquis of Camberwell Green' (Shrosberry–Boden, 1884) is a Viennese waltz. People often imagine that British music became subject to American influence only in the twentieth century. However, a transatlantic traffic in popular music travelled both ways in the nineteenth century. The English songwriter Henry Russell influenced the development of the parlour ballad in America (in the late 1830s); later in the century Gilbert and Sullivan influenced the development of American musical comedy; and British

---

[3] These are just two of more than half a dozen songs in the Dorian mode in Ralph Vaughan Williams and Albert Lancester Lloyds (eds), *The Penguin Book of English Folk Songs*, pp. 26 and 64.

[4] See ibid., 'The Banks of Newfoundland' and 'Lord Thomas and Fair Eleanor', pp. 16–17 and 62–3.

[5] David Hesmondhalgh, 'British Popular Music and National Identity', p. 284.

music hall influenced vaudeville. These influences were long lasting; indeed, there is still an obvious debt to Arthur Sullivan in George Gershwin's Broadway musical *Of Thee I Sing* (1931) – especially in the French ambassador's song. In return for the receipt of three British styles of music, America returned three nineteenth-century styles of her own: blackface minstrelsy (from the 1840s on) and, later, ragtime and the songs of the all-black musical.

This does not mean that these styles remained exclusively American. Ragtime of the 'When I'm Sixty-Four' variety has its legacy in British music-hall ragtime, which often included references to British localities, as in Marie Lloyd's 'Piccadilly Trot'. Note that the Beatles song mentions a cottage on the Isle of Wight. In contrast, the early American ragtime songs were often sung in blackface and almost invariably concerned subjects related to blackness, typically involving a lovelorn African American. Wilfrid Mellers remarks that 'When I'm Sixty-Four' has 'the raggy, twentyish music-hall style of George Formby'.[6] The Kinks' 'Afternoon Tea' also has the raggy feel of old-time variety. And, although it lacks the ragtime feel, the Who's 'Mary Anne with the Shaky Hand' (from *The Who Sell Out*, 1967) picks up on George Formby's appetite for innuendo, inherited from the music hall (where his father – also George Formby – had been a celebrated comic singer). Mellers has outlined various retrospective elements of *Sgt. Pepper*: the album opens 'with a "public" number (by Paul), inviting us to the show, and recalling Edwardian military music, the circus, and the working man's club';[7] Ringo takes over for his number 'in the manner of the old-fashioned music hall';[8] Paul's 'Getting Better' is 'a raggy music-hall song';[9] and 'She's Leaving Home' is a 'corny waltz',[10] although its phrasing is unusually asymmetrical, as Mellers acknowledges. It is really the cultural reference that makes it corny for someone of Mellers's generation, since it would have conjured up memories of parlour ballads. This nostalgic mood adds a layer of irony to the song, for, although it underlies most of the narrative, it can be interpreted as representing the old-fashioned and out-of-touch parents and their bewildered comments on their daughter's actions.

The Caribbean influence on British popular music began to increase in the late 1930s, when Ken 'Snakehips' Johnson & His West Indian Dance Band and others began to lend British swing a rather different character to American swing. In the 1940s, Edmundo Ros brought rumba and samba to London, and in the later 1950s, calypso became popular in Britain. The calypso rhythm is heard in the next decade in several songs by the Kinks (it even finds its way, in the shape of 'Monica', onto the album *The Kinks Are the Village Green Preservation Society*). Each decade brought further Caribbean styles across the Atlantic; but influences can travel back and forth, and it is obvious that the self-styled 'nutty sound' of Madness in the

---

[6]   Wilfrid Mellers, *Twilight of the Gods: The Beatles in Retrospect*, p. 94.

[7]   Ibid., p. 87.

[8]   Ibid., p. 88.

[9]   Ibid., p. 89.

[10]   Ibid., p. 92.

1980s adds a British perspective to Jamaican ska. 'Girls & Boys' (from *Parklife*) is not far off the rocksteady beat of 'Baggy Trousers' (1980), but remains a complex mixture of other musical ingredients – including disco and post-punk – and, in this, it is a song very much of its time. John Harris describes Albarn's voice on 'Girls & Boys' as 'mewling Cockney', and comments on his growing tendency to adopt this accent in his everyday speaking voice.[11] His mod style began to disappear and 'laddishness' took its place. The 'lad', whose worldview was dominated by lager, sex and football, was very much a 1990s phenomenon.

British Music Hall, Community Song and Cabaret

Neither the Beatles nor the Kinks write music-hall pastiche; instead, they rework this material. Even when Ray Davies writes a song with links to music-hall satire – 'Dedicated Follower of Fashion' (1966) could be said to update Arthur Lloyd's Cockney swell song 'Immenseikoff, the Shoreditch Toff' (1873) – he creates a typical Kinks song rather than a typical music-hall song, and does this while departing very little from the structure and harmonic style of music hall. It is significant, in this case, that the rhythm of 'Dedicated Follower' is closer to a foxtrot than to the polka rhythm of 'Immenseikoff'. Allan Moore comments on the Kinks' attempt to break with American influences, and cites the music-hall comic um-pah verse followed by chorus (a waltz) in 'All of My Friends Were There' from *The Kinks Are the Village Green Preservation Society*.[12] It is not common to find a change of metre between verse and chorus in music hall, but it does occur occasionally: for example, 'I'm Shy, Mary Ellen, I'm Shy' (Stevens–Ridgewell, 1910), a song made famous by Jack Pleasants, has a duple metre narrative verse with tonic-dominant bass followed by a waltz-time chorus. The Kinks and Beatles were not alone in incorporating music-hall elements; 'Rene' from the Small Faces' album *Ogdens Nut Gone Flake* (1968) has the typical music-hall form of narrative minor verse followed by a singalong major chorus. Yet this song, too, is no mere pastiche: the verse seems more indebted to Henry Mancini's 'Pink Panther' theme (1963) than anything out of music hall, and the chorus is in the tonic major, whereas music-hall songs with minor verses usually had relative major choruses.

The music-hall connection is also found in Blur: for instance, 'Parklife' has a narrative verse (spoken) with tonic-dominant-style bass, moving to a chorus that invites participation. Yet the 12/8 metre and 10-bar chorus are not typical of music hall. In fact, stylistically, the song might be thought more indebted to the music of Madness (for instance, 'It Must Be Love' of 1981). The lyrics, nevertheless, share the same high-flown expression of the mundane as those of Ella Shield's music-hall hit 'Burlington Bertie from Bow' (Hargreaves, 1916). The down-and-

---

[11]   Simon Hattenstone, 'Who wants to be a Drug Addict at 41?'

[12]   Allan F. Moore, *Rock: The Primary Text: Developing a Musicology of Rock*, p. 101.

out Bertie declares, 'I rise at ten-thirty and saunter along like a toff', while the protagonist of 'Parklife' rises when he wants, 'except on Wednesday, when I get rudely awakened by the dustmen'. The album *Modern Life is Rubbish* (1993) is often seen as signalling Blur's turn to the Kinks for inspiration, its very title announcing a Kinks-style rejection of modern life. Yet the epigraph to the printed lyrics of 'Sunday Sunday' makes clear that this is not to be taken as a readiness to embrace 'legislated nostalgia'. Moreover, 'For Tomorrow' is reminiscent of Bowie's harmonic style, rather than that of the Kinks, while the 'Intermission' is in the rhythm of that favourite nineteenth-century dance, the polka.

It is typical for a music-hall character song to be sung in the first person; for example, in the song 'Champagne Charlie', the singer announces, 'Champagne Charlie is my name'. Rock songs, however, tend to describe characters in the third person, though many of the characters have a Victorian, or Dickensian, ring to their names: for instance, 'Silas Stingy' (the Who) or Blur's 'Colin Zeal'. The latter is no doubt influenced in its lyrics by Kinks' songs such as 'A Well Respected Man' (1966) and 'Mr. Pleasant' (1967), but the influence does not extend to musical style. 'Star Shaped' is another Kinks-type satire, but without Kinks-type music.

Music hall is one element in the British sound (although it should not be assumed that British music hall and American vaudeville are wide apart stylistically). The songs of the music hall were heard regularly in the 1960s on the popular TV show *The Good Old Days*, broadcast from Leeds City Varieties Theatre (which still exists). Because of this, it is perhaps tempting to see music hall behind every singalong chorus; but you cannot say something is influenced by music hall simply on the grounds that you can sing along to it. You can also sing along to hymns, and some popular music is closer to the hymn than to music hall. Hymn references can be of three types: the uplifting anthemic style of hymn (the 'Jerusalem' type), the nonconformist hymn (or Salvation Army-type hymn), and the old austere hymn. Examples of each type respectively would be Rod Stewart's 'Sailing' (1975), Pink Floyd's 'Outside the Wall' (1979) and the Who's 'Silas Stingy' (1968) – the hymn-like connotations of the latter being enhanced by organ sounds in the accompaniment. The term 'anthemic' has, of course, been adopted for many popular songs that invite crowd participation, but the music-hall chorus could very rarely be described as anthemic.

Blur's *The Sunday Sunday Popular Community Song CD* (1993) points to another activity associated with Britain's musical past. It contains three tracks, one of which, 'Sunday Sunday', is also on *Modern Life is Rubbish*. The other two are 'Daisy Bell' (Dacre, 1892) and 'Let's All Go Down the Strand' (Castling–Murphy, 1909). In its heyday, 1926–29, community singing was a very British affair – songs from Wales or Scotland were fine, but American songs were shunned. Lord Beaverbrook had conceived the idea of a 'nation united in song' in 1926, the year of the General Strike. The newspaper he owned, the *Daily Express*, held the first Community Singing Concert in the Royal Albert Hall and went on to publish community songbooks. Predictably, the preference was for folksong, but more recent songs were tolerated if they had associations with patriotism – songs like

'It's a Long, Long Way to Tipperary' (Judge–Williams, 1912) that boosted morale during the First World War. A less-elevated form of community song is the 'pub song', the longevity of which is evident in Lonnie Donegan's 'My Old Man's a Dustman' (1960), and the songs of Chas & Dave in the 1970s and 1980s. It is also found with a rock character, however, in Ian Dury's 'Billericay Dickie' (1979), and in the Cockney Rebels' 'We Are the Firm' (1980), which quotes 'Knees Up Mother Brown' (Lee–Weston, 1938). The choruses of the Beatles' 'Yellow Submarine' and Blur's 'Country House' also have something of the character of the pub song.

Among other musical influences on 1960s rock, there is that of British cabaret: the Kinks' 'Sunny Afternoon' (1966) and 'End of the Season' (1967) seem indebted to Noël Coward. The former deals with the financial problems of the British aristocracy in a mock-serious minor key, as does Coward's 'The Stately Homes of England' (1937). 'End of the Season' is reminiscent of Coward's mood of resignation in 'The Party's Over Now' (1932). In the late 1940s, when radio was on the rise and variety theatres on the wane, the focus shifted to what was called British Light Entertainment (a concept that dominated TV and radio in the 1950s and 1960s). Side two of the original LP version of the Small Faces' album *Ogden's Nut Gone Flake* was given over to the tale of Happiness Stan; its use of songs interspersed with spoken narration is reminiscent of the latter days of variety as it moved to radio. The narration is, in fact, delivered by a famous mangler of the English language Stanley Unwin, who made his reputation on radio in the 1950s. The sound of British light music – a sound created by composers like Ronald Binge and Robert Farnon (actually Canadian) – is referenced between various tracks of *The Who Sell Out*.

Britpop and its Debt to Earlier British Pop

The sound of 1990s Britpop is that of the guitar-based band, and its musical structures typify the rock song (intro, verse, chorus, bridge, etc.). Britpop developed, most immediately, from indie, and was a reaction against grunge on one side and EDM (Electronic Dance Music) on the other. Making his voice heard in the debate about the origins of Britpop, Brett Anderson claimed that Suede led the way:

> … when we started we were trying to play songs about twisted English lives to rooms full of people obsessed with Pearl Jam … I wouldn't say we started Britpop because the Beatles, Bowie and the Kinks did that. But I think we were crucial in opening people's ears to British music again.[13]

In 2008, recollecting the events of the previous decade, Anderson said, 'I had always been fascinated by suburbia, and I liked to throw these twisted references

---

[13]   Quoted in John Harris, *The Last Party: Britpop, Blair and the Demise of English Rock*, p. 315.

to small-town British life into songs. This was before we had that horrible term Britpop. We were never really at the party [...] We could not have been more uninterested in that whole boozy, cartoon-like, fake working-class thing.'[14] Anderson was a fan of the Smiths, the Fall and the Happy Mondays, but the most readily perceptible influence on his output is David Bowie, especially Bowie's work from the first half of the 1970s, such as *Hunky Dory*. There is, however, little of the ironic detachment found sometimes in Bowie and frequently in Blur. The album *Suede* (1993) is a 'feel my suburban *Angst*' album, the band shifting 'constantly between the mundane and the apocalyptic', which Simon Frith regards as typical of the suburban sensibility in pop.[15]

It is unlikely that any one band can take credit for reawakening an interest in British music. It needs to be seen in the wider cultural context. Matthew Collings, for example, writes of the renewed interest in British visual art in the 1990s, and argues: '[t]he bridge between the awfulness of Bohemia in the 50s and the grooviness of Britpop in the 90s was Pop Art in the 60s'.[16] The artist Peter Blake, a key figure in Pop Art, was responsible for the cover of *Sgt. Pepper*. In the 1990s, Damon Albarn collaborated with artist Damien Hirst on the video for 'Country House'. The video made visual reference to British sexist (but now camp) comedy of the 1960s (the *Carry On* films, the Benny Hill Show), putting postmodern scare quotes around political correctness.

A variety of different styles and sounds were presumed to fit together as the Britpop style only because nobody was paying much attention to the music itself. The music of Blur, for example, rarely *sounds* like the Kinks. Elastica's song 'Line Up' might be thought a vicious version of the Kinks' 'Starstruck', but Elastica clearly drew upon punk more than any other style. Pulp displayed electronic influences in their style. 'Common People' (1995) made Pulp's reputation, a song widely admired at the time for being 'one of music's most accomplished treatments of class'.[17] Some listeners, however, may find that this scornful tale of the 'posh bird' seeking a bit of 'working-class rough' and being taught her lesson is an all-too-familiar fantasy of certain English left-wing misogynists. Ironically, if anyone associated with Britpop came close to behaving like the woman of this song and patronizing the working class, it was Damon Albarn during his 'Mockney' period.

Britpop was made possible in the 1990s by the emergence of a rock canon and, consequently, the idea of classic rock. The first university degree in popular music was successfully validated in 1993 (in Salford), and it is significant that rock music was finally included in the 2001 edition of the magisterial *Grove Dictionary*

---

[14]   Quoted in Michael Bracewell, 'I'm Surprised I Made it to 30', p. 27.

[15]   Simon Frith, 'The Suburban Sensibility in British Rock and Pop', p. 277.

[16]   Matthew Collings, *Blimey! From Bohemia to Britpop: The London Artworld from Francis Bacon to Damien Hirst*, p. 95.

[17]   Harris, *The Last Party*, p. xxi.

of Music and Musicians.[18] The interest in the 1960s is already evident in the La's eponymous album of 1990. The canonization of the Beatles was complete with the release of the three volumes of *Anthology*, 1994–95. The years 1965–67 saw the most striking development of a new English style (actually a mixture of ingredients both old and new, as all new styles are). It was a development that occurred because British bands in the mid-1960s began to move away from their initial preoccupation with either rockabilly or rhythm and blues. It needs to be emphasized that the Beatles and other bands were creating a distinctive popular style in the 1960s that would come to be recognized as British.[19] I know of no previous song, for example, that opens with either the first two chords or, indeed, the first few notes of Paul McCartney's 'Yesterday' (1965). John Lennon's 'In My Life' (1965) also has a most unusual melodic opening. Ray Davies was another songwriter helping to create a new English style: it is all too easy to imagine that the vein of English nostalgia in the lyrics of songs such as 'Waterloo Sunset' (1967) and 'Autumn Almanac' (1967) is matched by a retrospective musical style, yet that is not the case, or at least not predominantly the case. Other British beat groups of the 1960s (the Stones, the Who) became part of the rock canon, but so, too, did Bowie, the Clash and the Smiths. While Blur and Oasis frequently looked back to the 1960s, Elastica cultivated a post-punk idiom, perhaps because punk had given more prominence to women (three of the four members of Elastica were women). The influence of the Rolling Stones is more difficult to pinpoint because the influences on that band were so consistently American; however, they left their mark on the music of Shed Seven. It is evident, in short, that Britpop drew upon a rich diversity of former styles, and not just those from a single decade.

The glory days of Britpop were 1993–97, a high point being 1994 when both *Parklife* and *Definitely Maybe* were released. Media attention became frenzied in August the following year, when Blur's 'Country House' and Oasis's 'Roll with It', both released in August, raced up the charts (Blur achieved the number 1 spot, Oasis number 2). Part of the excitement about the Blur and Oasis battle was that it dovetailed neatly into the British fascination with class – art-school trendies versus working-class heroes, as the *Guardian* saw it.[20] Blur then seemed to abandon the competition. *The Great Escape* (Blur's fourth album) was disappointing, but so, too, was Oasis's *Be Here Now* with its over-grand ambitions. Pulp's *This is Hardcore* turned against Britpop, as did Blur's eponymous album of 1997, which put American models – even grunge (as in 'Song 2') – back on the agenda. Radiohead's *OK Computer* (1997) helped deal an end to Britpop: it had no 'in-your-face' attitude, no guitar focus, and employed layered harmonies and

---

18   Stanley Sadie (ed.), *New Grove Dictionary of Music and Musicians*.

19   Nobody has done more to reveal the musical originality of the Beatles than Walter Everett; see *The Beatles as Musicians: Revolver through the Anthology* and *The Beatles as Musicians: The Quarry Men through Rubber Soul*.

20   'Working Class Heroes Lead Art School Trendies', quoted in Harris, *The Last Party*, p. 230.

synths. It proved very influential. Meanwhile the media had become obsessed with the Spice Girls, whose first hit 'Wannabe' (1996) pointed in another new direction.

Oasis and the Beatles: Reworking the British Sound

Although it is apparent that the musical links are often tenuous between Britpop and British music of the 1960s, direct links have been made constantly between Oasis and the Beatles. I am therefore devoting the second half of this chapter to scrutinizing this relationship. The accusation that Oasis plagiarize the Beatles has never gone away; in 2008 Simon Hattenstone wrote, 'plenty of people can't stand the band, regarding them as crass copycats, playing 100 variants of the same song – when they're not ripping off the Beatles, they're ripping off themselves'.[21] Noel, the creative musical force behind Oasis, has said that he 'can't read or write music', and does not 'even know the chords' he's playing.[22] Whether this is credible, or merely an example of a familiar but enduring punk boast, is debatable. The first records he recollects hearing were the red and blue Beatles compilation albums, which, he says, 'taught [him] how to play guitar'. He has also stated that he learnt every riff on the Sex Pistols' album *Never Mind the Bollocks*.[23] The influence of punk rock is certainly evident in songs like 'Fade Away' and 'Headshrinker'.[24] His guitar hero from nearer home was Johnny Marr of the Manchester band the Smiths. The Stone Roses were also admired.[25] Harris claims that the Roses' 'Standing There' and Oasis's 'Cloudburst' are 'to all intents and purposes ... the same song'.[26] Surprisingly, some of the bands for which Manchester was well known – Joy Division, the Happy Mondays, and others who were signed to the Factory label – seem to have had no impact on him.[27] Noel has cited as influences the Beatles, the Small Faces, the Kinks, Elvis Presley and the Sex Pistols,[28] the first of these being all-pervasive: '[w]e can never remember life without the Beatles'.[29] However, I wish to make clear my contention that Oasis do not simply copy the Beatles, although I have no doubt that this erroneous notion constitutes

---

[21]   Hattenstone, 'Who Wants to be a Drug Addict at 41?'

[22]   *Oasis Interview* (included in a promotional *Definitely Maybe* singles box).

[23]   Mick St Michael, *Oasis*, p. 12.

[24]   Both songs may be heard on the album of Oasis B-sides *The Masterplan* (2000). They were originally released on the CD singles of 'Cigarettes and Alcohol' (1994) and 'Some Might Say' (1995) respectively.

[25]   The Stone Roses were 'an early inspiration to Oasis' (St Michael, *Oasis*, p. 62).

[26]   Harris, *The Last Party*, p. 392.

[27]   Noel mentions venues and the Factory label as reasons for Manchester's success as a pop music city; but Factory 'means nothing' to him – *Oasis Interview*.

[28]   Keith Cameron and Owen Morris, *Oasis Interviews*.

[29]   Ibid.

a major factor in the undervaluing of their music by many critics. My argument is that Oasis turn to those aspects of Beatles songs that might be regarded as a common pop language. Oasis make no attempt to imitate the harmonic and metric adventurousness of the Beatles;[30] to do so would result in crass pastiche.

Claiming that Oasis copy the Beatles is not so dissimilar to accusing Mozart of copying Haydn. The latter did not *own* the classical style, even though he developed a distinctive voice within it. Oasis seem to be interested in what, in Saussurean terms, may be understood as a distinction between *langue* and *parole* in the Beatles' musical style. Or, to put it another way, they appear to ask: what in the Beatles' style is a common musical language and what is the Beatles' individual articulation of that language? Perhaps, that is the reason their focus falls on 1965–67, before the Beatles moved too far into their own individual sound world. Another reason for such a focus is that Oasis are very much a live band, whereas the Beatles became a studio band after 1966.[31] The Beatles never performed 'I Am the Walrus' live, though Oasis have done so on numerous occasions.[32] Live versions of 'Supersonic' and 'Bring It All Down'[33] show that Oasis can effectively re-create their sound outside of a studio. The importance placed on live performance, which was crucial to their success – 'the Knebworth concerts represented the apex of Oasis's popularity', insists John Harris[34] – may stem from their early love of punk. Indeed, though Liam's and Noel's voices are both Lennon-like, Liam retains a punk sneer.

They believed that people had become tired of drum machines and sequencers and wanted to get back to 'the good old rock song'.[35] That Oasis returned to what they saw as classic rock is evident in the variety of source material they use: 'Cigarettes and Alcohol'[36] is indebted to T.Rex, but its eight-to-the-bar boogie-type start has a more distant ancestor in Chuck Berry's 'Johnny B. Goode'. It is to be distinguished from the kind of reworking given to this kind of material by Bowie and Eno in the album *Heroes* of 1977. 'Wonderwall'[37] begins by building

---

[30]   There are harmonic complexities in later Beatles' songs (e.g. 'Penny Lane' of 1967), but not always – 'Get Back' (1969) is built upon two chords only.

[31]   The only exceptions being their London roof-top gig, and the live performance on the album and film of *Let It Be*. In contrast, the Who were still a formidable live band when the 1960s ended, as the album *Live at Leeds* (1970) testifies.

[32]   A live recording from February 1994 can be found on *The Masterplan*. It was originally released on the CD single of 'Cigarettes and Alcohol'. On the CD single it lasts over eight minutes, whereas the recording on *The Masterplan* is made to fade out after six and a quarter minutes.

[33]   Released on the CD singles of 'Live Forever' and 'Cigarettes & Alcohol' respectively in 1994. Studio versions may be found on their first album, *Definitely Maybe* (1994).

[34]   Harris, *The Last Party*, p. 310.

[35]   Cameron and Owen, *Oasis Interviews*.

[36]   From *Definitely Maybe*, 1994.

[37]   From *(What's the Story) Morning Glory?*, 1995.

around a melodic motif in similar fashion to a song like the Lovin' Spoonful's 'Summer in the City'.[38]

Example 7.1   Excerpt from Oasis, 'Wonderwall'

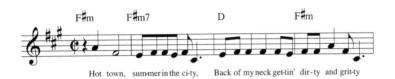

Example 7.2   Excerpt from the Lovin' Spoonful's 'Summer in the City'

Sometimes Oasis move uncomfortably close to an earlier melodic style: the tune of 'Shakermaker'[39] proved so reminiscent of Coca-Cola's 'I'd Like to Teach the World to Sing' that royalties have to be split with the latter's publishers.[40] Often, though, there is little more than the indefinable feeling that two songs share family resemblances, as happens with 'Roll with It'[41] and 'Ticket to Ride'.

'Don't Look Back in Anger'[42] can serve as a useful warning about making too facile a link to the Beatles: the opening piano figure[43] may remind us of 'Golden Slumbers'[44] or John Lennon's 'Imagine', but this sequence of chords has been around for centuries. It is heard in Pachelbel's *Canon*, Handel's *Arrival of the Queen of Sheba*, and Ralph McTell's 'Streets of London'. The melody, on the other hand, is reminiscent of 'Pretty Flamingo' (Manfred Mann).

---

[38]   'Summer in the City', however, remains closer melodically to the Beatles' 'Things We Said Today' than does the Oasis song.

[39]   From *Definitely Maybe*, 1994.

[40]   St Michael, *Oasis*, p. 37.

[41]   From (*What's the Story*) *Morning Glory?*, 1995.

[42]   From ibid., 1995.

[43]   The piano is played by Bonehead (Paul Arthurs), usually Noel's fellow guitarist.

[44]   From *Abbey Road*, 1969.

Example 7.3   Excerpt from Oasis, 'Don't Look Back in Anger'

Example 7.4   Excerpt from 'Pretty Flamingo' (Mark Barkan, 1966)

The acid-inspired 'Strawberry Fields Forever'[45] and related psychedelia on *Sgt. Pepper's Lonely Hearts Club Band* (1967) and later Beatles albums seem not to have had a great deal of impact on Oasis. The closest they have come is the song 'Magic Pie', complete with distorted voice, on their third album *Be Here Now* (1997). Neither have they taken up the idea of the 'concept album' initiated by *Sgt. Pepper*, or moved in the direction of transcendental meditation, the hippie lifestyle and 'summer of love'-type music. Yet, lyric-wise at least, Noel has probably been influenced on occasion by the quasi-surrealistic 'I Am the Walrus'.

The Beatles in 1963–64 typically opt for cut time (*alla breve*) with a Latin feel (for example, 'P.S. I Love You',[46] and 'And I Love Her'[47]).

Example 7.5   Typical cut time Latin rock

Sometimes there is a more marked Latin influence as, for example, in 'All I've Got to Do'.[48] A hard rock rather than Latin rock style begins to develop in

---

[45]   Released as a single, 1967.

[46]   From *Please Please Me*, 1963. The Latin beat is a characteristic of many of the songs of Jerry Leiber and Mike Stoller, and of Gerry Goffin and Carole King, with which the band would have been familiar.

[47]   From *A Hard Day's Night*, 1964.

[48]   From *With The Beatles*, 1963.

Rubber Soul of 1965. Oasis typically choose a hard rock style, the slower tempo of which allows a sixteenth- rather than an eighth-note subdivision of the beat. The basic rock rhythm heard in 'Supersonic' and 'Live Forever' is therefore more reminiscent of the early 1970s than the 1960s.

Example 7.6   Typical common time hard rock

'Hey Now!'[49] feels later still with its heavy punk drumming. There are, however, some Oasis songs in cut time, for example, 'Cast No Shadow'[50] and 'Wonderwall'. Ragtime vaudeville like 'When I'm Sixty-Four' or 'Maxwell's Silver Hammer'[51] may not seem typical of Oasis, but consider 'She's Electric';[52] it relates closely to this style in spite of its marked backbeat drumming.

'Wonderwall' has quasi-military drumming and a cello, bringing to mind 'Strawberry Fields Forever'. A more striking example of this military-style percussion is heard on 'Champagne Supernova', a song reminiscent of an LSD-influenced Beatles number.[53] Irregular metres, as found in 'Strawberry Fields Forever' and elsewhere rarely feature in Oasis songs. An exception is 'Stand By Me',[54] which contains a 'punctuating' use of a three-beat bar, after the manner of 'All You Need Is Love' (1967).

Where musical phrasing is concerned, the biggest difference between the approach of the Beatles and Oasis is in their treatment of hypermetre. This term refers to the larger metrical patterns that result from the tendency of phrases to form regular bar groupings, two- and four-bar phrases being the most common. The Beatles often clip phrases, creating an irregular hypermetre (for example, the irregular bar groupings of 'Strawberry Fields Forever'), whereas Oasis tend to extend one phrase and shorten the next, creating irregular phrasing within a regular hypermetre (as in 'Roll with It' and 'Don't Look Back in Anger'). Clipped phrases in Beatles songs can be found, for example, in 'Baby's in Black'[55]

---

[49]   From *(What's the Story) Morning Glory?*, 1995.

[50]   From ibid., 1995.

[51]   From *Sgt. Pepper* (1967) and *Abbey Road* (1969) respectively.

[52]   From *(What's the Story) Morning Glory?*, 1995.

[53]   The hallucinogenic connotations of this percussive feature, however, are also to be found on Jefferson Airplane's 'White Rabbit'.

[54]   From *Be Here Now*, 1997.

[55]   From *Beatles for Sale*, 1964.

(3+2+1½); 'Eleanor Rigby'[56] (4+1+4+1) and the chorus of 'All You Need is Love' (2+2+2+1½).[57] The verse of 'Every Little Thing'[58] seems a phrase short (2+2+2). 'Michelle'[59] has a more subtle six-bar verse, while 'Yesterday'[60] has an unusual seven-bar melody. Compare that to, say, the chorus of Oasis's 'Sunday Morning Call'[61] where a phrase may go on for a bar longer than expected, only to be followed by a one-bar phrase that restores symmetry. The result is that a refrain of twenty bars, falling into five hypermetric units of four bars each, has phrases that follow the pattern 2+2+2+2+2+3+1+2+2+2.

The vocal harmonies on the repeat of the chorus in 'Roll with It' have the distinctive harsh sound of parallel fourths found in some Beatles songs (for example, Harrison's 'If I Needed Someone' from *Rubber Soul*). Another striking example is found on the final cadences of 'Talk Tonight' (the B-side of the single they released of 'Some Might Say' in 1995);[62] here, the vocal harmonizing creates intriguing dissonances with the accompanying chords.

Example 7.7   Excerpt from Oasis, 'Talk Tonight'

A Beatles-influenced vocal harmony that includes falsetto and echoing of words is heard in 'Cast No Shadow'. 'Take Me Away',[63] an intimate Noel solo, uses a cadential phrase reminiscent of that in 'If I Fell'. The B flat–C–D cadence of 'P.S. I Love You' is heard in 'Fade Away' and 'She's Electric'.[64] Moving down to the bass part in Oasis songs, we find this is not as melodic or active as McCartney's (for example, 'Drive My Car', 'You Won't See Me', 'Nowhere Man',[65] plus the rock'n'roll covers 1963–64). A drone bass dominates much of 'Champagne

---

[56]   From *Revolver*, 1966.
[57]   Released as a single, 1967.
[58]   From *Beatles for Sale*, 1964.
[59]   From *Rubber Soul*, 1965.
[60]   From *Help!*, 1965.
[61]   From *Standing on the Shoulder of Giants*, 2000.
[62]   It can also be found on *The Masterplan*, 2000.
[63]   On the CD single of 'Supersonic' (1994).
[64]   From *(What's the Story) Morning Glory?*, 1995.
[65]   All from *Rubber Soul*, 1965.

Supernova',[66] reminiscent of 'Indian'-flavoured Beatles songs like 'Within You Without You'.

The production on an Oasis disc aims to create a saturated sound, which is achieved in large part by the use of synthesizer pads and multi-layering. Oasis records have a much fatter and louder sound than those of the Beatles, and are cut at a high level for good measure. Production values are also distinct from punk: the production on Oasis recordings cuts the treble and exaggerates the bass, whereas treble frequencies are emphasized in recordings of the Sex Pistols, the Clash and other punk bands. The production became excessively layered on the album *Be Here Now*, with as many as thirty guitar tracks sounding simultaneously (for example, on 'My Big Mouth'). Yet, in spite of this, the recording of an Oasis song does not convey the same sense of its being the definitive version of that song as does the recording of a Beatles song. The reason is that, as emphasized already, Oasis perform live. They have also released many live recordings. Even in their studio recordings, it is common for the recording to begin or end with extraneous noises that suggest we are eavesdropping on a live performance. 'I'll just take my watch off', says Noel before launching into 'Talk Tonight', thereby conveying, intentionally or not, a sense of immediacy about the performance.

The lyrics of several songs include Beatles references. 'Supersonic' contains the offer, 'You can ride with me in my yellow submarine'. 'Take Me Away' quotes 'I'd like to be under the sea' from 'Octopus's Garden', with the modification 'but I'd probably need a phone'. The words 'tomorrow never knows' appear in 'Morning Glory'. 'Don't Look Back in Anger' quotes from a tape of Lennon dictating his memoirs and referring to 'trying to start a revolution from my bed, because they said the brains I had went to my head'.[67] The title of 'Wonderwall' is taken from a film soundtrack album by George Harrison (the wonderwall was a wall with a hole through which a character in the film spied on a girl in an adjacent bedsit), and the drums enter on the word 'backbeat', which had been the title of a recent Beatles bio-pic.[68] The title of the third album, *Be Here Now*, is a quotation from Timothy Leary via the usual secondary source for Noel, a John Lennon interview.

Although Noel has stated that the music comes to him before the words do,[69] he tackles the thorny problems of word stress better than, say, the Manic Street Preachers, who accent the first and third words of 'A design for life'[70] among other oddities. The Beatles are not always faultless here, either – 'pride comes *be*fore a fall' in 'I'm a Loser'.[71] As for lyric content, Noel remarks that he said it all in 'Rock 'n' Roll Star', 'Live Forever' and 'Cigarettes and Alcohol', after which he

---

[66]   From (*What's the Story*) *Morning Glory?*, 1995.

[67]   St Michael, *Oasis*, pp. 87–9.

[68]   See ibid., pp. 82–4. Another flashback occurs in the video of 'Wonderwall', which contains an appearance by Patrick Macnee of the cult 1960s series *The Avengers*.

[69]   *Oasis Interview*.

[70]   From *Everything Must Go*, 1996.

[71]   From *Beatles for Sale*, 1964.

claims he has been saying the same thing in different ways.[72] 'Live Forever' was their first Top 10 hit, a deliberate counter-attack on grunge morbidity. After the individualist ideology of the Thatcher years, Oasis brought back enthusiasm for the collective. Oasis was part of a general mood that led to a revival in the fortunes of the Labour Party, bringing the Party to power in 1997. Those criticizing Oasis for lack of a political message should bear in mind that Paul McCartney once declared, '[w]e never get involved in politics because we don't know anything about it'.[73] Noel mentions his admiration for Beatles lyrics that remain a mystery, giving as examples 'I am the Walrus' and 'Bungalow Bill'.[74] He clearly lived uneasily with the label 'Britpop', since he contrasts the Englishness of groups like Blur with the universality of songs like 'Cigarettes and Alcohol'.[75]

It may be tempting to consider Oasis classic rockers, out of kilter with postmodernist values. In February 1996, Liam taunted the audience at the Brit Awards ceremony with the words, '[a]nyone tough enough to take us off the stage can come up now' (tough rock'n'roll talk 1950s/1960s style). At the same event a year later, 'Sporty Spice' (Mel C) threw out a challenge to Liam: '[c]ome and have a go if you think you're hard enough'. In the 1990s, unlike the 1960s, male bravado was easily seen through and mocked as a pose. During one of the innumerable Oasis interviews that are available on CD, the subject of Liam's aggressive stage behaviour was raised, only to be greeted with undisguised hilarity from Noel and his fellow guitarist Bonehead.[76] They did, indeed, regard it as nothing but posturing, and declared that Liam would be nowhere to be seen if anyone chose confrontation. Aggression, like revolt, has been turned into a style. In our postmodern times, every gesture made by a band like Oasis stands on the threshold of ironic reception rather than the 'shoulder [sic] of giants'.[77]

The Mike Flowers Pops cover version of 'Wonderwall' points up the historical differences between the 1990s and the 1960s in performing style, arrangements and technology, and reveals that you cannot escape your present. It assembles a syntagmatic chain of retro signifiers, but does so in the service of constructing a non-historically specific epoch. It is a mixture of 'Under the Boardwalk' (The Drifters, 1964), plus 1960s cinema intermission style strings, plus a revised harmonic vocabulary and Latin beat, and a host of other retro features, ranging from the 1950s guitar lick and the female choir to Herb Alpert's Tijuana Brass ('Spanish Flea') and the early 1970s hairstyle, large shirt collar and huge tie of Mike Flowers himself. Even the hiss and crackle of a vinyl 45rpm record is simulated.

---

[72] Cameron and Morris, *Oasis Interviews*.
[73] *The Beatles*, interview CD.
[74] *Oasis Interview*.
[75] Ibid.
[76] *Oasis Interview*.
[77] *Standing on the Shoulder of Giants*, Oasis's singularly titled fourth album, is a misquotation of Isaac Newton's words that encircle the British £2 coin.

It should not be forgotten that, despite the reputation the Beatles acquired for their involvement with psychedelic rock, they did not start out with the idea that the rock style might 'progress' through experiment and innovation. Paul explained in an early interview that they had gone along with trends rather than initiating them: '[w]e haven't tried consciously to start anything like a trend'.[78] John added: 'Everything we do is influenced by American music', mentioning Little Richard, Elvis and Buddy Holly.[79] The Beatles could well be labelled retro themselves, even in 1964, with their covers of 1950s rock'n'roll by the likes of Carl Perkins, Chuck Berry and Buddy Holly ('Honey Don't', 'Rock and Roll Music' and 'Words of Love' are all on the *Beatles for Sale* album). Moreover, they later became parodic as well as retro, as in the ragtime vaudeville songs, the 1950s four-chord riff of 'Octopus's Garden', Chicago bar blues in 'I Want You' and Fats Domino style R&B in 'Oh Darling' where McCartney's quasi-James Brown vocal may even be interpreted as a deconstructive strategy laying bare the representational code by which emotional crisis is signified.

Oasis arrived on the British pop scene at the time they did because a historical consciousness about pop had developed. The importance of British Beat to Britpop groups may be seen to have parallels with that of New Orleans jazz to those reacting against modernism in jazz after 1945. There is, after all, a similar generation gap. Should Oasis, then, be categorized as neo-classical or postmodernist? Noel claimed that there was 'no new direction' to be found on their second album *What's the Story*: 'It's not more poppy or more rocky. They're just rock'n'roll tunes.'[80] Such a postmodernist contempt for the idea of progress contrasts with the later Beatles, but also with later groups with modernist ambitions like The Prodigy or The Chemical Brothers. The Pet Shop Boys put their own position as follows: '[w]e come from a modernist tradition, believing that music progresses through technology and innovation'.[81] In that they are not attempting to progress or create an individual language for themselves, Oasis are postmodernist (that is, they reject pop metanarratives, and play down the role of 'originating genius'). The Beatles' concern with innovation, technology, progress and individuality marked them out as modernists, despite their occasional forays into postmodernist parody. However, since many critics still cling to modernist ideals as the last-ditch defence of Enlightenment values, there is a reluctance to offer Oasis aesthetic legitimation in the shape of artistic awards. The decision not to shortlist *What's the Story* for the Mercury Prize thus helped to show millions of Oasis admirers how passively they consumed music, how limited was their taste and how circumscribed were their musical horizons. It prompts a recollection of the old Broadway gag, 'nobody likes it but the public'. Even when reacting positively, critics were unreliable judges of Oasis: most initial reviews of the next album, *Be Here Now*, were good. It was

[78] *The Beatles.*
[79] Ibid.
[80] St Michael, *Oasis*, p. 73.
[81] Andrew Smith, 'A Tour of the New Pop Landscape', p. 4.

hailed on the front page of the *Observer*, 10 August 1997, as 'a triumph'.[82] Caroline
Sullivan wrote in the *Guardian* that the album captured Oasis 'at the peak of their
powers'.[83] As the dust settled a few days later, Andrew Smith asked, 'how far will
Be Here Now, with its dense, multilayered screes of guitar, bear repeated listening?'[84]
Disappointment set in as people began to feel taken in more by appearance
than substance. There was a sense of having reached a watershed. Paul Arthurs
(Bonehead) and Paul McGuigan (Guigsy) left the band in 1999, and Noel, putting
together a new line-up, was 'utterly dismissive about the idea of looking back'.[85]

Dig Out Your Soul, released in late 2008, and Oasis's most recent album at
the time of writing, shows no modernist trajectory of style. It is a return to greater
memorability of material but, at the same time, confirms that their style has never
changed. Noel is realistic about the contradictions of being a mouthpiece for a
generation: speaking of *Definitely Maybe*, he explains,

> I wrote that album when I was 21/22, and the people who picked up on that album
> were 21/22 year-olds ... we were the same as them. We had no money, the people
> in the crowd had no money. We're rock stars now ... [b]ut there's a point that lasts
> for about three years where you're in the same circumstances, you look the same
> and you dress the same as your audience, and that, my friend – you cannot buy.[86]

Paul Taylor thought Oasis's moment in pop history had passed: 'Oasis have added
little to their all-time greatest hits in the past decade', and as they rock on into
middle age, they look 'more like the new Status Quo'.[87] Actually, back in 1997,
'Roll with It' already sounded like Status Quo. Dan Cairns writing a review of
Oasis's live performance as part of the BBC Electric Proms in 2008, comments:
'[t]he six songs included from their only mildly diverting new album *Dig out Your
Soul*, reinforced the sense that Oasis these days trade chiefly in former glories'.[88]

Nevertheless, to end on a eulogistic note, let us acknowledge that Oasis
produced some of the most positive songs of the 1990s. In 'Cigarettes and
Alcohol', which could easily have been downbeat, the key words are 'You gotta
make it happen'. The sentiments of 'Live Forever' are also in marked contrast to
the 1960s mantra 'hope I die before I get old'. The typical Oasis song for Noel is
'Roll with It', and its message, 'shut up moaning and get on with it'.[89] Whatever
the debt to earlier British bands, it is important to recognize that times change, and
that the articulation of such sentiments, coming as they did in the wake of punk

82 Neil Spencer, 'Here at Last. Oasis Break the Drought', p. 1.
83 Caroline Sullivan, 'Never Mind the Bo***cks – Here's the Heart and Soul', p. 2.
84 Smith, 'A Tour of the New Pop Landscape', p. 4.
85 Jim Shelley, 'Oasis', p. 14.
86 Hattenstone, 'Who Wants to be a Drug Addict at 41?'
87 Paul Taylor, 'Are Rock's Big Hitters now Simply Quoasis?'
88 Dan Cairns, 'Oasis: Roundhouse, NW1'.
89 St Michael, *Oasis*, p. 67.

and grunge, needs to be distinguished from, say, a Beatles song like 'I Feel Fine'. Oasis consciously reacted against grunge misery.[90] Noel remarked trenchantly apropos of Nirvana, Pearl Jam, and their like, 'I think American youth has had enough of people telling them how crap their lives are, and I think that when they listen to our records we just tell them how good their lives could be.'[91] The lasting value of such Britpop optimism was revealed when demand for tickets exceeded expectations as the bands Shed Seven, Dodgy and Kula Shaker re-formed to tour in October 2007.[92] Perhaps, today, it is not unreasonable to see a band like the Kaiser Chiefs as inheriting the legacy of Britpop. As for Oasis, they were named Best British Band at the NME awards in February 2009 and were touring the world.

The protracted comparison of Oasis and the Beatles, with which this chapter has concluded, is intended to provide evidence to show that it is a mistake to dismiss Britpop as mere imitation. To make the point, it has been necessary to narrow the critical focus and scrutinize the most commonly cited example of such supposed imitation. The fact that Britpop groups did not create an innovative musical style for the later 1990s – in the sense that the Beatles and others did for the later 1960s (through harmonic adventurousness, novel modal inflections, metrical irregularities and unexpected phrasing) – does not mean that the music of bands such as Suede, Blur, Elastica and Oasis contained nothing new or exciting.

---

[90]   They would also probably reject words like 'I'm so glad that she's my little girl' (from the Beatles' 'I Feel Fine').

[91]   St Michael, *Oasis*, p. 96.

[92]   Dave Simpson, 'We're Bigger Now than Ever'.

Chapter 8
Britpop or Eng-pop?

J. Mark Percival

Introduction

Britpop in the mid-1990s, according to journalist and cultural commentator John Harris,[1] rapidly came to represent a peculiarly English form of Britishness in UK contemporary popular music. In this chapter I argue that there were two reasons for this. Firstly, Britpop despite its apparent openness to regional groups (Oasis from Manchester and Pulp from Sheffield, for example) was in reality London-centric and deeply exclusivist, particularly as mainstream crossover success transformed alternative sounds into significant record sales.[2] Secondly, a combination of the 'movement' being mainstream and its overwhelming Englishness meant that indie scenes in Scotland and Wales were simply not interested in associating themselves with 'Britpop'.[3] It is also important to frame any discussion of bands working outside of the Britpop milieu as not simply being a 'response' to Britpop. This has implications of a passivity clearly not present in 1990s Scottish and Welsh rock and pop.

Edwards[4] discusses signifiers of Welshness in late-1990s Welsh bands and, of her three-layer model (media discourse; the symbols of Welshness used by the bands; use of the music in public spaces), I focus here primarily on the *representation* of

---

[1]   John Harris, *The Last Party: Britpop, Blair and the Demise of English Rock.*

[2]   Or, in Blur's case, into significant record sales *again*, following their 1991 debut album *Leisure*, which reached number 7 in the UK sales charts, and their Top 10 single 'There's No Other Way'.

[3]   This chapter does not address Northern Irish popular music in the 1990s. This is not to suggest that there weren't significant developments in popular music in the province at this time, rather that Northern Ireland's relationship to notions of Britishness and Englishness is significantly more complex than that of Scotland or Wales. An example of this additional layer of complexity might be the use of the Union Jack flag in much Britpop iconography – contentious enough in an English/Scottish/Welsh cultural context, but symbolic of deep social, political and religious divisions in Northern Ireland. Two 1990s Northern Irish bands achieved significant national UK and international success: Therapy? and Ash. Of the two, Ash have had the higher profile career, though both bands were still active in 2009. Their relationship to Britpop is peripheral, reflecting the historic tendency for Northern Irish bands to develop in relative cultural isolation from the rest of the UK.

[4]   Rebecca Edwards, 'Everyday, When I Wake Up, I Thank the Lord I'm Welsh: Reading the Markers of Welsh Identity in 1990s Pop Music'.

Welsh and Scottish bands. I explore aspects of Scottish and Welsh popular music contemporaneous with *English* Britpop in the mid- to late-1990s and investigate how that music has been represented by the bands themselves and by journalists. The themes that emerge are identity, authenticity, place, community and (in Wales) language.[5]

This chapter, then, has three key aims: to show how representations of Scottish and Welsh bands in the 1990s Britpop era tended to attribute positive essentialist characteristics to the bands from Scotland and Wales, contrasted against negative essentialist characteristics of (English) Britpop artists; to argue that the explicit Englishness of Britpop was part of a cultural narrative that codified a pre-existing sense of Wales and Scotland as a distant 'other', increasingly culturally distinct from the London centre of the UK music industry; to suggest that simplistic discourses around national identity in Wales and Scotland fail to explain the processes through which new popular music emerges in these nations.

These aims are addressed first with a brief account of the cultural and historical context within which key bands were working, and from which the term Britpop emerged. There is then a discussion of place in relation to authenticity and to politics and identity, followed by two more extended sections on bands and representation. The Scottish bands covered are Travis, Mogwai and the Delgados. Welsh bands addressed are Stereophonics, the Manic Street Preachers and Super Furry Animals. Throughout the chapter I also draw, to an extent, on some of my own early interviews with, and participant observation of, indie bands in the Glasgow scene from 1997 to 2000 and in 2007.

Context

Tilley and Heath[6] argue that there has been a generational shift in which many of those who came of age from the 1980s onwards have significantly less attachment to notions of 'Britishness', and tend to emphasize their Welsh or Scottish identity. They identify several strands of evidence to support their argument, but perhaps of most relevance here is their suggestion that there was a stridently English version of Britishness espoused by both Thatcher and Major administrations (1979–1997). Scots in particular felt excluded by this discourse, and there is a reflection of this sense of exclusion in the formation of the Englishness of Britpop and the rejection of Britpop sounds and styles by many Scottish bands. The situation, and the discourse of Britishness, changed little after the 1997 election victory of Tony Blair's New Labour, which briefly declared support for the rebranding of the UK

---

    5   The music I'll be discussing is broadly pop and rock, generically and stylistically – I won't be considering Welsh and Scottish Celtic musics because these forms have their analogues in English folk and traditional music, rather than Britpop.

    6   James Tilley and Anthony Heath, 'The Decline of British National Pride'.

as 'Cool Britannia' (playing on the title of the eighteenth-century patriotic, nation-building song 'Rule, Britannia!').

Cool Britannia was an attempt to represent British popular culture as capable of world-beating leadership in music, film, contemporary art and fashion. Despite the ambitions of the campaign to replace established perceptions of Britain as rural, conservative and upper class with a celebration of outward-looking creative multiculturalism, Cool Britannia remained stubbornly English. McLaughlin[7] reports then Culture Secretary Tessa Jowell's 2001 assessment: 'the ... project had failed because it did not realise that "our national culture is something amorphous, something changing, and something complex", defined by and open to external influences'. Implicit in McLaughlin's work is the point that when a Prime Minister tells the nation that something is 'cool', any vestige of subcultural coolness will be thoroughly erased.

There is also an historical perspective to the use of the term 'Britpop' as a signifier of national identity. An early instance of the use of the descriptor 'Britpop' has an international dimension. In 1977 'Britpop' is used in an NME Sex Pistols feature by Charles Shaar Murray. Although this is an English journalist writing for a London-based national UK music weekly, he describes how the Sex Pistols were perceived by their Swedish hosts, during their Scandinavian tour: 'At home The Sex Pistols are public enemies. In Sweden, they're an important visiting Britpop group.'[8] This use of the term 'Britpop' illustrates my point about British/English synonymy, but it also alludes to the existence of broader issues around authenticity and the pop/rock differentiation so important in British popular music discourse, academic or otherwise. In 1977 the notion of the Sex Pistols as pop would have been considered absurd by British punk fans, yet Shaar Murray suggests that in the Scandinavian context there was little if any distinction between pop and rock, or between Britishness and Englishness. Elsewhere in the same article there is a recurring theme of the tedium of Sweden (weak beer, polite people, and so on), so this lack of ability to make such distinctions is both ridiculed ('they don't understand our culture'[9]) and celebrated ('the Pistols are treated like a *proper* band by Swedes'[10]).

Matt Snow, in a 1983 NME review of the fourth Gang of Four album *Hard*, uses 'Britpop' to describe the Thompson Twins, Talk Talk and 'quasi-Brits Icehouse'.[11] Here the British bands in question are again English, but the sounds are more clearly and explicitly 'pop'. It wasn't until 1993 that 'Britpop' became a 'movement' – that year, English music journalist Simon Reynolds used 'Britpop' in a US-based interview with Brett Anderson for *Melody Maker*, but in the context

---

[7]   Eugene McLaughlin, 'Re-branding Britain'.

[8]   Charles Shaar Murray, 'The Social Rehabilitation of the Sex Pistols'.

[9]   Ibid.

[10]   Ibid.

[11]   'Quasi' in the sense that the band were in fact 'British'-sounding Australians; see Matt Snow, 'Gang of Four: Hard (EMI)'.

of establishing an historic lineage to Suede's 'Britpop forebears, from Roxy Music to The Jam to The Smiths'.[12] Reynolds's situating of Suede as part of a canon of great British (English) bands is also central to a mid-1990s Britpop tendency towards nostalgia and arguably even pastiche – Blur (David Bowie, Syd Barrett, the Kinks); Suede (David Bowie again; 1970s Glam Rock); Elastica (late-1970s punk and new wave); Oasis (the Beatles). Each of Reynolds's chosen points of reference has their own particular nostalgic tendency: the Jam and 1960s mod and soul; the Smiths and kitchen-sink post-Second-World-War tragi-drama; Roxy Music, whose name alone connotes a British dance-hall past. 'Britpop' by 1993/1994 then had become attached to a 'movement' (in reality a rather disparate assemblage of bands and sounds), lost its quote marks and became an unproblematized Britpop.

Place and Authenticity

Several Scottish and Welsh bands achieved commercial success alongside Britpop contemporaries – Travis and Stereophonics, for example, had both become high-sales, major-label bands by the end of the 1990s. However, for most bands the mainstream quality of Britpop and its Englishness worked to underline a pre-existing sense of *not*-Englishness in Scottish and Welsh bands and the unwillingness of those bands to be perceived as part of a mainstream culture of rock and pop production. In short, it emphasized bands' sense of their own authenticity in the face of Britpop's perceived *inauthenticity*. This process can be seen at work even in bands like Travis and Stereophonics whose commercial success equalled their Britpop peers. The success of Travis and Stereophonics was often framed by the bands themselves and by journalists in terms of their Welshness or Scottishness, and associated national stereotypes of self-deprecation, Celtic passion/sentimentality and an authenticist appeal to their regional and class origins.

The perceived inauthenticity of Britpop bands reflected also on those Scottish or Welsh bands that attempted to hitch their careers to Britpop image and sound. A band that suffered particularly from this characterization was Glasgow-based five-piece The Gyres, whose attempts to break through from 1995 onwards on their own label (Sugar) included tours with Oasis, Cast and Echobelly. Stuart Braithwaite of Glasgow post-rockers Mogwai contrasts his positive, authenticist view of the creativity and innovation of Glasgow's underground bands in the mid-1990s, against bands he and others perceived as derivative and commercially-driven:[13]

---

[12]   Simon Reynolds, 'Suede: The Best New Band in America?'

[13]   To a degree, the antipathy to the London-based mainstream record and media industries built bridges between Scotland and Wales in the form of the closeness of bands like Mogwai and Super Furry Animals, and the personal affection between their de facto leaders, Stuart Braithwaite and Gruff Rhys – Rhys has written and sung lyrics on the Mogwai track 'Dial: Revenge' from their third studio album, *Rock Action* (2001). As Super Furry Animals keyboard player Cian Ciaran put it on the eve of a 2001 UK tour: 'We are

Part of the reason that there was a burst of bands [in Glasgow] around about the time we started [1995], was that Glasgow got no attention at all from the media. So the bands were finding their feet without any labels coming to see them or journalists writing about them. When we started with The Yummy Fur, Urusei Yatsura, Pink Kross, Bis ... [we] weren't the bands that [the London-based national UK media and the record industry] were interested in ... [they] wanted bands that were pale imitations of Oasis [like the Gyres].[14]

So in this case a band from the Lanarkshire town of Blantyre that made explicit sonic and visual references to Oasis is perceived as inauthentic by the indie/alternative scene, despite having solid roots in a Scottish working-class community. What is perhaps ironic is that at least part of Oasis's success appears to have been connected to the Gallaghers' unashamed and obvious pastiche of Beatles' sounds and styles. The Gyres' authenticity is compromised by an apparent attempt to sound like a successful contemporary English band, whereas Oasis's authenticity is emphasized through their many references to the Beatles as one the most important and recognizable (English) sounds in popular music history.[15]

Place, Politics and Identity

It isn't really possible to address this period in Welsh and Scottish popular music history without at least briefly considering the broader political and cultural context in which these bands emerged. Despite the apparent similarities between the Scottish and Welsh political situations in the mid- to late-1990s, as Scotland moved towards a devolved Parliament and Wales towards having an Assembly, things were rather different on the ground. Nationalism had always been a much stronger force in Welsh culture and politics than in Scotland. Davies argues that changes in the meaning of Welsh 'national identity' were significant in bringing

---

good mates with the Mogwai lads and although we are not playing in Glasgow we might still meet up with them for a few beers' – W. Miller, 'Furry Cool: Super Band are Animal Magic', p. 16.

[14]   Author's interview with Stuart Braithwaite, 2007. An example of the length of time this sentiment has survived was still visible as late as October 2009 – keyword tags applied by Last FM users to The Gyres included, amongst others, 'a disgrace to Glasgow', 'Britpop' and 'shite' (see Last.FM, 'The Gyres'). 'Shite', as opposed to 'shit', is used in many regions around the UK, outside of London and the Home Counties, but is often associated with Scots and Northern Irish dialect.

[15]   It is probably worth making the point that Oasis have had a strong popular following in Scotland since they were signed by Creation Records' Alan McGee after a 1993 gig in Glasgow venue King Tut's Wah Wah Hut. The problem for some Scottish music fans was not Oasis's Englishness, but The Gyres' perceived attempt to sound like them.

about what she refers to as a 'pro-devolution shift'.[16] This shift in Welsh attitudes to devolution is evident in the contrast between the 1979 referendum on a proposed Welsh Assembly (rejected by a vote of around four to one), and the 1997 referendum in which a Welsh Assembly was approved by a narrow margin of 50.3 per cent to 49.7 per cent. In Wales, then, the 1990s were characterized by an increased national self-confidence that became the cultural backdrop to more significantly politicized pop and rock.

In Scotland, outside of the more explicitly political songwriting of traditional folk performers, there is little evidence of politics (and the significance or otherwise of devolution) in the bands that emerged in the mid-1990s. My empirical work with some of those bands has convinced me that Elisabeth Mahoney was absolutely right in an *Independent* newspaper feature on music in Scotland in the spring of 1999, as the inauguration of the Scottish Parliament approached.[17] Mahoney's point is that external (in this case, English) perceptions of Scotland tend to be deeply inflected with broad stereotypes:

> In these momentous days of imminent political change in Scotland, you might expect to find ... be-kilted balladeers penning sentimental hearts-on-sleeves numbers, songs with 'Braveheart' in the title, or at least the chorus; you're probably expecting a Big Country revival any minute now. But no, something strange is happening, or not happening, in Scottish pop right now. No one, musically, is taking much notice of the political goings-on. This isn't to say individual musicians aren't interested or passionate about political change. But so far, there's been little crossover between devolution and pop, and that has a lot to do with the very healthy state of music in Scotland these days.[18]

Implicit in this argument is the sense that by the early 1990s it became less important to explicitly *perform* Scottishness in popular music. This does not mean that issues of identity and some of the essentialist/nationalist arguments had disappeared, merely that their expression was significantly more understated. It is here that I feel there are problems with some accounts of popular music and the

---

[16]   Rebecca Davies, 'Banal Britishness and Reconstituted Welshness: The Politics of National Identities in Wales', p. 106.

[17]   Some of this empirical work appears in a chapter of my 2007 PhD thesis (Percival, 'Making Music Radio: The Record Industry and Popular Music Production in the UK'), addressing the relationship between local music scenes and specialist indie and alternative radio shows. My interest in this area came in part from my parallel career as BBC Radio Scotland DJ, playing indie pop and alternative rock 1988–1994, and electronica 1997–2000. Between 1993 and 1998 I ran a regular club night at venue The 13th Note, where I met and worked with many Glasgow's new indie-scene bands. In the late 1990s and early 2000s I interviewed several of these bands for research papers presented at a number of academic conferences.

[18]   Elisabeth Mahoney, 'Rip it Up, Start Again', p. 11.

politics of identity. The problems are rarely with the work itself, which is often thorough and revealing, but with what it is that is studied. Stokes[19] approaches the argument largely in terms of the association of folk, traditional and community/ regional music with conflict, violence, oppression, imperialism and resistance to dominant cultures and ritual. This doesn't help us understand what's going on with contemporary rock and pop in the UK in the ways that Cohen's contrasting account of local music-making in Liverpool does.[20] Of the aspects of local music Cohen addresses (ritual, belief, convention, authenticity and the city), it is the other-ing of Manchester as Liverpool's cultural and economic competitor that has resonances with the situation in Scotland and Wales in the mid- to late-1990s, where the 'other' is embodied in the English centres of Britpop, most notably London.

Of course, the association of popular music and place is far from straightforward. Connell and Gibson argue that 'distinctive national styles are … marked by strategic essentialism, marketing and local boosterism',[21] and that:

> … linking music to physical places or ethnic groups can only be a contested enterprise. Boundaries are porous, constantly being broken, necessitating … new attempts to sustain imagined communities in the face of transnational flows. National sounds are retrospective and nostalgic, markers of a less fluid, more local era: a wider scale of the fetishisation of locality.[22]

Britpop then was a 'deliberate media construction of national musical style',[23] which resonates with Regev and Seroussi's argument that 'the existence of a constructed national culture in which narratives of ancestry and origin are presented as objective history is widely accepted'.[24] Whether there was a sense of shared style in the big names of Britpop is not as important, though, as the argument that 'national' sounds are both retrospective and nostalgic.

Bands and Representation 1: Scotland

The Scottish and Welsh bands I discuss here illustrate the central argument of this chapter – that Britpop (with its core emphasis, explicitly or otherwise, on various constructions of Englishness) served to emphasize a self-identified otherness in

---

[19] Martin Stokes, 'Introduction: Ethnicity, Identity and Music'.

[20] Sara Cohen, *Rock Culture in Liverpool: Popular Music in the Making.*

[21] John Connell and Chris Gibson, *Sound Tracks: Popular Music, Identity, and Place*, p. 124.

[22] Ibid., p. 143.

[23] Ibid., p. 124.

[24] Motti Regev and Edwin Seroussi, *Popular Music and National Culture in Israel*, p. 3.

Scots and Welsh bands. This otherness is largely part of Scots and Welsh musicians' sense of identity as it functions in an industry dominated by London-centred production and media institutions. It also seems to be a constant across genres and contrasting levels of economic and critical success, which often appear to be in opposition. While there is a long-standing popular discourse placing creativity in opposition to commerce, Frith observes that it is the fusion of the creative and the commercial that has created industrialized popular music as we know it.[25] Consider Mogwai, a post-rock band with its roots in Glasgow's independent scene of the early to mid-1990s.[26] The band had critical success with their earliest releases, but became commercially successful enough to sell out a live show at the Royal Albert Hall in 2006. Yet Mogwai, despite this evident and ongoing popularity, retain their critical cachet. Four-piece guitar pop band Travis formed in Glasgow a year or two before Mogwai, but moved to London in 1996 to pursue commercial success. Travis were embraced by a mainstream audience, but were treated more equivocally by music critics. Take Scottish journalist Keith Cameron's comment about Travis front-man Fran Healy in a 2001 *Guardian* feature:

> Healy's ... arch populism – he happily admits to being one of the 90 percent of the population who don't avidly buy records, who don't read many books, who don't care very much about politics – [has] ensured Travis pariah status among those who believe music ought to represent something more than a sop to the masses ... [27]

So, by one construction of authenticity, that of opposition by an innovative minority to a culturally conservative mainstream, Travis fail. Healy nevertheless often refers to his ethnicity as a signifier of difference from the English music industry. In an October 2003 press release accompanying the album *12 Memories*, Healy comments on the band's response to their fame: 'Being Scottish, we're very reticent about being famous pop stars; it's encoded into our DNA that we can't be brassy or show off. But suddenly, we weren't this little band in Glasgow any more'.[28] Healy emphasizes the notion that one key characteristic that distinguishes Scots from the English is a modest self-awareness that is at odds with the requirements of being famous, and is reflective of the essentialism that tends to dominate popular

---

[25]   Simon Frith, 'The Industrialisation of Music'.

[26]   The term 'post rock', allegedly coined by *Melody Maker* journalist Simon Reynolds, refers to a number of bands that began releasing albums in the early-1990s. Although using for the most part conventional rock instrumentation, songs are frequently instrumental and extended in length, drawing influences from earlier experimental rock movements and sounds. Bands described by music journalists as post rock include US groups Slint and Tortoise, and Bark Psychosis from the UK.

[27]   Keith Cameron, 'Songs in the Key of Life'.

[28]   Fran Healy, 12 Memories: press release.

discourse on national identity.[29] From considerably further to the critical left of Travis, Mogwai's Stuart Braithwaite pulls together place, authenticity and the creativity/commerce bi-polarity:

> It's important that Glasgow's not London. I know when I've been in London, around the music scene, there's a different atmosphere. It's all talk about who's cool, or who's going to be really big, because it's an industry, it's all about money. The scene we emerged from wasn't concerned about money.[30]

The geographical space between London and Glasgow is also, for Braithwaite and other Scots musicians, a cultural distance that re-enforces the sense that Scotland is in some way better or more authentic than England. Mogwai have a more direct relationship with Britpop, though. In 1999 the band had T-shirts printed with the legend 'Blur: Are Shite', and developed the concept across several press interviews. Following the announcement of Blur's summer 2009 reunion shows, a blog on Mogwai's official website suggested that they were considering a new line of T-shirts bearing the message: 'Blur are shite once again'.[31] Perhaps to their credit, Blur did not respond in kind to Mogwai's 1999 critique, but it's clear that Mogwai's T-shirts were about more than simply representing Blur as mainstream and creatively bankrupt. The shirts were parodic, using an accurate reproduction of the typeface and graphic design of then-current Blur promotional material. Further, their use of the regional term 'shite' and the obvious humorously provocative intentionality reflect an irreverence to authority and to dominant mainstream culture. Initial stocks of the 1999 T-shirt sold out quickly and Mogwai reported that they'd had requests for more stock from US alternative rock band Pavement and from Welsh long-time friends Super Furry Animals, which suggests that the humour of the T-shirt worked well beyond Mogwai's west of Scotland home. Leading Britpop bands, during the mid-1990s height of the 'movement', were many things (commercially successful, melodic, nostalgic, clever, dumb) but with the exception of Pulp's Jarvis Cocker, somewhat short of public displays of wit or humour. In this example then, humour becomes an additional signifier of difference, emphasizing the cultural and geographic distance between Glasgow and London.

The cultural distance remains intact, however, even when the geographic separation is no longer there, as was the case with Travis living and working in London. Music journalist Keith Cameron, in his 2001 *Guardian* feature on the band, framed its 1999 breakthrough in terms of the fallout of Britpop.

> Here … was a band with the universal musical pedigree of, say, Oasis, but without the bad attitude, the humble hangover after Britpop's hedonistic binge

---

29 Richard Kiely, Frank Bechhofer and David McCrone, 'Birth, Blood and Belonging: Identity Claims in Post-Devolution Scotland'.

30 Author's interview with Braithwaite, 2007.

31 *NME*, 'Blur: Are Shite Once Again'.

> ... Unlike Oasis, with whom they have shared stages as well as an entrenched
> faith in the traditional values of honest songcraft, Travis shuns the conspicuous
> trappings of success.[32]

Here Cameron rather adeptly wove together several strands of authenticity, at
least as perceived by, as he put it, 'the people charged with deciding what music
we hear'.[33] In the broadest sense, those 'people' are gatekeepers throughout the
popular music and media industries, and it is those notions of 'musical pedigree'
and 'honest songcraft' that draw around themselves an aura of positive and
apparently desirable values. Travis and Oasis are connected through these positive
associations, through these authenticities. Yet the Scots are distinguished from
the Mancunians through the former's apparent humility and lack of demonstrable
hedonistic excess. The commercial success of Travis is characterized, at least in
part, as being a consequence of a disillusionment with Britpop and its seemingly
English drug- and alcohol-fuelled extroversion, perhaps even its arrogance. Later
in the same piece Cameron describes the willingness of Travis as a band to work
unselfconsciously *with* the music and media industries' publicity machinery.
He compares Travis with Welsh art-punk-rock anthemicists the Manic Street
Preachers' reluctance to do the same, yet both bands are, in Cameron's own italics,
real. In this case he was referring to a then-popular Saturday morning children's
ITV show, *CD:UK*:

> *CD:UK*'s base currency is pop [but] occasionally ... a 'proper' band slips
> through the net. Several months ago, it was the Manic Street Preachers,
> mumbling and squirming in the face of their bright-eyed inquisitors, clearly
> mortified to be there at all. By way of contrast, Travis are garrulous naturals.
> Healy and bassist Dougie Payne play the game, sign autographs, smile for
> pictures, and generally accept their role of token scruffs with far more grace
> than it warrants.[34]

In this piece, however, it isn't clear where Cameron's own sympathies really lie.
On one hand, he represents the apparent normality and down-to-earth-ness of
Travis as a positive value (they display 'grace' as they participate in the media
process). Yet, in Cameron's description of the Manic Street Preachers as somewhat
embarrassed to be seen on a mainstream Saturday morning television show, there
is both critique of rock authenticity (the band looked ridiculous) and celebration
(it is *natural* that a 'proper' band will feel like that when placed in the context of
a 'pop music' show).

This perspective assumes readers' knowledge of the Manic Street Preachers'
1990s history as provocateurs, polemicists and latterly major rock artists capable

---

[32]   Cameron, 'Songs in the Key of Life'.

[33]   Ibid.

[34]   Ibid.

of selling a large number of anthemic rock albums. It also invites the reader to consider the humour, even the absurdity, of a band whose seriousness is underwritten by a disappeared, presumed dead guitarist, having been interviewed by future mainstream media stars Anthony McPartlin, Declan Donnelly or Cat Deeley.[35] The historical contrast between Travis and the Manic Street Preachers might be further emphasized by comparing their most noteworthy Glastonbury appearances. In 1994 the Manic Street Preachers' bass player Nicky Wire announced to a main stage crowd that there should be a 'bypass built over this shithole'.[36] In contrast Travis at Glastonbury 1999 were remembered because of the real rain that accompanied a performance of their hit single, 'Why Does it Always Rain on Me?', a happy coincidence that helped garner them coverage across the UK national media. As Travis guitarist Andy Dunlop put it:

> There are points in your career that you would include in the ... film of it. Bits of luck that made the band take off. Like when we were doing Glastonbury and it rained as soon as *Why Does it Always Rain on Me* started. Everyone was talking about how we made it rain.[37]

Travis then emerged from the end of the Britpop decade as the fourth biggest-selling UK band of 1999[38] with positive public perceptions of their Scottishness intact. The band's association with Oasis, on stage and off, appeared to re-enforce particular generic rock authenticities like honesty, song craft and 'connection' to audience. Yet their embodiment of Scottish stereotypical values of humility and self-deprecation distanced them from the apparent arrogance of the late Britpop scene in general, and Oasis in particular. A 1999 *NME* live review, discussing the Travis album *The Man Who*, sums up these representations rather succinctly, noting that the songs on the album 'retain a humble simplicity and candour that is entirely Travis' own'.[39]

The Delgados formed in 1994 when vocalist and guitarist Emma Pollock, from a small town in south-west Scotland, joined vocalist and guitarist Alun Woodward, bass player Stewart Henderson and drummer/producer Paul Savage, all three from Hamilton, 15 miles south-east of Glasgow. They released their first full-length album, *Domestiques*, in 1996 and split up in the spring of 2005, following the 2004 release of their fifth and final studio album (*Universal Audio*). They continue to jointly own and run Chemikal Underground, an independent label based in Glasgow.

---

[35] The Manic Street Preachers' rhythm guitarist and lyricist, Richey Edwards, disappeared in 1994 and was pronounced legally dead in 2008; see *NME*, 'Manic Street Preachers' Richey Edwards Officially Dead'.

[36] *NME*, 'Nicky Wire says Glastonbury "Shithole" Comment was a Joke'.

[37] Quoted in Emma Pinch, 'Travis: New Album's Creative Process was Liberatingly Unstructured'.

[38] British Phonographic Institute, 'Yearly Best Selling Albums 1999'.

[39] *NME*, 'Glasgow Garage'.

The Delgados, with Mogwai, Bis and a number of other disparate bands, were part of the 13th Note café-bar-venue scene that began to coalesce in 1993–94, around the same time as Britpop emerged south of the Border. My own work in the past on this scene suggests that, while there was little or no sense of these young Scottish bands *responding* to Britpop, it was clear that they saw themselves as clearly distinct from the Englishness (and in particular, the *London-ness*) of Britpop.[40] For the 13th Note-scene bands, this distance conceptually and geographically was frequently played out in reviews, features and interviews. As early as 1997, just as the 13th Note-scene bands were putting out their first records, Charlie Porter, in a *Times* piece on new bands, noted: '... most of the new British talent does not care for attempts at commercial success ... Glasgow's ... Mogwai will continue to gain support, as will Arab Strap and the Delgados, two of the best bands in Britain with none of the Gallagher hype.'[41] Porter flags the authentic values inherent in ideologies of independent music, and contrasts the authenticity of the Glasgow bands with the media 'hype' surrounding Oasis. On one hand Oasis were a massive commercial success at the centre of a new rock establishment. For bands and journalists who subscribe to the notion that independence from a commercially driven mainstream industry is intrinsically a good thing, Oasis were inauthentic, and worse, not cool. On the other hand the Gallagher brothers were working-class boys made good; they were from the industrial north of England; they made records that strongly recalled the holy grail sounds of the Beatles (though not, for the most part, the Beatles' ability to innovate and experiment). For many Oasis fans these latter qualities bestowed an undeniable aura of authenticity to the band.

For some journalists and critics, Glasgow had by 1998 become a place where important and innovative new music was being made, and stood in stark contrast to the evils of Britpop. Tom Cox of *The Guardian* suggested that:

> Glasgow has stepped forward as Britain's undisputable second musical city, leaving competitors Manchester and Liverpool in a cloud of sub-Oasis dust. With [its] 'Who, us?' demeanour disguising a quiet determination, the Glasgow attitude nestles light-years from its mouthy counterpart south of the border. 'There was a nationalism in Britpop that you wouldn't get here. Because we live in a smaller country, we tend to think more internationally', [Stephen] McRobbie [of the Pastels] points out ... [The city is] honest and vibrant.[42]

---

[40]   See J. Mark Percival, 'Time, Space and Identity and Indie Music Production in West Central Scotland'. It is true that none of the big three Britpop bands (Blur, Oasis and Pulp) was actually *from* London, but their labels were based there, as were most of the musicians involved during the height of Britpop.

[41]   Charlie Porter, 'Songs for the Soul, Not for the Sales List', p. 15.

[42]   Tom Cox, 'West End Pearls: Scottish Bands used to be Pompous Arena Queens, but since Glasgow became European City of Culture, a Remarkable Renaissance in its Pop Scene has Occurred [...]', p. T012.

Glasgow here is framed as a place that not only is *not* London but which is also socially intimate, characteristically modest and generally unconcerned with the economic drivers of the English centre of the music industry in the UK. More importantly, Stephen McRobbie of Glasgow band the Pastels, who formed in 1982 and were still active in 2009, contrasts the English nationalism of Britpop against the internationalist attitude of Scottish independent/alternative bands. This correlates with journalist Elisabeth Mahoney's argument that devolution at the end of the 1990s had little or no cultural impact on independent music-making in Scotland – bands were much more likely to be interested in a much less explicit and more subtle notion of national identity.[43]

This relaxed attitude to contested notions of national identity is also reflected in Chemikal Underground's notion of pragmatic independence. Stewart Henderson, after only three years of running the label alongside the other Delgados, had already developed a principled sense of ambition for future success: 'We're not precious at all about any indie ethic. We want to keep the label independent because it is a good thing to do, but we want Chemikal Underground to out-perform all the majors'.[44] This is balanced by a practical conceptualization of the relationship between Glasgow and London. Emma Pollock of the Delgados and Chemikal Underground makes a clear and unsentimental distinction between the cities:

> We need the press and radio and distribution based in London. But as far as the creative side of music is concerned, we can do that in Glasgow. Any time people go to London [from here] it's because they have to. Glasgow's big enough for me to have an element of anonymity, but small enough to walk around.[45]

Pollock knows that Chemikal Underground works in the same business environment as the rest of the record industry, and that, in order to continue to function sustainably, the label must engage with the same media and distribution networks as their competitors. There is also here a clear statement of why Pollock believes Glasgow to be a better place to both live and work than London.

The first big-selling album on Chemikal Underground was Mogwai's *Young Team* in 1997 (reissued in a deluxe re-mastered format in 2008), an album that established both the label's financial viability and its cultural influence. Mogwai's music is predominantly instrumental post-rock and so the band stand in particularly stark contrast to some of their Welsh contemporaries for whom language itself was a contested arena in which notions of national identity were played out. In a 1999 *Guardian* review of Mogwai's second studio album *Come On Die Young*, John O'Reilly sees no explicit reference to traditional notions of Scottish national identity in Mogwai and the band's peers, but he does attribute to them some of the distinctive traits frequently associated with Scots and Scotland:

---

[43] See Elisabeth Mahoney, 'Rip it Up, Start Again'.

[44] Quoted in Charlie Porter, 'Balancing Act', p. 10.

[45] Author's interview with Emma Pollock, 2007.

> It's not nationality or record label that binds together Mogwai, [Falkirk band] Arab Strap and the Delgados. What marks out their sound is a musical honesty that is also utterly self-effacing. It is the same dry existentialism that is often disguised in a writer like Irvine Welsh by his tales of chemical excess. But Mogwai's *Come On Die Young* has taken self-effacement to the point of disappearance.[46]

O'Reilly associates Mogwai's music with the authenticity bound up in 'honesty',[47] but also the modesty of the musicians involved in making the record. Both of these signifiers have been deployed around other Scottish bands, including those like Travis whose fame and commercial success far outstrips that of Mogwai, Arab Strap or the Delgados. In a 1999 feature on Mogwai in *The Independent*, Ben Thompson allows the band to simultaneously debunk writers who have situated the band in a stereotypically Scottish, working-class milieu, and to demonstrate again the authenticity of honesty, and also in this example, humour:

> Those uneasy about the band's instrumental bent have been inclined to exaggerate their social realist tendencies – as if proximity to dour Scottish housing estates somehow excused them from lyric duty. 'That's rubbish', says Stuart cheerfully. 'We're all middle class. Just because we swear a lot and get pissed occasionally doesn't stop our families living in nice houses ...'[48]

Class here appears to be less important than less measurable signifiers of authenticity such as honesty and modesty. The same may not always be true for Mogwai's Scottish peers, but honesty and modesty are still central to many representations of Scottish indie bands. It is, then, in Welsh popular music of the mid- to late-1990s that the significance of place and class and particularly language are more clearly evident.

Bands and Representations 2: Wales

For both journalists and academics it has been rather too easy to dismiss the significance of Stereophonics when considering Welsh pop and rock: they don't exhibit the headline-grabbing sloganeering of near contemporaries the Manic Street Preachers; their sound is mainstream pop-rock; they've sold hundreds of

---

[46]   John O'Reilly, 'Tunespotting: The New Offering from Young Scottish Band Mogwai is a Masterpiece of Understatement', p. T017.

[47]   See, for example, Guy Peters, 'Trainspotting: Music from the Motion Picture (1996)'.

[48]   Ben Thompson, 'Come on, Feel the Noise', p. 12.

thousands of albums; coming from South Wales, they don't speak Welsh.[49] The band is, however, quietly, resolutely Welsh and many of their early lyrics address their depressed small-town origins. Stereophonics formed in 1992 and developed a career against the backdrop of Britpop in the mid-1990s, releasing their debut album *Word Gets Around* in 1997. Like Travis, they display some aspects of rock authenticity: they are proficient musicians; in interviews they are represented as, and represent themselves as, down-to-earth and approachable; they profess their commitment to traditional rock-song writing and performance. From some popular critical perspectives, again like Travis, Stereophonics are characterized as unimaginative and conservative. In a review of Stereophonics' album *Language. Sex. Violence. Other?*, *Guardian* journalist Alexis Petridis, in a generally positive 3-star review, suggests that somewhere in the world the band 'will always be doggedly grinding away, dishing up their soul-destroying Britrock chug'.[50]

Yet Stereophonics' development as a band had taken place in much the same environment as that of the Manic Street Preachers and Super Furry Animals in Wales, or Mogwai and Travis in Scotland. The distance from the English centre of the UK music industry sustained a clear space in which sounds and musicians could develop – a distance characterized by Mogwai's Stuart Braithwaite elsewhere in this chapter as clearly beneficial to local scenes. Music journalist Ian Fortnum, in a 1998 *Vox* magazine feature, captures the sense of value in this distance, while explicitly contrasting Stereophonics' authenticity and humility against a contemporary Britpop arrogance and nostalgia, identified as English:

> They've all the anthemic hugeness of the Manic Street Preachers, yet none of their over-intellectualised nihilism. Kelly Jones' lyrics have an honest realism untainted by Morrissey's kitchen-sink feyness or the Gallagher's Champagne-swilling self-aggrandisement, and like so many of their Welsh counterparts they've been allowed a priceless, press-free, Beatles-in-Hamburg-style live apprenticeship which has seen them hone their craft to a quite stunning degree.[51]

Fortnum's journalistic specialisms are hard rock, classic rock, and alternative rock – broad generic categories in which there is particular emphasis on constructions

---

[49]   It is worth noting that neither do the Manic Street Preachers speak Welsh. There is a linguistic North–South divide in Wales – first-language Welsh or bilingual Welsh/English speakers in the North and English speakers in the South. Stereophonics and the Manic Street Preachers are both from South Wales, so there has never been an expectation, domestically or elsewhere, that they would record in Welsh. Super Furry Animals were formed in Cardiff, South Wales, and led by a Welsh speaker, Gruff Rhys from North Wales, so there is also some geographical mixing.

[50]   Alexis Petridis, 'CD of the Week: Stereophonics, Language. Sex. Violence. Other?'

[51]   Ian Fortnum, 'The Stereophonics'.

of authenticity that emerged in the mid- to late-1960s: honesty, integrity, live performance skills, and so on. It is not surprising, then, that a comparison to Hamburg-era Beatles is used to signify not only the importance of an equivalent geographic and conceptual distance from London, but also a particularly mythologized musical purity, uncorrupted by the evils of the record industry. It also places Stereophonics in a more generalized rock narrative of 'due-paying', in which the penury and general unpleasantness of hard gigging and practice are repaid through justified success. Fortnum's praise of Stereophonics is also framed by a clear disdain for the perceived arrogance of Oasis, a band that signed to Creation Records in 1993, allegedly after only a handful of gigs, thus not having served an appropriate dues-paying 'apprenticeship'.

Elsewhere, Stereophonics frontman Kelly Jones further distances himself and his band from 'these twats in [London] bars … Some people are arrogant by nature, but we could never be cocky even if we tried. It's not in our nature.'[52] In the same article, however, Jones describes a late-night, post-show chance meeting and jam with Liam Gallagher in a London hotel: 'he was really cool with none of the attitude'. It is possible, then, that the shared experience of music industry success (and in this case, a working-class background) trumps geographic difference, perceived values and mediated images. Yet the socio-cultural roots of Stereophonics are frequently referenced, particularly in their early media coverage, making explicit a connection to a place that is *not*-urban and *not*-English. Myers quotes *South Wales Echo* journalist Alison Stokes talking about her reaction to an early Stereophonics demo: 'because I'm from the Valleys myself I could relate to the songs, Stereophonics were singing about the people I grew up with'.[53] Here, Myers emphasizes a very rooted localness, implying that the Jones/Gallagher encounter appears to be a somewhat unlikely aberration, rather than a regular celebrity-club experience for Stereophonics.

Fortnum's anti-intellectualist critique of the Manic Street Preachers positions Stereophonics as their unpretentious peers. Yet both bands have a similar background in depressed, rural South Wales villages only around 40 miles from each other, and Stereophonics have shared stages with the Manic Street Preachers on many occasions. In this example, the same shared socio-cultural environment is used to denote two different authenticities. The first of these represents adherence to working-class values and mainstream rock ideology as highly valued (Stereophonics). The second authenticity represents working-class aspirations as achievable through education and intellectual development (the Manic Street Preachers). The rock ideologies to which both Welsh bands subscribe are ultimately no less nostalgic than the values and sounds of Britpop, but other contextual signifiers of authenticity, not least their Welshness, serve to distance them from the Englishness of Britpop:

---

52   Ben Myers, 'Stereophonics: Three Local Boys Go Global'.

53   Ibid.

The band hark back to a bygone age of rock classicism for their legion musical influences: Deep Purple, Aretha Franklin, Led Zeppelin, Stevie Wonder, Black Sabbath, Sam Cooke, Creedence Clearwater Revival and, above all, AC/DC. Yet unlike such latter-day copyists as Oasis, Ocean Colour Scene, and the ubiquitous Weller fella, the Stereos inherited the essential simplistic spirit and Trojan work ethic of their schoolyard heroes. Thankfully they decided against a tiresome campaign of slavish imitation.[54]

For a classic rock or soul fan, the first set of names represents a litany of quality, credibility and authenticity. Fortnum knows also that fans of both broad genres may also see Oasis and their Britpop contemporaries as 'copyists', despite those musicians themselves professing admiration for many of the same classic artists of the 1960s and 1970s. This was a period that included, perhaps ironically, Paul Weller's first band, the Jam, formed in 1972 and signed to Polydor in 1977.

The Manic Street Preachers are, for Fortnum at least, the anti-Stereophonics, but their career arc – formed 1986, debut album 1992, playing and recording in 2009 – is more broadly analogous to that of Blur – formed 1989, debut album 1991, re-formed for gigs in 2009. Both bands were well established by the time Britpop emerged as a 'movement', but Blur were central players and the Manic Street Preachers cast as outsiders.

In an early 1991 Simon Reynolds *Melody Maker* feature, there is already emphasis from the Manic Street Preachers' bass-player Nicky Wire on the twin authenticities of working-class roots and a rejection of particular representations of Englishness in music.

> 'Where we come from in Wales, it's very working class, but there is a tradition of bettering yourself. Our parents never wanted us to go down the pit. Self-education is a really big thing. The work ethic is just massive' … For the first six months, they adored The Smiths, 'until we realised that there was no point in just standing on stage saying life hurts you'.[55]

The group's relationship with Wales appeared contradictory at times – they seemed to want to reject what some might think the perfectly understandable tendency of some fans to see the band as ambassadors for Welsh music:

> You get the Welsh ones who think you're trying to do something good and important for Wales. Why do they bother? We've never said good things about where we come from. All we've said is, 'we're from Wales, from a town where

---

[54]   Fortnum, 'The Stereophonics'.

[55]   Quoted in Simon Reynolds, 'Manic Street Preachers'.

there's nothing to do'. We've never felt any sense of pride in where we come from.[56]

To have a Welsh band breaking out into national UK success was unusual in the early 1990s. For Bradfield to publicly confess a lack of affection for the band's local roots was consistent with their alignment to aspects of 1970s punk ideology, including lack of concern for established norms of social order.

Super Furry Animals formed in Cardiff in 1993 and, like the Manic Street Preachers and Stereophonics, were still releasing new music in 2009. Unlike their more mainstream contemporaries, however, Super Furry Animals have had a long and explicit association with a more politicized vision of Welshness. An early tour saw them supporting Welsh anarchist collective Anhrefn, and their members' pre-Super Furry Animals history included time in Welsh-language bands like Pobol Cryff. Often described in UK national media coverage as 'fiercely nationalist',[57] the band emerged against a background of a politicized Welsh-language popular music movement whose origins stretched back to the 1960s.[58] In an early music press interview, Super Furry Animals front-man Gruff Rhys explains the significance of language in the band's work: 'Because of our background … everything we do takes on a political dimension, and we have to take responsibility for it. For example my brother thinks we should only sing in Welsh.'[59] The practice of singing in English is seen by some in Welsh popular music as a capitulation to the hegemonic power of both the language and the economic power of Wales's next-door neighbour. Thompson[60] refers to a 1996 Welsh television documentary that suggested that, by writing and performing songs in English, Super Furry Animals, Catatonia and Gorky's Zygotic Mynci were 'killing the [Welsh] language'. Rhys has often had to justify his band's position on language, as in this example from a 2003 interview in the *Daily Mirror*, in which he recalls early gigs and recordings in the Welsh language:

> We never thought of anything else – it is our first language so it was a natural thing to do. We toured pubs around Wales for 7 years but we reached a point where we thought we could take our music and audience further. It was made easier for us because people like Catatonia had gone before us, we weren't the first to jump.[61]

---

[56] Singer/guitarist James Dean Bradfield quoted in Tom Hibbert, 'Manic Street Preachers: Pathetic…'.

[57] J. Gluck, 'Super Furry Animals'.

[58] Sarah Hill, *'Blerwytirhwng?': The Place of Welsh Pop Music*.

[59] Quoted in Ben Thompson, 'Super Furry Animals'.

[60] See Ben Thompson, *Ways of Hearing: A User's Guide to the Pop Psyche from Elvis to Eminem*.

[61] Quoted in Gavin Martin, 'Rings around Cardiff: Super Furry Animals'.

Rhys was able to call on an entirely separate narrative of authenticity when he first heard John Cale's 'The Gift ' from the Velvet Underground's second album *White Light/White Heat*.[62] Cale's performance of the song is in English with an undeniably Welsh accent. It seems likely that the haze of (sub)-cultural capital around the Velvets was, for the young Rhys at least, sufficient to counterbalance the weight of expectation around language, Welshness and the sense that musicians should remain somehow true to their social roots and cultural traditions. As Rhys puts it: 'I thought [John Cale] was a Welsh rock heritage I could pick up without being frowned upon'.[63]

Notions of Welshness were often deployed in media coverage of Super Furry Animals and their peers as a clear signifier of their *not*-Englishness, particularly in comparisons with the Britpop bands of the mid- to late-1990s. Thompson[64] describes Super Furry Animals as working in a 'realm of zest and intelligence the bulk of their Brit-pop peer group will never even visit'. Since their English-language debut album *Fuzzy Logic*, Super Furry Animals have occupied a remarkable cultural space. Not only do their songs, in both Welsh and English, seem equally lauded by fans in Wales and elsewhere in the world, but they are in a sense both Britpop and *not* Britpop. They were signed to Creation Records, run by a Scot (Alan McGee) in London and record label of perhaps the quintessential Britpop act, Oasis. Yet to a significant extent, they remained outside of Britpop's overtly English Britishness:

> We didn't really like the imagery of people flying Union Jacks, we've never flown flags ourselves because I think music is really an international thing. I felt Britpop was a very parochial thing, a few good bands and a lot of misguided bands who weren't as sharp following them.[65]

Similarly, Welsh journalist Tryst Williams quotes Carmarthenshire-based live events publicist Joe O'Neil in 2006: 'There's a certain parochialism about British guitar rock which the Welsh bands don't contribute to. It's much more of an international sound. I think they're looking for a bigger market than the UK'.[66] Rhys and O'Neil reaffirm Stephen McRobbie (of the Pastels)'s argument[67] that bands from smaller countries tend not to conceptualize their cultural production as constrained by notions of national identity and understand their work as situated in an international context. This tendency for bands in Scotland and Wales to be outward-looking is partly a response to the limited economic possibilities offered by small domestic markets. It also, however, indicates a willingness in

---

[62]   See Thompson, *Ways of Hearing*.
[63]   Quoted in ibid.
[64]   Thompson, 'Super Furry Animals'.
[65]   Gruff Rhys, quoted in Martin, 'Rings around Cardiff'.
[66]   Tryst Williams, 'Is it Cool Cymru – Again?'
[67]   See Cox, 'West End Pearls'.

creative communities like those of independent musicians in smaller countries to conceptualize their identities in cultural terms, rather than by understanding themselves in terms of the politically bounded nation-state.

Conclusion

The first of this chapter's aims was to show how representations of Scottish and Welsh bands in the 1990s Britpop era tended to attribute positive essentialist characteristics to the bands from Scotland and Wales, contrasted against negative essentialist characteristics of (English) Britpop artists. In popular critical discourse from the mid-1990s to the early 2000s there are many examples of deployment of just such essentialist characteristics, but the argument is complicated by the fluid nature of constructions of authenticity.[68] In one case, Scottish band The Gyres' claim to authenticity in the form of their socio-economic background and tour associations with successful Britpop bands is trumped by the inauthenticity of their apparent willingness to adopt the look and sound of Britpop, rather than pursue the appearance of innovation so valued in alternative and indie rock scenes. In another case, the same economically depressed, working-class Welsh rural village background spawns conflicting authenticities. Stereophonics' adherence to a class-based work ethic and celebration of mainstream rock ideology in both sound and lyrics plays to a traditional construction of authenticity based around honest expression of a true lived experience. The Manic Street Preachers rejected expectations that they would represent Welshness to the world and advocated a traditional socialist argument that working-class aspirations could be achieved through education and intellectual development. Britpop bands generally, and Oasis specifically, were associated with excessive behaviour, arrogance and a particularly English form of flag-waving. Essentialist characteristics attributed to Scottish and Welsh bands were a mixture of broad national stereotypes such as Scottish humour and work ethic, emphasis on Welsh language as signifier of Welshness, and less commonly addressed traits of the Scottish and Welsh, such as modesty and self-deprecation.

The second aim of the chapter was to argue that the explicit Englishness of Britpop was part of a cultural narrative that codified a pre-existing sense of Wales and Scotland as a distant other, increasingly culturally distinct from the London centre of the UK music industry. The broad essentialist attributes identified above have worked to re-enforce notions of Welsh and Scottish 'difference' from a very English Britishness. Tilley and Heath[69] describe this process as a decline in British national pride, accompanied by an increase in the number of younger people who saw their primary national identity affiliation as Scots or Welsh. A central component of their argument is that this process was in part driven by the

---

[68]   Peters, 'Trainspotting'.

[69]   Tilley and Heath, 'The Decline of British National Pride'.

English version of Britishness promoted by successive Conservative governm... from 1979 onwards, alongside policies that increased the contrast in wealth between the south-east of England and the so-called 'Celtic fringes'. For indie and alternative musicians in Wales and Scotland, the other-ing of London-as-England is sometimes dismissive (Kelly Jones's description of metropolitan bars full of 'arrogant twats'), sometimes pragmatic (Emma Pollock: '[a]ny time people go to London – it's because they *have* to').

The third aim of the chapter was to suggest that simplistic discourses around national identity in Wales and Scotland fail to explain the processes through which new popular music emerges in these nations. Unlike the folk and Celtic music movements, Scottish and Welsh indie and alternative contemporaries of Oasis, Blur and Pulp were less concerned with making a 'national' music and more with the creative opportunities offered by the London-centricity of Britpop and its geographical and cultural distance from Scotland and Wales. The deployment of the union flag in much Britpop and 'Cool Britannia' iconography simply re-enforced Welsh and Scottish perception that Britpop was indeed Eng-pop. As Gruff Rhys of Super Furry Animals notes: '[w]e didn't really like the imagery of people flying Union Jacks, we've never flown flags ourselves because I think music is really an international thing. I felt Britpop was a very parochial thing.'[70] Similarly, Stephen McRobbie of the Pastels suggests, '[t]here was a nationalism in Britpop that you wouldn't get [in Scotland]. Because we live in a smaller country, we tend to think more internationally.'[71] The codified Englishness of Britpop, then, was not accompanied by equivalent emphasis on essentialist expressions of Scottish or Welsh national identity in indie and alternative scenes. There was instead an explicit rejection of the perceived inward-looking parochialism of Britpop and an understanding of alternative music in Scotland and Wales as internationalist, free from the constrictions of narrow nationalism.

---

[70] Quoted in Martin, 'Rings around Cardiff'.
[71] Quoted in Cox, 'West End Pearls'.

Chapter 9
Unsettling Differences: Music and Laddism in Britpop

Stan Hawkins

Victorious and flagrantly bloke-ish, Britpop stormed in. History was repeating itself, this time in the form of a resistance to Nirvana, who since 1992 had ruled the world. The grey backdrop of Britain in the late 1980s would offset the colourful ascension of Britpop in the 1990s, and, in retrospect, much of this felt somehow predestined. That Britpop had positioned itself against grunge, as well as the outside world, was evident in Suede's debut single 'The Drowners', released at the same time Blur toured the US, over-emphasizing their Englishness to the point of self-ridicule. Pulp's popularity, meanwhile, was put down to a bunch of introspective songs, while Oasis delivered their music in a loutish manner.

It was as if Britpop held up a mirror to all that was quintessentially British, its musical influences impossible to conceal: the Mod movement (the Who, the Kinks, the Small Faces), 1970s glam (David Bowie, T.Rex, Roxy Music), punk and the New Wave (the Jam, the Buzzcocks, Wire, Madness, Squeeze, Elvis Costello), the Stone Roses, the Smiths, and, of course, the Beatles. At any rate Britpop's crafty blend of style and coolness harked back to the late 1960s, reconstructing a national style of bonds and boundaries.

A new, feisty generation would emerge through big hits like 'Some Might Say', 'Country House', 'Common People' and 'Stay Together' (in order, Oasis, Blur, Pulp and Suede), reinforcing notions of Britishness in a society still reeling in the aftermath of Thatcherism. It certainly helped that the UK's most popular radio station, BBC Radio 1, now refurbished, had replaced middle-aged hosts with younger ones, who favoured a musical style that redefined old values.

So what, then, were the effects of this musically? Why did people need reminding of their heritage, and, most of all, how did Britpop frame this? The central aim of this chapter is to consider Britpop as a juncture between music and gendered subjectivity. Turning to various artists and their recorded performances, I address issues of masculinity in lad culture and consider how vocality offers a way into understanding the aesthetics of this musical trend. I have chosen this approach as a means for raising the issue of the artist's presence in the recording, as well as the conditions of vocal performance that determine musical style. I argue that musicologically this is a matter of significance as vocal presence in songs attests to a cultural context that feels 'real', thus becoming a site for identification. Because vocal intimacy is primarily mediated through recordings in Britpop, some critique of vocality seems necessary in order to identify vocal types.[1] Singing, after all, is the most intimate inscription of subjectivity, allowing fans access to pleasures unattainable in the spoken voice. For the purpose of this study, I have selected frontmen Jarvis Cocker, Damon Albarn, James Dean Bradfield and Noel Gallagher to usher in a range of ideas. With the aid of musical examples, lyrics, images and anecdotal material, my aim is to expose various performance strategies and the ways these privilege norms and ideals.

Given the Britpop star's construction is about a particular form of gender performance, a prime objective of this chapter is to tease out some of the more elaborate formations that underpinned the New Lad in the 1990s, making him the subject of nostalgia and cultural expression. Integral to this 1960s revivalism was the media hype involving references to a bloated sense of Britishness. Michael Bracewell puts this down to nostalgia – in the form of a pop heritage that positioned a group like Oasis as 'a *cultural hologram* of their heroes'.[2]

The Manic Street Preachers' song 'A Design for Life', released in 1996, the first track from the *Everything Must Go* album, was inspired by Joy Division's EP record, *An Ideal for Living* – a collection of songs dealing with class, ethnicity and socialist conviction.[3] And one year earlier, heavily influenced by the theme of 'slumming', 'Common People', by Pulp, from their *Different Class* album, picked up on similar influences. In the same year Oasis's 'Wonderwall', from their second album *(What's the Story) Morning Glory?*, would draw its inspiration from George Harrison's first solo album *Wonderwall Music*, released in 1968.

The year 1994 was when 'Girls & Boys', off Blur's third album, *Parklife*, came out, parodying the trendiness of pansexuality, satirizing the hedonistic party culture of British youth going on holiday to places in the sun, with the sole intention of picking up, getting drunk and brawling in the local nightclubs. Notably, this track aped (by reversal) the album title, *Boys & Girls* (1985), by Britain's smooth crooner Bryan Ferry. All told, these four recordings remain to the present day poignant cameos of a bygone era.

In its heyday, Britpop signalled a distinct reaction to the new trends of masculinity that emerged in the 1980s and the set of liberal politics the New

---

[1]   In an earlier study I have taken up the discussion of vocal tailoring in pop music, considering the controlling role of the recording process and the aesthetic implications of this. By reference to a range of technical and stylistic elements I argue that the pop voice is a powerful transmitter of subjectivity through attitude. See Stan Hawkins, *The British Pop Dandy: Masculinity, Popular Music and Culture*, pp. 121–51.

[2]   Michael Bracewell, *England is Mine: Pop Life in Albion from Wilde to Goldie*, p. 229 (my emphasis).

[3]   The Manic Street Preachers are stylistically more Britpop-related than specifically Britpop, and have been classified as part of the second wave of Britpop. My reason for selecting them is that their imagery and catchy lyrics and hooks helped frame the backdrop for something decidedly British and working class. James Bradfield's vocal style is unabashedly gruff and raucous, conjuring up associations of laddishness.

Male upheld.[4] Stylistically, an offshoot of alternative rock, Britpop displayed the idiosyncrasies of male behaviour within a British context. Those of us who were around will recall the hype surrounding this phenomenon, whose very appeal rested upon a 'situated knowledge' of being British, and, at all costs, un-American. Undoubtedly, the inheritance of a style, prevalent in the aesthetics and sensibility of the music, symbolized a defiant sense of nationhood, with the dramatic red, white and blue colours of the Union Jack depicting a patriotic landscape.

Any critique of Britpop cannot bypass the significance of patriotism, whose referents lie in a subculture fixated on football, fast cars, alcoholic beverages (especially lager) and men's magazines such as *Maxim, FHM* and *Loaded*. What earnestness drove the Manics as they yelled out, 'We don't talk about love, we only want to get drunk', or when Oasis waxed lyrically, 'Said maybe, / You're gonna be the one that saves me'. And what lay behind Blur's take on fashion and sex, epitomized in the phrase, 'Girls who are boys / Who like boys to be girls, / Who do boys like they're girls', which had an uncanny similarity to Pulp's xenophobic, embittered response to Greek middle-class girls, 'You'll never watch your life slide out of view,/ And then dance, and drink, and screw / Because there's nothing else to do'.

Notwithstanding a range of attitudinal similarities in the four songs I have selected, there are also vast differences when it comes to personal style and musical expression. Characterized by a frenetic search for original, back-to-basics music, these songs are introverted and egotistical in their own way. And, as a musical trend, Britpop can provide a useful space for considering issues of class, ethnicity and culture, extending debates on male behaviour into the public arena. With this in mind I shall turn to aspects of musical versatility, male subjectivity, and the matter of vocal delivery.

Voicing One's Position: Four Songs

Known affectionately as the Manics by their fans, the Manic Street Preachers have produced songs that are undercut by an intellectual and political lyrical style. Growing up during the tough miner's strike of the 1980s,[5] they would emerge as the most successful pop act from Wales since Tom Jones. 'A Design for Life', written by Nicky Wire and sung by James Bradfield, became a working-class anthem for the group, putting them on a par with Oasis. With this hit, however, the band's image was easily confused with loutish behaviour (much

---

[4]   Lad Culture in the 1990s has also been referred to as New Lad culture and a direct backlash against feminism. Humour in lad culture has much to do with the reclaiming of sexist language rather than just functioning as parody. See an account of this in Germaine Greer, *The Whole Woman*.

[5]   Notably, they would dedicate one of their awards to the leader of the National Union of Mineworkers, Arthur Scargill.

to the indignation of their fans).[6] A referent for this appears in Bradfield's vocal timbre and singing technique, a muscular, raw and hyper-energized force. I am referring here to a sound that vocalizes attitude, depicting something boyish that harnesses that special moment of 'arrested development' between adolescence and adulthood. With all its inflections, his singing style in the rock anthem 'A Design for Life' comes across, for its time, as dramatized. Let me explain. Strenuous and full-throated in its high range, Bradfield's exertion is discernible when he hits the highest pitches, B and C, in the melodic line. Intensifying the sentiments of the song, his intervallic leap to a high B is registrally risky, theatricalizing his 'ordinariness'. This is because major seventh intervals are notoriously demanding for 'untrained' singers to pitch when singing loudly. Falling on the first word of the hook, 'a design for life', this major seventh interval results in pitch-slippage around the pitch B, heightening the sense of effort invested on the part of the singer. Furthermore, the tautness of Bradfield's hoarse voice produces a timbre that is in stark contrast to the bombastic instrumental backing. As if lost in the grand scale of the arrangement, Bradfield's voice reflects the bloke histrionics of an era, a voice that is disoriented and rebelliously weary.

So what lies behind the disciplinary forces that drive such vocal delivery and make Bradfield's performance empathic? Granted, my use of the term empathic relates to presumptions of normalcy that are rooted in gendered representation and behavioural aspects. On this note let's turn to Noel Gallagher and his brother Liam, whose performance style exemplifies Britpop.

'Wonderwall', perhaps Oasis's most popular song and only smash hit in the US, was recorded at Rockfield Studios in Wales.[7] Compared with Bradfield's voice, Gallagher's is less gruff and decidedly nonchalant. Prominent in the mix, it comes over as aloof and yet intimate. His Mancunian accent blends into a register and timbre that works the gestural contours of the melody and lyrics. Poignant in expression, his voice is exposed within the mix. In particular, its pseudo-live quality is elegantly executed against the backdrop of a simple rock guitar riff (accompanied by long, sustained notes on the cello). Sticking to the beat, he stresses key words, employing a vocal tone that implies indifference. Owen Morris, who produced this track (with Noel) in half a day, employed an engineering technique called 'brickwalling', which involved turning all the instruments on the album to full volume, making the song especially loud. Notably, Gallagher's voice is foregrounded to the point that it appears to grow out of the mix as the song's arrangement develops.

Of all the stylistic characteristics that define the vocality in 'Wonderwall', it is the lyrical enunciation and the melodic treatment that produce a sense of affectation.

---

[6]   The song, which focuses on themes of solidarity and of working-class identity, especially concerning young men, has also been perceived as a raucous drinking anthem, with Bradfield epitomizing the lad absorbed in drinking alcohol, sport and sex.

[7]   Gallagher has confessed that singing this hit makes him feel sick every time. From Starpulse, 'Liam Gallagher Hates "Wonderwall"'.

Phrasing is achieved through a great deal of vocal stretching and inflection. For instance, in the final chorus (2:39–3:42), on the phrase, 'I said maybe, / You gonna be the one that saves me', Gallagher, characteristically, hyperbolizes the rhyming of 'maybe' and 'save me', prolonging the 'eeee' sound over several beats. The major third interval (C sharp–A) on these 'eeee' vowels is underpinned by a harmonic shift of chords F sharp minor to A major, and in such moments Gallagher's over-personalized style serves to play on his vulnerability with a touch of irony.[8] The result of this is a beautiful sense of sentimentality that bespeaks the despondency of a generation. It is as if Gallagher's sneering singing style provides a point of identification that heaps scorn on others; this occurs through the narrative structure of the song, vocal production, and the conventions of the singer's cultural context. And by the end of the song, we are left wondering who is 'wonderwall' – a friend, a lover, an imaginary person, a girl, a boy? Indeed, we might ask is there anyone who can indeed save *him*?

Less introspective than 'Wonderwall' is Blur's 'Girls & Boys', which is without doubt more tacky, as its production (not to mention its sleeve cover) suggests.[9] Albarn's estuary English accent, exaggerated at times to sound cockney (or, better, mockney), enables him to pelt out his lines crisply. In contrast to Gallagher, his voice is mixed to the fore of the recording to enable precision and clarity. Seldom does Albarn strain up to his high notes in the same way as Bradfield and Gallagher. Rather he soars into the high register via a well-controlled falsetto that helps him neatly pitch the top C (and, in comparison with Bradfield, there is little slippage). Energized by a thumping bass, the bulk of the material is overlaid by a catchy guitar riff (which includes a plectrum glissando) with cheap-sounding synth interjections. Throughout the musical arrangement this instrumentation comes across as chirpy and superficial as Albarn's playful delivery, with a mock disco feel connoting musical fooling around. Jeeringly, Albarn enacts his own position as something resistant, crazy and inane.

Each chorus in 'Girls & Boys', as I read it, is a template for quintessentializing the Britpop performer. Comprising an extravaganza of quips and snide retorts as the rickety instrumental accompaniment parodies Euro-disco, post-Duran Duran, Albarn's sung lines, 'Girls who are boys, / Who like boys to be girls …' are

---

[8]   For a discussion of ironic intent see my study of Morrissey in Chapter 3 of Stan Hawkins, *Settling the Pop Score: Pop Texts and Identity Politics*. There is a striking parallel between the video performance of 'Wonderwall' and the song, where, shot in monochrome, the video oozes with a nostalgic glance back to the 1960s. Another feature involves Noel Gallagher's non-smiling gaze back at the camera for a good deal of the video's duration: his attitude is nonchalant and defiant, mirroring the laidback aesthetics of the song.

[9]   Iconography in pop tells us much about a songwriter's intentions, contributing to the effect and reception of songs. Consider the schmaltzy front cover of 'Girls & Boys', which was taken from a pack of Durex condoms, featuring a girl and boy on a beach facing one another, silhouetted against a sunrise or sunset.

essentially snide in their social critique of British culture. Exploiting the content of the lyrics and using pitches that are close to one another, he maintains a tight control of the tune during the chorus sections. Thus, by regulating the nuances of melodic shaping, Albarn's singing style extracts the satire of a narrative that deals with working-class holidaymakers in Greece and Ibiza wanting to get drunk and have sex with strangers. In no uncertain terms, the song scoffs at the generation of the 1990s – the dance-oriented, multicultural British youth – who gender-bended with little concern for where this might lead or whom it might offend.

Cynicism aside, many entertaining features prevail in this Britpop song that warrant attention. In particular, the voice, mapped against the jaunty synth hook, carries with it an idealized construction of the ego. Ostensibly aware of his subject-matter, Albarn highlights the wry lyrics and parodies the trashiness of lad culture through self-send-up. Intentionally, mannerisms of this kind are directed towards silliness, idiocy, futility, scorn, disparagement, and all that.

I want now to shift my focus over to Pulp, another proponent of Britpop.[10] Jarvis Cocker's performance in 'Common People', not unlike Albarn's, Gallagher's and Bradfield's, prompts a more quirky, brooding and self-conscious singing style that is loaded with connotations. All the way through, the memorable hook in 'Common People' builds up fervently to a powerful rush of emotions towards the end of the song. Cocker's vocality in this moment cleverly depicts that of the male hysteric. Inducing a manic, shouting technique he yodels wildly on the words 'you' and 'la-la-la-la', his unrelenting scat straining to breaking-point as his voice splits between his natural and falsetto register. Catching the single syllables and vowel sounds of 'you' and 'la' in an aggressive yowling manner, he turns to pitch embellishment, dynamic swells and melodic licks, where pronunciation, accent, pitch, timbre, melisma and physical release contribute to an unleashing of frustration. As in 'Wonderwall' and 'Girls & Boys', 'Common People' builds on a long cadential-type chorus, serving as a vehicle for discharging pent-up emotions. In sum, the foregrounding of the vocals in such an overtly mannered way musicalizes the lyrical content through a weighing-down of the vowels rather than the words. As in each of the other songs I have considered, Cocker's vocal delivery is distinct and defiant, with him holding out with his tune and driving his message home.[11] Attentively and emotively, Cocker knows he has to engage us as much as his fellow band members, his prime goal being to position himself at the helm of the group. Naturally, there is a price to pay for this, as we will later see.

---

[10]   As Allan Moore has insisted, it is often the way rock-singers sing rather than what they sing about that most attracts listeners (see *Rock: The Primary Text: Developing a Musicology of Rock*, p. 49). Of course this does not diminish the significance of the lyrics, but rather raises the issue of how empathy is invoked in a performance.

[11]   Conversely, see Matthew Bannister's critique of indie rock singers, where he points to singers' inability to hold a tune. This is commonly interpreted as a virtue, heightening the singer's credibility (read: authenticity) (*White Boys, White Noise: Masculinities and 1980s Indie Guitar Rock*, pp. 75–7).

Music Analytic Reflections

Interpretations of songs are conjoined to music and biography, and, moreover, the social and cultural conditions that surround any performance. The relationship between artist and fan is about negotiation, suppression and intervention. What, then, do our four male singers secure as bonds of common interest through the mannerisms of singing? And how are their words and phrases intensified musically in ways that entice the listener into the singer's world? One answer lies in Britpop's ideal as a coercive mechanism of cultural, social and political engagement, through which displays of self-indulgence are dramatized.

During the performance of Britpop songs specific control is exerted over the musical reinforcement of the lyrical content, often to the point of exaggeration. Somewhat deceptively, Britpop tends towards simple musical structures. In the four songs discussed above there is evidence of easy minor-modal scales, triads and simple suspensions that support catchy tunes. In melodic terms, the songs favour repetitive devices, where the main melodic hooks are underpinned by straightforward chord progressions (this is in stark contrast to songwriting, where more complex, angular melodies tend to rival or unhinge chord structures). Undoubtedly, Britpop songs are appealing through their 'ordinariness', and this has much to do with how the voice is performed and inserted into the mix. This calls into question music's expressivity through vocal practice, and, in particular, the devices employed to connote subject-matter. Effectively, musical authority in Britpop is conveyed through a sense of frankness that unashamedly recycles the past.

Given the wealth of elements that distinguish one song from the next, it is vocal presence that mostly connotes aspects of identification. For sure the pop voice is out to lure the fan; sophisticated vocal productions, such as those I have looked at, are masked cunningly to define the vulnerability of the lead singer. Inevitably, the voice discloses the 'realism' and credibility of the singer as frontman. This is why the aesthetics of Britpop are contingent on the lead singer's performance on- and off-stage; of course, the pressures of such roles are demanding. Deena Weinstein, in addressing this, claims that the prime goal is to be a 'team player'. 'Singers', Weinstein points out, 'are less likely to be seen as dicks if they indulge in backstage clowning, joke telling, or getting out of their heads on drug or alcohol binges off stage – and many of them resort to these measures'.[12] Authenticated by the 'ordinariness' of the vocals on display, the singer's role is mitigated by the built-in tensions between band members. This returns us to the qualities inherent in vocal delivery. If singing evokes powerful empathic responses, how does it achieve this?

Certainly, the sonic quality of the Britpop voice can be interpreted as a veritable cliché; it is uptight, self-deprecating and defiant in its performative ambition. Furthermore, it includes a range of inflections, embellishments and

---

[12] Deena Weinstein, 'All Singers Are Dicks', pp. 325–6.

gestural traits that are gendered by association. As we have seen, the Britpop voice adheres to a genealogy of British bands, its referents historically entrenched and defined by a brusque quality that is codified by a spectrum of sonic signifiers. Stroppiness, defiance, contempt, self-deprecation are frequently revealed in the timbral, rhythmic and gestural qualities of vocal delivery. Furthermore, Britpop consists of musical formulae that are shaped by the sub-styles of melodic, guitar-laden pop and/or a synthesizer-dance pop that are in contrast to more serious 'pure' rock styles. Individual vocal techniques are the prime carriers of attitude, communicating to the fan what the singer is all about. And instrumental and vocal backing serve to frame the lead singer convincingly: consider Pulp's and Blur's use of synthesizers and Oasis's and the Manics' employment of guitars. In the end, the Britpop sound is mediated by the full effect of the idea of 'local production', conveying codes of gender behaviour that are self-regulatory.[13] This is defined by a musical style that fuses lyrical flair with the inferences of musical function and gendered behaviour.

Inscriptions of Laddism: A Discourse of 'Ordinariness'

At this stage I want to expand on some of my previous ideas by concentrating on behaviour patterns in British pop culture at the dawn of the twenty-first century, which have shown little sign of letting up. In the wake of Britpop laddism has remained in the media spotlight. An article from 2006 ran the caption, '[l]ad culture corrupts men as much as it debases women'. Journalist Alok Jha would take issue with 'lad magazines', asserting that they go so far as to incite date rape. Jha's underlying assertion was that lad culture has completely distanced young men from real life. By telling lads how to get the girls they want and watch them fall at their feet, lad magazines have played a divisive role:

> These magazines claim to give young men the confidence they need: an insight into the skills they require to navigate a path through their romantic lives and an understanding of the qualities that women find attractive. Instead, impressionable young men have been sold a distorted image of who women are and what masculinity is about – an image that does nothing but frustrate, degrade and humiliate them.[14]

Somewhat less moralistic in tone, Laura Baldwin probes into what happened to the 1990s lad (in a piece for the UK feminist journal, *the f-word*). Did he finally grow up into a man? Did he indeed ever want to be a man? Baldwin considers the

---

[13]   For an in-depth cultural debate on the relationship between indie and other genres, as well as questions of authenticity and 'local production', see David Hesmondhalgh, 'Indie: The Institutional Politics and Aesthetics of a Popular Music Genre'.

[14]   Alok Jha, 'Lad Culture Corrupts Men as much as it Debases Women'.

development of 'ladette' culture, girls whose behaviour turned sexual relations into something antagonistic. Identifying a feminist backlash, she argues that lad culture emerged because young men felt threatened and belittled by women's increasing dominance in society.

> We are told men are from mars [*sic*], women are from venus [*sic*]. Women snigger at men for having a small dick, [m]en snigger at women for having no boobs. Women snigger at men for being unable to work a washing machine, men snigger at women for being bad drivers. The list of stereotypes go[es] on and on until you can almost see both genders at either side of the field ready to charge into each other with swords![15]

Fuelled by TV shows like *The Battle of the Sexes*, *Love on a Saturday Night* and *Joe Millionaire*, lads are the males British society loves to 'endure', their idealized representations aligned to anti-feminism in a non-threatening albeit abusive manner. For the gendered identity ascribed to Britpop draws on a vocabulary that underscores hegemonic masculinity.

This account goes some way to explaining why Britpop acts have been so popular. It is almost obligatory that lads conform to patterns of gender behaviour that are safe and familiar; for laddism is about gender policing and therefore self-regulatory. Robert Heasley has argued that males who confirm their straightness 'are rewarded for not breaking the norms',[16] his point being that the disruption of gender norms bears a heavy burden that the majority struggle with. Understandably, there are penalties for breaking loose:

> The psychological diagnosis of gender dysphoria has been used to label boys who show signs of being 'sissies', encouraging parents and teachers to see boys (and girls) acting outside of traditional gendered norms as needing intervention based on the child's presentation of self, not necessarily on any harm or threat the child poses to himself or anyone else.[17]

Slotting into a hetero-masculinized discourse, then, laddism is supported by binary perceptions of gender; it is dependent on a form of compulsive gendered behaviour that is reinforced by homophobia and anti-femininity.

In another piece entitled, 'The Dark World of Lads' Mags', Kira Cochrane opens up a similar debate around chauvinism:

> The worst crime of lad culture as a whole was that it took old-fashioned sexism (chauvinism), served it up in exactly the same format – endless pictures of

---

[15]   Laura Baldwin, 'Why [i]t's Time for the "Battle of the Sexes" to End'.

[16]   Robert Heasley, 'Crossing the Borders of Gendered Sexuality: Queer Masculinities of Straight Men', p. 113.

[17]   Ibid., p. 114.

scantily clad women, for instance, beside captions about how 'up for it' they were – and slapped the label 'irony' on it.[18]

Cochrane goes on to insist that chauvinism reigns in the guise of laddish irony, and once a woman has claimed this as 'sexist' she is accused of lacking humour and can be shut down instantly. Describing lad culture as a 'blokelash', Cochrane, like Jha, criticizes the role of the male magazine sector, noting, however, its recent dramatic slump in sales.

Homosociality in pop performance is complex and central to an understanding of the politics of performance. One might say that the performativity of the Britpop star is predicated upon the concerns of emasculation, where there is a heightened awareness of the risks involved on the part of the performer. Matthew Bannister throws light on this, describing how the star can be conscious of how emasculating his role is when positioned as an object of desire. In fact, his bond with the group's fans can be seen as a betrayal of his relation to the rest of the band and lead to conflict: 'A lot of men are uncomfortable with this kind of attention – certainly it gets you more sex, but it also risks losing the respect of your masculine peer group.'[19] Existing in a band situation is about being socially attuned and letting others know you are 'only performing'. Good examples of this are Morrissey and Michael Stipe, who, as Bannister points out, are 'continually forced to remind the audience that their "real" self is not available for public scrutiny'.[20] Thus, the public display of a band affects the internal relationships of a band in intricate ways. Britpop, like most rock, is therefore shaped by special relations that have to do with homosocial solidarity and rivalry – all part of the symbolic order that governs masculinity.

Endemic in all pop is the gendered body, whose desirability pushes sexuality to the fore. Over time Britpop artists have emerged as icons of desire and are inevitably subjected to what I would describe as the multifaceted 'gaze', a gaze that instantly implores recognition and respect from many perspectives. As part of this empathic process, the gaze is about empowerment socially, politically and culturally.[21] And, as endless accounts of feuds between Britpop band members in the 1990s testify, unruly behaviour is integral to performances off-stage and legitimized through this prescription.

Conspicuously, Bradfield, Albarn, the Gallagher brothers and Cocker all communicate the normative rules of gendered practice through their performances. They remind us that the stakes are high when it comes to their representation. In fact, the sheer amount of interest generated by biographical anecdotes relating

---

[18]   Kira Cochrane, 'The Dark World of Lads' Mags'.

[19]   Bannister, *White Boys, White Noise*, p. 106.

[20]   Ibid.

[21]   See Susan Fast, *In the Houses of the Holy: Led Zeppelin and the Power of Rock Music*; Philip Auslander, *Performing Glam Rock: Gender and Theatricality in Popular Music*; Hawkins, *The British Pop Dandy*.

to them in the British tabloids during the mid- to late 1990s would fuel an avid fascination at national level. Moreover, the rigidity of institutionalized laddism was the result of the pressures of a media-saturated industry opposed to the softening-up of an earlier male generation: Morrissey, Boy George, George Michael, the Pet Shop Boys, Prince, David Bowie, et al.[22]

Perhaps the main challenge of working out the links between Britpop and gender lies in identifying the details of a straight masculinity. Stevi Jackson insists that heterosexuality 'can be used in relation to the erotic or to denote an institution involving a much wider social relation between men and women'.[23] If we go along with the idea that this dominant paradigm is a dense, ideological institution, with varied norms and traditions, then the difficulties of defining it are all the more daunting.[24] This is partly why Jackson gets into deep water when suggesting that masculinity is about being '(hetero)sexually *active*', where femininity is about being 'sexually *attractive* to men'.[25] Obvious exceptions to this weaken Jackson's claim, especially with regard to his positioning of sexual *attractiveness*. After all, lifestyles, iconography and attitudes precariously condition the display of sexuality through the variable structures of gender. This needs to be grasped when it comes to understanding the popularity of all-male bands and the gendered body on display.

Another point worth considering is the positioning of nationhood alongside the body in Britpop. As much as class struggle, it is the construction of the male prototype as white, straight and very British that counts. Simon Reynolds's critique of Britpop in 1995 and the British media links the music industry to a cunning marketing strategy:

> The music press is buzzing because Britpop's aesthetic base – the mid-60s, filtered through its late 70s echo, New Wave – had hitherto been strictly an indie style, and thus the province of the inkies. At the same time, the bands are overtly anti-experimental and pre-psychedelic; they combine playsafe

---

[22]   See Simon Reynolds and Joy Press, *The Sex Revolts: Gender, Rebellion and Rock 'n' Roll.*

[23]   Stevi Jackson, 'Sexuality, Heterosexuality and Gender Hierarchy: Getting Our Priorities Straight', p. 25.

[24]   Concepts of heterosexuality as an institution are located in the work of scholars from the late 1960s to the early 1970s. See Jackson, 'Sexuality, Heterosexuality and Gender Hierarchy'; Heasley, 'Crossing the Borders of Gendered Sexuality'; Stephen M. Whitehead and Frank J. Barrett (eds), *The Masculinities Reader*. Defining masculinity easily becomes essentialist, which is evident to varying extents in the work of theorists such as Judith Butler, Eve Sedgwick, Steven Seidman and Angela McRobbie. Given that heterosexuality is afforded its meaning as a given of everyday life, assumptions about it abound that deal with the confirmation of masculinity.

[25]   Jackson, 'Sexuality, Heterosexuality and Gender Hierarchy', p. 30 (original emphasis).

1966-meets-1978 aesthetics with an almost doctrinal ethos of ambition and stardom-at-all-costs.[26]

The significance of ethnicity, exclusion and nationhood, as Reynolds points out, is symbolic in that Britpop turned its back on the black sensibility associated with dance music in the 1990s. He goes on to describe the specific socio-historical context:

> For Britpopsters, the 60s have a mythic status as a lost golden age which is alarmingly analogous to the Empire for football hooligans and the BNP. Even more than the insularity of Britpop's quintessentially English canon (Kinks, Jam, Small Faces, Buzzcocks, Beatles, Smiths, Madness), it's the sheer whiteness of its sound that is staggering.[27]

In previous studies I have undertaken, I have theorized British white masculinity from a variety of angles, emphasizing how agency and the queering of sexuality becomes part of mainstream musical entertainment.[28] Casting a glance back to the period of Cool Britannia, notions of nationhood were certainly behind redefining a set of politics concerned with gender, ethnicity and sexuality – hence Britpop's reflection of the struggles of male identity through countless hit songs: Blur's 'She's So High', Pulp's 'My Legendary Girlfriend', Oasis's 'Slide Away', the Manics' 'Your Love Alone is Not Enough' and Suede's 'Stay Together', all of which thematize, albeit ironically, love, despair, romance, hopelessness, gloom and heartache.

As a result, 'ordinariness' through the sound and image of the stroppy Britpop lad is predicated upon the privilege of the 'visible invisibility that is accorded to heterosexuality'.[29] And, as Chris Brickell points out, the 'normativeness' of straightness through the tropes of the 'ordinary person' serves to signify a social order type that is constructed as 'essentially neutral'.[30] Yet many artists are positioned outside such norms in popular music, where their inversions make them the oppressors, winning them 'special rights'. In no uncertain terms, countless British pop acts fall into this category, often masking or deregulating the realities of heterosexist cultural domination.[31] This position, however, seems diametrically opposed to the Britpop lad, who, as I have argued, is skillfully hyperindividualized to appear straight and bloke-ish. Again, how come?

---

[26]   Simon Reynolds, 'Reasons to Be Cheerful'.

[27]   Ibid.

[28]   See Hawkins, *The British Pop Dandy*.

[29]   Brickell, 'The Transformation of Heterosexism and its Paradoxes', p. 101.

[30]   Ibid.

[31]   Brickell defines the newer forms of heterosexism as *cultural heterosexism*, where mainstream culture is presented on the one hand as neutral and equal, while, on the other hand, constructed as heterosexual and defended to the hilt on this basis (ibid., p. 86).

Robert Heasley insists that to branch out of the idealized structure of the hetero-masculine is to put oneself at risk with the accusation of being a 'homo in waiting'.[32] Tabloid gossip surrounding Britpop artists bears this out time and time again, one case in point being an article published in *Select* magazine in 1999. 'The Death of a Party', by Stuart Maconie, critiqued the behavioural antics of Blur through a multitude of amusing anecdotes. Interviews with band members Alex James, Graham Coxon, Damon Albarn and Dave Rowntree revealed that drugs, booze and girls underscored squabbles, fall-outs and acrimonious assessments of one another. Underpinning this was a tacit necessity to state the band's heteronormativity, hence Coxon's rueful outpouring:

> I ended up being the milkman [in the 'Country House' video]. If I'd done what I was supposed to I would have had a lobotomy by now. I was supposed to do all sorts of nasty things – getting bottoms in my face and chasing girls … It was so stupid. Alex thought it was great. Damon thought it was cheeky … I felt like a real stick in the mud or a monk or something. I was scared people thought I didn't like girls. I do. But I don't think you have to be rude about them. So I wasn't a proper bloke.[33]

Such anecdotes are useful for underlining the nature of interrelationships between band members, and the angst around sexuality. From this one might conclude that being a 'proper bloke' is determined by a social dynamic that operates as a shield for protecting assumptions of normalcy. In turn, this is tied up with the consumption of pop, which, contingent on marketing tactics, is equally dependent on the hegemonic arrangement of gender. For in Britpop the strategy is to reduce anxiety around male representation. However, to what extent this achieves its goals remains debatable.

Fulfilling the requirements of the 'proper bloke', through performances off-stage as much as on-stage, formalizes rituals of courtship, family, parenting and romance. I would further suggest that the sign system of showcasing misconduct spells out the reassurance of 'normality', a powerful source of entertainment in its own right. Foregrounding the elements of misbehaviour might therefore be interpreted as a containment of masculinity in a controlling manner; as if the very display of the Britpop lad becomes the function of an enforced materialization of the sexualized body. In other words, when reduced to the normative, the gendered body must maintain some security. In this light, it is inscribed within the hetero/homo binary, adumbrating a wide range of safe desires.

What laddism provides us with, then, is an opportunity to gain some insight into male power and oppression, as well as its relation to music. Moreover, the platform it offers up can help identify the processes of idolization in pop, a critical factor for evaluating musical experience as much as performance practice.

---

[32] Heasley, 'Crossing the Borders of Gendered Sexuality', p. 112.

[33] Stuart Maconie, 'The Death of a Party', p. 3.

My arrival point is: if popular music studies is to critically view masculinity as a bundle of practices and ideologies, then it needs to attend to men's positionings within the structures of musical performance.

Conclusion

White, straight and working class, Britpop lends its full weight to gender politics; Bradfield, Gallagher, Albarn and Cocker, albeit in different ways, exemplify the preservation of a singing tradition articulated by the social values of national pride. I am referring specifically to their musical style as an organizational element, something that glamorized the working-class ideals that had virtually vanished from a British landscape in the mid-1990s. Fetishized by glories of the past, Britpop mourned the loss of class, ethnicity and gender at the same time. Moreover, it gave young male singers the opportunity not only to rebel against the new codes of gender behaviour that had emerged during the 1980s, but also to register their group identity through a musical style that consolidated and expressed an implied opposition to mainstream international pop. Most obviously, Britpop was constructed around young male performers who celebrated the body as a site of entertainment – music thus provided the materiality for transforming the structures of laddism into pleasure. For all this, the new lad of Britpop based his identity around what Mark Simpson has described as 'an implicit repudiation of homosexuality', where its reassurance was dictated by 'an exhausting schedule of boozing, shagging babes, and fighting over football scores ... a hysterical attempt to ward off any suggestion of poovery and keep the homo tag at bay'.[34]

The voices of the four artists I have considered in this chapter pathologize a generation insecure about their masculinity, where wanting to belong and forgetting one's own problems was of central concern. Because the different kinds of vocal delivery found in Britpop testify to a patriotic sense of pride, they fly, at the same time, in the face of the processes that were already afoot towards a transformation of class, ethnicity and culture in the UK. Signifying a renaissance, Britpop involved an intense, short-lived nostalgic moment in time. The culture connected to laddism is rooted in other more rebellious British bands from the 1960s, and, not least, the 'realism' associated with the Britpop voice is a result of a set of conventions that are defined through musical connotations that drew on ideological, historical and cultural relationships.

Assimilating the cultural effects of Britpop and its mod influences highlights the politics of gender relations on the basis of redevelopment and reconstruction. In its yearning for the era of the British Invasion in the mid-1960s, Britpop was a rebuke of US grunge bands dominating mainstream pop in the UK. Against the backdrop of new political hope, Britpop offered the promise of cultural rebirth and, moreover, a flattering snapshot of Britain's imperial past.

---

[34]   Mark Simpson, *It's a Queer World: Deviant Adventures in Pop Culture*, pp. 7–8.

Tempting as it might be to dismiss Britpop as a simple, no-nonsense replica of the past, the debate around this is more elaborate. As I see it, laddism is a historical outcome of various phases within contemporary popular music, both in the UK and US. It pinpoints a problem area of display as manifested in the subordination of the young white male of the late twentieth century. Turning to music to seek modes of expression that helped them define themselves, Britpop artists reinvented the 1960s. This trend became documented through strong musical personalities that depicted a vitality and flamboyance in pop during the mid-1990s. In an extraordinary manner, Britpop's cartoonish songs would integrate a wide range of influences in a whirl of sonic imagery, of jangly guitar hooks, synth-pop riffs, orchestral fanfares, tuneful refrains, all evoking a romantic glimpse of the UK, its charm, its bygone glories and its inevitable downfall. Into this equation entered the voice of laddism, giving rise to structures of behaviour and reminding us that music is a matter of convention and *not* a given or something guaranteed. For this reason alone, the idiosyncrasies of Britpop need to be laid bare.

SECTION 3
Post-Britpop

Chapter 10

Devopop: Pop-Englishness and Post-Britpop Guitar Bands

Ian Collinson

The cultural nationalism of 1990s Britpop has been generally regarded as 'a circling of the wagons', a defensive reaction against the perceived threat of multiculturalism and American cultural hegemony.[1] These tensions have not dissipated, and in the last decade they have been augmented by concerns about devolution, greater European expansion and integration (the spectre of the Euro), and, in the aftermath of 9/11, wars (on Iraq and 'terror') and their impact on thinking about multiculturalism. Where Britpop was implicated in the production of a nostalgic, hybridity-erasing and appealing form of Britishness (even if it was Englishness 'writ large'), identity politics in Britain have in the interim changed to include a debate about Englishness. Citing the proliferation of scholarly and general publications on this topic, David McCrone argues that there has never 'been such interest in the English question as there is today'.[2] As the 'old hegemonies which secured taken-for-granted meanings for the terms "British" or "English"'[3] have fragmented, so 'the English are for the first time having to confront seriously the question faced previously by many nations: who are we?'[4] Formulating an answer to this English question is difficult for a number of interrelated reasons: the English are not used to thinking about this question; Englishness is often subsumed by Britishness; regional identification is still very strong; and there are a variety of possible 'Englishnesses' from which to choose.[5] In this chapter, I want to look at this range of possible Englishnesses in the context of the new generation of English guitar bands that sprouted almost exactly a decade after Oasis released *(What's the Story) Morning Glory?*

The music media have made many attempts to situate this new generation of guitar bands within the tradition of Britpop. Such a comparison has reached the

---

[1]   Nabeel Zuberi, *Sounds English: Transnational Popular Music*, p. 23.

[2]   David McCrone, 'A Nation that Dare Not Speak its Name', p. 267.

[3]   David Morley and Kevin Robins, 'Introduction: The National Culture in its New Global Context', p. 6.

[4]   Krishan Kumar, 'Nation and Empire: English and British National Identity in Comparative Perspective', p. 593.

[5]   Christopher Bryant, 'These Englands, or Where does Devolution Leave the English?', p. 394.

point where some groups have been identified as a second generation of Britpop. Here, I would like to examine these new guitar bands by looking at some of the continuities and discontinuities between them and first-generation Britpop. Within this debate, I want to pay particular attention to the nostalgic renderings of pop-Englishness that connects the current crop with both the Britpop bands of the 1990s and an older English popular music tradition. In order to focus this debate I shall concentrate on the music of three of the most commercially successful groups within this current generation: Kaiser Chiefs, Arctic Monkeys and Bloc Party.

Déjà Vu Again: Britpop Nouveau

In the second edition of *The Last Party: Britpop, Blair and the Demise of English Rock*, John Harris offers a gloomy prognosis for the future of English rock music. According to Harris, English rock music is dead because 'the fires that once fuelled the best British music have, for the moment at least, been snuffed out'.[6] Disconsolate, Harris points to the Libertines as an example of 'British rock music regaining its old strengths ... quite the most important group to have emerged since the fall of Britpop'.[7] However, within 12 months Harris's gloomy forecast was to be proved wrong. Instead of marking a period of decline, the five years between 2003 and 2008 witnessed a proliferation of new guitar-based indie-pop/rock bands in the UK pop music scene. As Sutherland and Straw have noted, in 2006 'popular music fans in Great Britain once again felt a sense of energetic generationalism, as a host of young rock bands, like the Arctic Monkeys or Kaiser Chiefs, rode waves of hype and genuine enthusiasm to the top of the sales charts'.[8] Along with the aforementioned Kaiser Chiefs and Arctic Monkeys, Razorlight, Kasabian, Bloc Party, the Wombats and the Futureheads are representatives of this new, and as is normally the case, unanticipated generation.

In a comparison that is no doubt encouraged by the tenth anniversary of Britpop, and a nostalgia among journalists for a time when mainstream music newspapers and magazines operated as arbiters of taste and success, the music press has been keen to promote Britpop's apparent second coming. Writing for the BBC's *Top of the Pops* website, Stephen Dowling asks, 'are we in Britpop's second wave?', because, he claims, 'British groups seem to be taking the world by storm again'.[9] The bullish mood about the future of British pop music is also expressed by journalist Neil McCormick in a *Daily Telegraph* article entitled 'How Keane, Snow Patrol, Kaiser Chiefs and Razorlight Followed Oasis to Revive Britpop'. In

---

[6]   John Harris, *The Last Party: Britpop, Blair and the Demise of English Rock*, p. 377.

[7]   Ibid.

[8]   Richard Sutherland and Will Straw, 'The Canadian Music Industry at a Crossroads', p. 143.

[9]   Stephen Dowling, 'Are We in Britpop's Second Wave?'

his article McCormick asks, 'Is this the return of Britpop?', before then making the connection between the new wave of guitar music and new hope for the music companies: '[i]t is a wave of homegrown rock bands on whom the UK record industry is pinning hopes of revival, each ripe with the potential for multi-million international sales'.[10] *Q Magazine*, in a special edition celebrating '50 Years of Great British Music', goes so far as to assert that the 1990s 'were a time for heroes, when alternative indie scenesters took the charts by storm under the guise of Britpop ... Now in the '00s, here we go again.'[11]

'Brit-pop nouveau', 'Britpop V.2', 'second generation Britpop', 'Brit-pop's next generation' and, in the US, 'Brit-sound',[12] are all labels that have been applied to these new guitar bands, labels that at least some of the bands seem to embrace. When asked what it felt like to be at the head of 'Brit-pop mark II' by a BBC interviewer, Ricky Wilson, the lead singer of Leeds band the Kaiser Chiefs, replied, 'It's not mark II mate, it never stopped ... we're just revving it a bit.'[13] In its efforts to create this 'second wave', the music press has tried to replay the rivalry between Blur and Oasis, itself a resurrection of the media-fuelled competition between the Beatles and the Rolling Stones, with the Kaiser Chiefs and the Arctic Monkeys cast in the role of antagonists. On occasion, the music press connects the old and the new music not to boost the new but to disparage it. For example, Robinson writes that the 'Godfathers of landfill Indie', like Razorlight, the Pigeon Detectives and the Wombats, are doing for the new generation of indie-guitar bands what Menswear and Sleeper did for Britpop.[14] In a neat and ironic reversal afforded by such generational discourse, Britpop's moment of unoriginality has now been recast as an originary moment. Rather than frame Britpop bands as shameless appropriators of the 1960s' British popular music canon (Beatles, Rolling Stones, Small Faces), Oasis, Supergrass and Blur are transformed into the pathfinders of this second generation. As Tom Meighan of Kasabian put it, 'Oasis did the job ten years ago and now it's us',[15] or more succinctly: '[f]irst there was Britpop'.[16]

As was the case with Britpop, which was a discourse as much, if not more, than it was a genre or a distinct sound,[17] these new-generation guitar bands exhibit a musical diversity that is always occluded when commentators move from, on the one hand, identifying a new generation of bands demographically to, on the

---

[10]   Neil McCormick, 'How Keane, Snow Patrol, Kaiser Chiefs and Razorlight Followed Oasis to Revive Britpop'.

[11]   Jo Whiley, 'The '00s'.

[12]   This term is quite broad musically as it also encompasses performers like Amy Winehouse and Lily Allen.

[13]   Ian Youngs, 'Sound of 2005: Kaiser Chiefs'.

[14]   Peter Robinson, 'All Killer No Landfiller'.

[15]   Cited in Osley, 'Britpop is Back ... and This Time even the US Charts Can't Ignore it'.

[16]   *Later with Jools Holland 2 – Cool Britannia 2*, liner notes.

[17]   David Hesmondhalgh, 'British Popular Music and National Identity'.

other, placing them within a new and discrete musical generation or movement. Overall, the new bands operate within the indie tradition, of 'guitar rock or pop combined with an art-school sensibility'.[18] These post-Britpop bands do seem less reliant on the 1960s popular music canon than their predecessors. Instead, it is English popular music from the 1970s that holds sway, along with Britpop itself.[19] The influence of Britpop is evident too in the 'singalong' pop sensibility displayed by nearly all the new-generation guitar bands I have mentioned. This 'singalong sensibility' is also something that should be seen as a legacy of the English pop music tradition as a whole. Moreover, such a sensibility might also be related to a renewed interest in what could be thought of as literate and intelligent lyric-writing, a phenomenon that *Guardian* journalist Alexis Petridis suggests is 'the most interesting thing about British rock music in recent years'.[20] But while the musical antecedents might be a little more diverse, and their lyrics more interesting, this new wave continues the gender, ethnic and racial exclusivity of Britpop.[21] With the odd exception, like the now-defunct the Long Blondes and racially hybrid Bloc Party, the new generation is male and white.

Pop-Englishness and the New Guitar Bands

I shall now focus on the music of just three of these acts – Kaiser Chiefs, Arctic Monkeys and Bloc Party. There are three reasons why I have selected these particular bands for more in-depth consideration. Firstly, of all the new-generation bands, these three are the most prominent and commercially successful. If album sales are still a valid indicator of popularity, then these three bands are indeed extremely popular. The first Arctic Monkeys' album, *Whatever People Say I Am, That's What I'm Not*, sold 363,735 copies in the first week of release, and it became the biggest-selling debut album ever in Britain. The second album, *Favourite Worst Nightmare*, sold 500,000 units in the same time period. Similarly, *Employment*, the Kaiser Chiefs' debut album, sold 1.8 million copies in its first year and has now sold over 3 million globally, while *Silent Alarm* has also given Bloc Party a million-seller at its first attempt. There is something anachronistic about such mainstream popularity in an age, supposedly, of musical fragmentation, a time

---

[18]   Wendy Fonarow, *Empire of Dirt: The Aesthetics and Rituals of British Indie Music*, p. 40.

[19]   For example, Razorlight are indebted to early U2; Kasabian to the Stone Roses, Oasis, the Chemical Brothers and glam rock; and the Futureheads draw on the Jam, XTC and punk-period Elvis Costello.

[20]   Alexis Petridis, 'The Soundtrack'.

[21]   See Nick Baxter-Moore, '"This is Where I Belong": Identity, Social Class and the Nostalgic Englishness of Ray Davies and the Kinks'; Tara Brabazon, 'Robbie Williams: A Better Man?'; Michael Bracewell, *England is Mine: Pop Life in Albion from Wilde to Goldie*; and Steven Quinn, 'Rumble in the Jungle: The Invisible History of Drum'n'Bass'.

when such sales are thought to be only within reach of the musical products of reality television programmes like *Pop Idol*.[22] Secondly, each of the three bands has a different relationship with its Britpop antecedents: the Kaiser Chiefs are the most reliant on the Britpop idiom, Bloc Party the least. Thirdly, each offers a different articulation of pop-Englishness.

(i) Kaiser Chiefs: 'What do you want for tea? I want crisps'

Of the new-generation guitar bands, the Kaiser Chiefs are perhaps the band most directly influenced by Britpop. With their 'laddish gang mentality, sixties musical sensibility and witty lyrics about modern British life',[23] the Kaiser Chiefs have built their short career on a traditional formula of anthemic pop-rock and social observation. Lead singer Ricky Wilson recounts how 'Blur, Supergrass and the 90s Britpop scene exploded when we were just 16 and that time set us on the tracks for what we have become. I remember being inspired by Supergrass' first album as they were only just older than us, but writing such great songs ...'.[24] This willingness to follow, or to admit following, the Britpop template has led one reviewer to comment that their 'song-writing is oddly dated, lacking any of-the-moment urgency. You don't have to look too hard today to find bands in thrall to the Strokes and the Libertines ... the Kaiser Chiefs, however, are even less modern'.[25] Others are more succinct but no less critical, describing them as 'old-timers peddling a nostalgic rehash'.[26] The Britpop influence is continued by the choice of producer on the first two albums, Stephen Street, known for his work with Blur and prior to that, Morrissey and the Smiths. And it is with Blur that the Kaiser Chiefs are most often compared. Although the musical comparison is a valid one, the relationship to Blur's articulation of Englishness is less clear cut. The Kaiser Chiefs seem to vacillate between two of Martin Cloonan's five modalities of pop-Englishness: 'ambivalent Englishness' and 'hip little Englishness'.[27]

As inheritors of the English 'droll-pop tradition',[28] the Kaiser Chiefs' songs often articulate an ambivalent attitude towards England, an ambivalence modulated through irony, sarcasm and humour. For example, the single 'I Predict a Riot', released at a time when then-Prime Minister Tony Blair was formulating

---

[22]   Simon Frith, 'Does British Music Still Matter?: A Reflection on the Changing Status of British Popular Music in the Global Music Market'.

[23]   McCormick, 'How Keane, Snow Patrol, Kaiser Chiefs and Razorlight Followed Oasis to Revive Britpop'.

[24]   *The Times*, 'Kaiser Chiefs Talking Point'.

[25]   Victoria Segal, 'Kaiser Chiefs: Yours Truly, Angry Mob'.

[26]   Dan Cairns, 'The Prolific Kaiser Chiefs on Off with Their Heads'.

[27]   Martin Cloonan, 'State of the Nation: "Englishness", Pop, and Politics in the mid-1990s', p. 53.

[28]   McCormick, 'How Keane, Snow Patrol, Kaiser Chiefs and Razorlight Followed Oasis to Revive Britpop'.

his 'respect agenda', satirizes the moral panic surrounding 'binge drinking', 'anti-social behaviour' and the British folk devil of the early twenty-first century, the yob. For Wilson and his collaborators, modern life in Britain is, once again, rubbish, whether it is the superficiality of everyday life in 'Modern Way' ('This is the modern way / Faking it every day'); the drudgery of a customer service job ('My God'), or the general malaise of 'Ruby' ('Due to lack of interest / Tomorrow is cancelled'). It is the appropriately titled 'Everything is Average Nowadays', however, that best exemplifies this sense of national ennui: 'And everything is going down the pan / And everyone is following the craze / Of everything is average nowadays'. Such complaints are themselves part of a long national tradition of criticizing modernity, what Michael Bracewell has dubbed 'English inertia' in the face of apparent national decline.[29] It is this type of social observation that has no doubt led *Rolling Stone* writer David Fricke to describe the Kaiser Chiefs as 'Britain's most political pop group at the moment ...'.[30]

On other occasions, though, like Albarn and Blur a decade before them, a 'fondness for the nation generally shines through'.[31] In a BBC interview Wilson indulges in the cultural nationalism and anti-Americanism that was a feature of Britpop's ideology:

> It [Britpop] gave me so much pride to be British ... There's some great bands that have come out of America and Australia, but we don't have to rely on them to give us our music, to fill our charts. The British have always done it best, from Franz Ferdinand back to the Beatles.[32]

Even the normally reticent Simon Rix, the band's bassist, told an interviewer that he'd 'rather be in Meanwood in Leeds than in Hollywood any day'.[33] When the band played the BBC's Electric Proms in 2007, they closed their set with a version of *Land of Hope and Glory* as either, or perhaps both, a parody and/or homage to the Last Night of the Proms, an event that, despite numerous attempts at reform, still seems to many like 'an uncomfortable and inappropriate display of deluded, mindless and escapist [nationalist] nostalgia'.[34]

Britpop bands of the 1990s celebrated 'hackneyed narratives, images, musical tropes, and ways of representing England'.[35] Likewise, the pop-Englishness of the Kaiser Chiefs is mobilized through nostalgic means. Unlike Oasis and Blur, the Kaiser Chiefs look back to the 1970s, rather than the 1960s, for their musical

---

[29]   Bracewell, *England is Mine*, p. 47.

[30]   David Fricke, 'Off with Their Heads review'.

[31]   Cloonan, 'State of the Nation', p. 53.

[32]   Quoted in Youngs, 'Sound of 2005: Kaiser Chiefs'.

[33]   In Steve P., 'Every Day I Love the US Less'.

[34]   David Cannadine, 'The "Last Night of the Proms" in Historical Perspective', p. 340.

[35]   Zuberi, *Sounds English*, p. 23.

models. Although the main riff of their hit 'Ruby' is filched from the Faces' 'Stay with Me', a band that is a standard Britpop reference, the Kaiser Chiefs' sound owes much to David Bowie, Roxy Music, the Stranglers, Sham 69, XTC, Madness, and even early Spandau Ballet. The band's sonic nostalgia is buttressed by references in lyrics, interviews and promotional material to Leeds United Football Club and its glory days of the 1970s, venerable children's comics like *The Beano* and its grown-up eighties' parody *Viz*, children's television programmes (like *Jim'll Fix It* and *Screen Test*), red buses, and the satire of Monty Python. However, what appears at first to be a break between musical generations becomes a marker of continuity between the Kaiser Chiefs and their Britpop predecessors as their cultural cartographies of England are similarly drawn from the music and popular culture of a period not directly experienced by their respective generations, a period that would most likely be part of their parents' adolescence. And just as this nostalgic thread connects the first- and second-generation Britpop bands, so it also ties both to 1960s bands, like the Kinks, who were similarly obsessed with an England that had just dropped below the horizon.[36] At this moment it would be difficult not to agree with Ruth Adams when she writes that nostalgia has 'a constant presence in British culture'.[37]

Like the Kaiser Chiefs, Sheffield's Arctic Monkeys are also retrospective in their pop-Englishness, but whereas the Kaiser Chiefs offer a collage of quotations – sonic, textual and epitextual – that index Englishness through its past popular culture, the Arctic Monkeys work within a nostalgic idiom.

(ii) Arctic Monkeys: 'Your name isn't Rio, but I don't care for sand'

Aided by a strong live following, word of mouth and a novel MySpace marketing strategy, which marked either the end or the rejuvenation of the music industry, the spiky sixties-tinged pop-punk of the Arctic Monkeys became a national phenomenon in 2005. A representative of music retailers HMV told a *Times* journalist: '[p]eople rightly draw comparisons with Oasis, but in terms of sheer impact, where a band has come from virtual obscurity to achieve huge, overnight success, we haven't seen anything quite like this since the Beatles'.[38] Such was their popularity that the then-Chancellor of the Exchequer and later Prime Minister, Gordon Brown, was embarrassed publicly by his inability to name any of the songs on the Arctic Monkeys' first album.[39]

Although he once actually wanted to be in Oasis, and is an admirer of the ubiquitous Morrissey, Alex Turner (singer, guitarist, lyricist)'s songwriting is

---

[36]   See Baxter-Moore, "'This is Where I Belong'".

[37]   Ruth Adams, 'The Englishness of English Punk: Sex Pistols, Subcultures, and Nostalgia', p. 483.

[38]   In Adam Sherwin, 'Arctic Monkeys Race to Top of the Tree'.

[39]   Gaby Hinsliff and Ned Temko, 'What I Really Mean about Liking the Arctic Monkeys, by Gordon Brown'.

influenced by both Britpop and rap. In his own words he walks 'the tight-rope between Mike Skinner [the Streets] and Jarvis Cocker [Pulp]'.[40] It is social realism that links Turner to Jarvis Cocker and then to English writers like Alan Bennett, Alan Sillitoe, Stan Barstow, the 'kitchen-sink' dramatists of the late 1950s and early 1960s, and soap operas like *Coronation Street*. The title of the Arctic Monkeys' debut album *Whatever People Say I Am, That's What I'm Not* is taken, no doubt knowingly, from a line of dialogue in Sillitoe's archetypal social-realist novel *Saturday Night and Sunday Morning* (1958).[41] While the reference to Cocker is to be expected, not least because he and Turner come from the same city, acknowledging the influence of Mike Skinner and the Streets is significant because it reveals a highly attenuated nexus between the Arctic Monkeys' post-punk and black musical forms. This punk–rap combination shows up particularly in Turner's rhythmic vocal phrasing (see 'From the Ritz to the Rubble', for example), although this phrasing could also register the influence of punk poet John Cooper Clarke. That rap enters the debate via a white rather than black performer, Mike Skinner rather than, say, Dizzee Rascal, is an indicator of the overwhelming whiteness of Britpop, new and old.

Unlike the romantic imperative of the shabby-genteel Morrissey, Turner writes observational lyrics about the travails of everyday life in a northern English city. An interest in the everyday is the second link between Turner and Skinner, and a salient feature of contemporary English pop music more widely.[42] Turner speculates that *Whatever People Say I Am* might be a 'day-in-the-life-of' concept album: 'it almost were a bit conceptual, is that the right word? It were a day, a weekend'.[43] As a social observer, Turner writes of altercations with nightclub bouncers: 'He's got his hand on your chest / He wants to give you a duff / Well secretly I think they want it all to kick off' ('From the Ritz to the Rubble'); stand-offs with the police ('Riot Van'); fickle girlfriends ('Mardy Bum'); boozy nights out and the taxi home ('Red Light Indicates Doors Are Secured'); of prostitutes and 'scummy' men ('When the Sun Goes Down'); and of the promise of an illicit one-night stand ('Still Take You Home'). By drawing on the routines and rituals of everyday northern English life, routines and rituals that are commonplace in other parts of the British Isles, Turner is working in the tradition of the Kinks' Ray Davies who took similar everyday 'images, sentiments and feelings' and 'arranged them in such a way that their reference to British society is

---

[40]   Quoted in Collins, 'They're Big and they're Clever: the Success of the Arctic Monkeys Marks the Return of Brainy Pop'.

[41]   This social-realist aesthetic in Turner's writing is developed cinematically by Paul Fraser's 2006 short film *Scummy Man*. Inspired by the Arctic Monkeys' 'When the Sun Goes Down', extracts from *Scummy Man* were later used for that song's video.

[42]   Rafael Behr, 'It May be a Golden Age for Pop Lyrics, but Is Amy Really That Good?'

[43]   Quoted in Craig McLean, '21st-Century Boy'.

both unmistakable and highly novel'.[44] Ray Davies's 'roast beef on Sunday' ('Autumn Almanac') has been replaced by Turner's fast food (curry, kebab) on Saturday night.

In crafting his social vignettes, Turner draws on a stockpile of words and their attendant images that connote a particular type of urban and authentic working-class Englishness. Words and phrases such as 'gagging for it', 'Mecca Dobba' (marker pens used in bingo halls), 'birds' (young women), 'tracky bottoms' (tracksuit pants), 'wagging school' (playing truant), 'scummy', 'duffed-up' (beaten-up), 'naughtiness', 'have a laugh', 'banging tunes' (good music) and 'kick off' (begin) are supplemented by Yorkshire dialect words, like 'mardy' (moody) and 'dunt' (didn't), and references to English pop culture – Sherlock Holmes, Frank Spencer, the Police, Duran Duran. The English affect of such references is multiplied by Turner's strong Sheffield accent. As the *Guardian*'s Simon Armitage remarked, 'I can't think of another singer whose regional identity has been so unapologetically and naturally intoned through his singing voice'.[45] Like the Kaiser Chiefs' Ricky Wilson, but much more so, Turner's singing is a marker of a specific class and regional identity and, in turn, this identity becomes a synecdoche of the nation. As it did for Britpop in the 1990s, the local provides a site for the articulation of pop-Englishness.[46]

Despite claiming not to want 'to sleep in a city that never wakes up / blinded by nostalgia' ('Yellow Brick'), there is nevertheless something retrospective and nostalgic about the Arctic Monkeys, from their mod fashion to their reliance on the rock trinity of guitar, bass and drums. Keyboards feature only on one track ('505') of *Whatever People Say I Am* and they have a distinctly analogue (pre-1980s) tone. A reverence for the styles and sounds of the past is even more evident in Turner's side project, the Last Shadow Puppets, whose first album, *The Age of the Understatement*, has been described as a collection of theme tunes for 1960s James Bond films that were never made.[47] It is worth noting that the Arctic Monkeys have also been known to perform a live cover of Shirley Bassey's James Bond theme tune 'Diamonds are Forever'.[48] So, although the band is lauded for their 'gritty' (read 'authentic') narratives of everyday life, they are nonetheless narratives without references to work (or unemployment), politics, multiculturalism, or panics about national security and border protection. Indeed, remove the scant references to ringtones ('There's only music / so there's new ringtones' ('A Certain Romance') and text-messaging, and it is hard to see what in the Arctic Monkeys' lyrics is truly contemporary. Taking this into account, if *Whatever People Say I Am* has, according to *Q* magazine, 'helped 21st-century

---

[44] Andy Bennett, 'The Forgotten Decade: Rethinking the Popular Music of the 1970s', p. 23.

[45] Simon Armitage, 'Foreword', *Great Lyricists: Alex Turner*, p. 8.

[46] Cloonan, 'State of the Nation', p. 65.

[47] Sam Wolfson, 'The Last Shadow Puppets, the Age of Understatement'.

[48] McLean, '21st-Century Boy'.

Britain gain a fresh perspective on its own ever-fluid identity',[49] then it has done so in a way that overlooks many of the complex social and cultural issues that define contemporary British society. Through the use of an anachronistic social realist aesthetic, albeit robbed of its political edge, Turner has created a vivid but monochromatic urban English pastoral that elides tensions about ethnicity, race and religion. Turner seems to have adopted the colour blindness that was a feature of the novels and films of the 'Angry Young Men' of the late 1950s and 1960s,[50] while he registers class only as an amalgam of leisure, language and libido. If Pulp's 'Common People' harked 'back to a world where people were much surer of their identity regionally, nationally and in terms of their class position and overall place in the scheme of things',[51] then the same can be said of Turner's lyrical rendering of pop-Englishness.

(iii) Bloc Party: 'This tommyrot and flag waving is just getting me down'

Nostalgia might be a recurrent theme in the articulation of pop-Englishness, but its influence is not total. Of the three new-generation guitar bands I have discussed here, London's Bloc Party offer a singularly nostalgia-free engagement with ideas of Englishness. While lead singer, guitarist and main lyricist Kele Okereke cites proto-Britpop band Suede as an early musical influence, Sonic Youth, Joy Division, Pixies, DJ Shadow, Gang of Four and, in the case of lyrics, Morrissey are also influential. Bloc Party's music is greatly influenced by black Atlantic musical forms, an influence heard most immediately in Matt Tong's stuttering drum-and-bass inspired percussion on the band's first album, *Silent Alarm* (2005). On the second and third albums (*A Weekend in the City* [2007] and *Intimacy* [2008]), the band move further into the realm of dance music and other electronic genres that have, in the past, had 'little to do with Englishness and everything to do with multiculturalism'.[52] Standard guitar-band instrumentation is increasingly augmented by a range of electronic instruments and effects, including keyboards, drum machines and samplers. The dance aesthetic is underlined by Bloc Party's release of remixes, a move that jettisons the monadic rock authenticity that was so integral to Britpop's legitimacy. Technology combined with a dance aesthetic gives Bloc Party's music an immediate sense of twenty-first-century modernity. A combination of indie guitars and the rhythmic urgency appropriated from drum and bass imparts the sensations of 'social and cultural dislocation'.[53] Yet, paradoxically, this debt to dance forms also places the band firmly within the

---

[49]   Pat Gilbert, 'Whatever People Say I Am, That's What I'm Not', p. 89.

[50]   Caryl Phillips, 'Kingdom of the Blind'.

[51]   Bennett, 'The Forgotten Decade', p. 29.

[52]   Bracewell, *England is Mine*, p. 233.

[53]   Quinn, 'Rumble in the Jungle'.

context of London's recent musical heritage: jungle especially is 'claimed by its innovators to be specifically a London product'.[54]

Popular musical avant-gardism is not normally associated with pop-Englishness. Bennett has noted, for example, that the Beatles' keenness to experiment marks them out as, surprisingly perhaps, less English than their contemporaries.[55] Bloc Party's desire to experiment musically and technologically has brought down the ire of Noel Gallagher, who described them as 'a band off University Challenge', a comment that Okereke rebutted by calling Oasis 'repetitive Luddites'.[56] Bloc Party's dance-inflected music aesthetic acknowledges and incorporates a wider range of influences than either the Kaiser Chiefs or the Arctic Monkeys. As Okereke makes clear in an interview, '[t]here are certain musical forms that I hold very dear that are not straightforward, that are not part of rock music history and that affects how we put things together'.[57] While it is problematic to equate a difference in aesthetics of sound to a difference in notions of Englishness, Bloc Party's engagement with 'the nation' is the most critical of the bands discussed here. They are the least reliant on the English pop music tradition and they are the new generation's only multi-racial band.

Cloonan has written that, 'while black English-born (or resident) artists have, inevitably, commented about the state of England, they have seldom been identified with it'.[58] Despite this lack of identification, much of what has made British popular music British, rather than American, has been the creativity of non-white immigrants. So, while British pop music has developed in *dialogue* with America, it

> ... has been since the 1950s a *multilogue*, a mixture of musics intersecting in the various urban centres to produce among other things various forms of British reggae; two-tone; Bhangra and Indi-pop; and indeed skiffle, punk and Indi-pop; with all these being constantly subject to interactive evolution and reworking.[59]

Bloc Party operate within this tradition of 'non-identification', but they do so by deploying a *critical cosmopolitanism* that manifests itself in the aforementioned musical experimentation and a willingness to confront the socio-cultural tensions of contemporary British society.

Much like the Arctic Monkeys' *Whatever People Say I Am*, Bloc Party's second album, *A Weekend in the City*, described by one journalist as 'a great leap forward for British music',[60] is a quasi-concept album where the local is once again a proxy

---

54   Andrew Blake, 'Re-placing British Music', p. 220.
55   Bennett, 'The Forgotten Decade', p. 22.
56   BBC, 'Bloc Party Blast "Stupid" Oasis'.
57   Cited in Alexis Petridis, 'This is Going to Look Really Bad'.
58   Cloonan, 'State of the Nation', p. 59.
59   Blake, 'Re-placing British Music', p. 219.
60   Craig McLean, 'Hey, Hey it's the Arctic Monkeys'.

for England. Rather than Turner's urban pastoral, or the familiar and comfortable ambivalence of Hodgson and Wilson, Okereke writes about 'life in London: drugs, suicide, racism, gay sex, violence, youth in hoodies and white vigilantes. This is London, it says, and this is now.'[61] Social observation remains a lyrical staple, but the kinds of observations made differ radically. In the track appropriately entitled 'England', Okereke makes a statement about the state of the capital and, as a corollary, the state of the nation. Now the territory of white vigilantes who video assaults on their mobile phones, London wide, 'From Ilford to Ladywell / The streets have become cruel' ('England'). Elsewhere, he writes of East London as 'a vampire' that 'sucks the joy right out of me' ('Song For Clay (Disappear Here)').

Unlike either the Kaiser Chiefs or Arctic Monkeys, Bloc Party places England and Englishness in a global geo-political and social context. 'Price of Gas' and 'Helicopter' are commentaries on the Iraq War, and in 'Hunting for Witches' Okereke writes of 9/11 ('Airplanes crash into towers'), the London public transport bombings ('As bombs explode on the 30 bus'), the media scare campaign of their aftermath ('The Daily Mail says the enemy's among us') and its consequence ('Fear will keep us all in place'). Similarly, they acknowledge the existence of the 'great unspoken' of pop-Englishness: multicultural Britain and its lived tensions. In 'Where is Home?', Okereke speaks of the alienated experience of second-generation migrants to Britain who are endlessly reminded that Britain is not home. And whereas both Turner and Wilson sing about the encounter between adolescents and the police in comic 'laddist' terms, about 'wind[ing] the coppers up' ('Riot Van') and 'Here comes the referee (the light's flashin')' ('Never Miss a Beat'), Okereke wants only 'to stamp on the face of every young policeman' ('Where is Home?'). In light of their troubled relationship with England and hegemonic forms of Englishness and Britishness, a parallel might be drawn between Bloc Party and the musical practitioners of the 'dissident diaspora'.[62] Musical outfits like the Asian Dub Foundation, also from East London, offered a political rejoinder mobilized through a fusion of jungle, punk and the sounds of the post-colonial margins, to the xenophobic and commodified patriotism of Cool Britannia. However, in comparison, Bloc Party seems satisfied to witness Britain's inequalities and injustices rather than offer a political alternative. The overwhelming sense of alienation is caught in *A Weekend in the City*'s cover art, an aerial photograph of a major road in West London immortalized by the Clash in *London Calling*, the Westway, populated only by the ghostly trails of car head- and tail-lights, an anti-postcard for the non-space of the metropolis.

---

[61]   Ibid.

[62]   Koushik Banerjea, 'Sounds of Whose Underground? The Fine Tuning of Diaspora in an Age of Mechanical Reproduction', p. 64.

Answering the English Question (or Not)

In their articulations of Englishness, the Kaiser Chiefs', Arctic Monkeys', and Bloc Party's music offer three imagined answers to this English question. While the first decade of the twenty-first century might be marked by a 'choice of Englishnesses',[63] the three bands I have examined here have shown little imagination in their selection.

Kaiser Chiefs and the Arctic Monkeys answer the English question by looking unapologetically backwards. Like the Britpop bands before them, Kaiser Chiefs and Arctic Monkeys exhibit a 'displaced nostalgia' for cultures that they are too young to have experienced directly themselves.[64] This 'displaced nostalgia' might be diagnosed as a symptom of Fredric Jameson's cultural amnesia, a manifestation of the cannibalistic tendencies of a culture that is able, like no culture before it, 'to transmit, store, retrieve, reconfigure and invoke the past in new and specific ways';[65] or, more conventionally, a sign of youthful longing for an always gone 'golden age' of English popular music, be it the 1960s, 1970s or any other period. More positively, nostalgia might be implicated in recognition that 'aspects of the past' could operate 'as the basis of renewal in the future'.[66] However, in terms of questions of Englishness, such 'displaced nostalgia' has important consequences.

Raymond Williams uses the appealing but slippery term 'structure of feeling' to describe the felt quality and pattern of life as it is engendered by a particular culture. A structure of feeling is not directly accessible to those who have not experienced it, but a form of access is granted by 'the arts of a period ... For here, if anywhere, this [structure of feeling] is likely to be expressed'.[67] Therefore, in retrieving past sounds and styles, sounds and styles that are already part of the 'selective tradition' of English popular music, the Kaiser Chiefs and the Arctic Monkeys, like Oasis and Blur before them, evoke a structure of feeling that cannot help but be haunted by the ghosts of England's past. Moreover, the incredible commercial success of these two bands might in some way be derived from their evocation of a time when questions about national identity could be answered more easily, even though in reality the 1960s and 1970s were periods of intense debate about the county's future in light of decolonization, the influx of Commonwealth migrants, economic stagnation and Britain's relationship with Europe.

Whereas Williams refers to the 'well-known habit of using the past ... as a stick to beat the present',[68] here it seems that versions of the past are used to avoid pressing issues in the present. Hence the Kaiser Chiefs' answer to the

---

[63] Bryant, 'These Englands', p. 394.

[64] Toby Young and Tom Vanderbilt, 'The End of Irony', pp. 6–7.

[65] Paul Grainge, *Monochrome Memories: Nostalgia and Style in Retro America*, p. 28.

[66] Michael Pickering and Emily Keightley, 'The Modalities of Nostalgia', p. 921.

[67] Raymond Williams, *The Long Revolution*, pp. 64–5.

[68] Raymond Williams, *The Country and the City*, p. 21.

English question is to deploy familiar tropes of commodified Englishness that could stand and have stood, simultaneously, for Britishness. Groom highlights this problem by suggesting that connotations of Englishness are largely inseparable from connotations of Britishness: '[t]he celebration of landscape, poetry, music, democracy, radicalism, and humour is, however, hardly likely to distinguish what is specifically English, from what is more generally British'.[69] He goes as far as to suggest that the reason for this is that Englishness 'is the key component of Britishness';[70] or expressed differently, Britishness cannot function as the other of Englishness. Seen in this light, Kaiser Chiefs are the inheritors of Britpop, where questions of Englishness do not arise because Englishness dominates British identity, and so one is subsumed by the other.

On the other hand, I would argue that the Arctic Monkeys do offer a sense of Englishness separable from a generic Britishness. Turner and company achieve this feat by articulating Englishness through the local, as it is expressed through a constellation of territorializing English affects. But undeniably rooted as they are in a particular English place, the band nonetheless relies on a nostalgic idiom to articulate the experiences of England's Gen-Y, an idiom that provides a 'touch of the real' at the cost of purging their music of most contemporary references, musical and lyrical. So even as he evokes a highly territorialized Englishness, Turner appears to have slipped into the imagined past to do so, an act that seems to suggest that thinking of England in such a fixed, stable and bounded way is not a possibility *in the present*.

Significantly, of the three bands I have examined here, the one that is least reliant on Britpop as an inspiration, Bloc Party, offers the most contemporary and critical engagement with British and English culture and society. Criticizing the question, however, is not the same as answering it – to be against something is not necessarily to be in favour of something else. Despite their obvious differences from Kaiser Chiefs and Arctic Monkeys, Bloc Party similarly fail to imagine what an Englishness-to-come might look like. There are no new hegemonies here.

Conclusion

Over the last five years there has been a proliferation of new British guitar bands. By representing these new bands as the 'second wave' of Britpop, the music media has attempted to re-create the excitement and optimism, and hopefully record sales, of that increasingly mythologized period of British musical history. However, in positioning these new bands as the successors of the class of 1995, it is easy to avoid the differences between the various bands, not necessarily in terms of musical style or genre, although these are apparent, but in their articulation of pop-Englishness. Rather than attempt a survey of this putative second wave

[69]   Nick Groom, *The Union Jack: The Story of the British Flag*, p. 311.
[70]   Ibid., p. 313.

en masse, I have instead looked at three of the most prominent and commercially successful of these new groups. This approach is taken not to use a part to represent a whole but to demonstrate the different forms of pop-Englishness evinced by these post-Britpop guitar bands. The Kaiser Chiefs, Arctic Monkeys and Bloc Party all have different relationships to their Britpop antecedents, and each offers a different variety of pop-Englishness: the 'ambivalent-little-Englishness' of the Kaiser Chiefs; the urban-pastoral Englishness of the Arctic Monkeys; and the non-identified critical cosmopolitanism of Bloc Party. It would seem that, while these representatives of the 'second wave of Britpop' do offer a slightly wider range of possible answers to the English question than the first, none offers an emergent Englishness that might influence national perceptions in the context of a devolved, integrated, globalized and multicultural Britain. Of course, it might be asking too much to expect popular music to provide emergent forms of Englishness when broader political and cultural domains seem unable to provide an answer either, although performers like Billy Bragg[71] (2006) have tried to do just that. Then again, perhaps a totalizing English identity is not an answer to the conditions that prompted the English question in the first place.

---

[71]   See Billy Bragg, *The Progressive Patriot: A Search for Belonging.*

Chapter 11

Worries in the Dance: Post-Millennial Grooves and Sub-Bass Culture

Nabeel Zuberi

One of the most disturbing aspects of the UK in the new century, at home and abroad, has been its international partnership with the US in the wars and occupations of Afghanistan and Iraq. In response, British Islamists have continued to plan and carry out terrorist attacks on civilians. According to the human rights lawyer Gareth Peirce, the British state's strategies of internment, deportation and endorsement of torture owe much to the treatment of the Irish as a 'suspect community' in the twentieth century.[1] The last decade has witnessed an exaggeration of threats to the national way of life posed by immigrants, asylum seekers and British Muslims. Successive Labour governments have stressed Britishness as a unifying set of ideas to deal with these 'problems'. As Sanjay Sharma and Ashwani Sharma put it, 'The troubled discourse of liberal multiculturalism is ambivalently split and caught between the celebration of cultural diversity and a heightened manifestation of cultural racism and Islamophobia.'[2]

This chapter focuses on some of the black humours in dance music during the last decade. My examples include MCs/rappers Dizzee Rascal, Sway and M.I.A., as well as recordings from electronic genres such as Dubstep. They foreground surveillance of the racialized subject and the evocation of 'troubled' spaces. The sounds, images and commentary circulate affective energies and sensations that are dark and pleasurable. They offer social critique but are also integrated into the contemporary economies and hierarchies of cultural difference. The star musician, the transnational collaboration, the genre or local scene all mediate affects and geographies strongly marked by fear and paranoia, anger and melancholia. They do this through figures such as criminals, zombies, ghosts, hooded figures and other scary monsters. The modes of the gothic and horror, gangsterism, science fiction and tabloid news reportage are deployed, sometimes with earnestness but more often than not through carnivalesque humour, unruly gestures, postcolonial mimicry and pantomime.[3] Hip-hop, dancehall and grime rely on microphone techniques, stylized urban realism and aggressive articulations of the self. Dub,

---

[1] Gareth Peirce, 'Was it Like This For The Irish?'

[2] Sanjay Sharma and Ashwani Sharma, 'White Paranoia: Orientalism in the Age of Empire', p. 8.

[3] John Hutnyk, 'Pantomime Terror: Diasporic Music in a Time of War'.

techno and other types of electronica are renowned for immersion in repetitive sound, their spatial imaginaries or virtual spaces. The music has its vocabulary of sound effects designed for club sound systems and personal music players: hooks like gunshots, helicopters, heavy metal guitar riffs, 'foreign' vocals, funky synths, sub-bass lines, and spatializing techniques like echo and reverb. I am interested in how these recordings and associated videos, CD packaging and music writing *mediate* affects such as paranoia in this period, and how these affects are marked by racial and ethnic differences. I do not seek to argue that this popular music reflects the zeitgeist.

This music is testament to the agonistic 'conviviality', as Paul Gilroy terms the 'processes of cohabitation and interaction that have made multiculture an ordinary feature of social life in Britain's urban areas and postcolonial cities elsewhere'.[4] All this music has 'roots and routes' in Afrodiasporic and electronic music cultures. But these recordings also incorporate musical codes from multiple genres and even more dispersed sources, and have themselves been repeatedly modified, remixed, edited and sampled in other genres. While it has been highly mobile, much of the commentary on this music in journalism and websites centres on 'placing it', situating it, marking its boundaries, and making critical claims about its authenticity, success or failure based on its belonging to a place or places. Popular music discourse, inside and outside academia, manifests a territorializing imperative and desire for enclosure that is integral to the boundary-making of music cultures, but may also be linked to wider anxieties about aliens and borders.

Popular music assemblages intersect and play off the other mediations that make bodies and landscapes psychically and physiologically legible, visible and audible. Media technologies have been integral to the expansion of security and surveillance. Clive Norris, Mike McCahill and David Wood have accounted for the peculiarly high presence of CCTV in the UK as a result of rapid structural adjustment:

> ... the aggressive deregulation pursued by Conservative governments from 1979 onwards, coupled with the economic recession of the early 1990s combined to produce a crisis in British city centres ... It is the destabilising effects of transformation and restructuring which heighten perceptions of risk and create more visible polarisation. This in turn facilitates a climate receptive to increased levels of surveillance especially if it promises increased security.[5]

Media texts like forensic drama series (such as the *CSI* franchise) and reality television formats (such as *Big Brother*) have made surveillance mundane, intimate and pleasurable. They have complicated the separation of public and

---

4   Paul Gilroy, *After Empire: Melancholia or Convivial Culture?*, p. xi.

5   Clive Norris, Mike McCahill and David Wood, 'Editorial. The Growth of CCTV: A Global Perspective on the International Diffusion of Video Surveillance in Publicly Accessible Space', pp. 120–21.

private domains and disclosures, and generated the enjoyment of watching the policing and judging of ourselves and others. Ethnic differences and resemblances have been a source of anxiety in these media texts as elsewhere. Patricia Clough argues that, with the development of digital media technologies, we are witnessing the forging of a new kind of body, the biomediated body,

> ... which allows the raced body to be apprehended as information. Here the very technologies of surveillance and security, which presently operate to race populations, do so by monitoring bodily affect as information, ranging from DNA testing, to brain fingerprinting, neural imaging, body heat detection and iris or hand recognition.[6]

Media generate corporeal information across many sites, in many codes and with particular intensities and sensations. Music cultures and their media reproduce and respond to these processes of articulating affects or structures of feeling. In his book on British (South) Asian music in the 1990s, Rehan Hyder suggested the degree of reflexivity with which musicians use ethnic signs and knowledge, or 'ethnic resources' in their work, encoding them in several modalities.[7] Jan Nederveen Pieterse extends this observation more generally to argue that producers and consumers in a 'global multiculture' practise a *flexible acculturation* that 'deploys flexible methods (switching and mixing cultural vocabularies and alternating circuits of affiliation) towards the general aim of belonging and being at home in the world'.[8] These forms of 'code switching', supremely common to popular music, test the lines between the ironic and the insulting, the 'politically correct' and the profane.

Inglistan is a Bitch

'Inglan is a bitch / There's no escapin' it', pronounced dub poet Linton Kwesi Johnson on his track about English racism and the exploitation of the black working class on the album *Bass Culture* (1980). LKJ's offensive phrase was still resonant in 2009 when the electronic musician Luke Vibert sampled it several times for his track 'Batting for England' on the album *We Hear You* (2009). The cut opens with the sample 'Inglan is a bitch fi true / Is whey wi a goh dhu 'bout it?' The title of Vibert's track suggests the now residual cricketing metaphor that marked national loyalty and service. Yet with the next sample, you realize the bat in question is more likely to be a baseball bat. The loop we hear is 'I'll beat that bitch, I'll beat that bitch, I'll beat that bitch with a bat' from Farley Jackmaster Funk's 'Ghetto

---

    [6]   Patricia T. Clough, 'The Affective Turn: Political Economy and the Biomediated Body', p. 19.

    [7]   Rehan Hyder, *Brimful of Asia: Negotiating Ethnicity on the UK Music Scene*, p. 3.

    [8]   Jan Nederveen Pieterse, 'Global Multiculture, Flexible Acculturation', p. 74.

House' track from 2000. Also repeated through most of the second half of this track is the sample of a screeching and wavering heavy-metal guitar.

One often wishes to take a bat to the hollow piñata of national identity, but I wonder if what Gilroy calls an 'emphatically non-national account of the development of diaspora culture' is a utopian dream.[9] Though I have contributed in small measure to the academic literature, the focus on *Britishness* and *Englishness* may limit the ways we understand the identifications, aesthetics and politics associated with music because we are so desperate to attach them to the territory of the UK.[10] This is the case whether we brand culture as national, make the national culture more inclusive or attempt to break up the idea of England or Britain. To distinguish or disarticulate England and Englishness from Britain and Britishness may not solve some problems. Devolution doesn't substantially shift the terms of national identity for many England dwellers since for pragmatic reasons of immigration, settlement and movement across national borders, to be 'British' is directly tied to the status of citizens and legal residents. There is no such thing (yet?) as an English passport. The state also continues to advocate a *British* national identity. Arun Kundnani points out that, in the new century, the political centre-left and New Labour in particular have adopted 'Britishness' as part of a discourse of *integrationism*. He cites Gordon Brown's appearance at a Fabian Society conference on national identity in January 2006, where he argued for the need for 'core values' of Britishness to be reinforced.[11] In seeking to construct an elusive British national identity, the pronouncements of ministers and commentary in the press have slid easily between different groups blamed for the particularities of their own 'cultures'.

From the middle of the decade, black youth crime came increasingly under the spotlight with the growing number of teenage deaths in knife and gun violence. Young men of any ethnic background that wore their hoodies up (the hooded tops associated with hip-hop culture) were subject to scrutiny. Politicians used this (in)visibility to score points with the public through their tough attitude to crime as well as their sensitivity to young people's problems. Anxieties about the sartorial choices of the population here were mirrored in 2006 by the amplification of the issue of British Muslim women covered head to toe and 'faceless' in *niqab*. Sara Ahmed has suggested that the affective economy of fear depends on a 'stickiness' between the objects of fear: 'fear does not reside in a particular object or sign, and it is this lack of residence that allows fear to slide across signs, and between bodies'.[12]

---

[9]   Paul Gilroy, 'Multiculture, Double Consciousness and the "War on Terror"', p. 443.

[10]   Nabeel Zuberi, *Sounds English: Transnational Popular Music*.

[11]   Arun Kundnani, *The End of Tolerance: Racism in 21st Century Britain*, pp. 121–2.

[12]   Sarah Ahmed, 'Affective Economies', p. 127.

On his way out of 10 Downing Street as Prime Minister, in April 2007, Tony Blair gave a speech in which youth crime was blamed on a *distinctive* black culture of gangs and dysfunctional families:

> We need to stop thinking of this as a society that has gone wrong – it has not – but of specific groups that for specific reasons have gone outside of the proper lines of respect and good conduct towards others and need by specific measures to be brought back into the fold.[13]

Cultural studies academics might have reached for their old copies of Stuart Hall et al.'s *Policing the Crisis* (1978) on the racial panic generated around mugging in the mid-1970s, but a Canadian Muslim blogger responded more immediately and succinctly: '[t]hat's a bit rich coming from someone who has caused the death of tens of thousands with an illegal war'.[14]

Critics of the techniques of nationalism are caught in the paradox of having to cite Englishness and Britishness in order to refute them. This repetition is one sign of what Paul Gilroy has called 'postcolonial melancholia', a desire to return to 'the morbid core of England and Englishness in remorseless decline, the same strain that feeds interminable and increasingly desperate speculations about the content and character of the shrinking culture that makes England distinctive'.[15] For example, the seventy-fifth anniversary of J.B. Priestley's *English Journey* (1934) took *The Guardian*'s Sarfraz Manzoor on another expedition from the south to the exotic north and Priestley's hometown to ask 'what "Englishness" means today in a city like Bradford'.[16] To which one might respond: why must the quest for national identity function as the discursive regime through which the voices of people already marginalized in English-British society are articulated?

The spectre of Britishness couldn't keep away from a November 2008 exchange between BBC TV *Newsnight* anchor Jeremy Paxman and MC Dizzee Rascal (Dylan Kwabena Mills). Unable to bridge the generational, class and racial divide, and failing to take seriously Dizzee's assertion that hip-hop helped Obama win the US presidency through its mobilization of American youth, Paxman asked, '[c]ould it happen here?' But before Dizzee could answer, he interjected, 'Mr Rascal, do you feel yourself to be British?' To which Dizzee replied, '[o]f course I'm British. It doesn't matter what colour you are. I think a black man, a purple man, a Martian could run the country, as long as he does right by the people.' Impishly, Paxman went on to ask Dizzee, '[d]o you believe in political parties?' To this, *Mr Rascal* gave one of the most appropriately understated statements about the state

---

[13]   Patrick Wintour and Vikram Dodd, 'Blair Blames Spate of Murders on Black Culture'.

[14]   Crescent Canuck, 'So it's the Blacks Who Are at Fault?'

[15]   Paul Gilroy, 'Joined-up Politics and Postcolonial Melancholia', p. 162.

[16]   Sarfraz Manzoor, 'Sarfraz Manzoor Asks What "Englishness" Means Today in a City Like Bradford'.

of contemporary parliamentary politics: 'They exist.'[17] In the media commentary that followed, there was criticism of Paxman's questioning but also of Dizzee for not representing young black Britons and musicians in an appropriate way.[18] The objections revealed the gulf between Dizzee's vernacular and an establishment BBC register, even though Dizzee was now a successful pop star. Paxman's out-of-the-blue question about Dizzee's Britishness also demonstrated that mainstream media organizations were happy to use national identity and race to stimulate controversy for higher ratings.

Black Criminals, Illegal Immigrants and Terrorists

From Bow, London E3, Dizzee Rascal had become a Mercury Prize-winning and chart-topping celebrity through a life of grime, a British composite of US Hip-hop, Jamaican dancehall, with a genealogy that takes in jungle, drum 'n' bass and UK garage. Where garage was more R&B-influenced in its lyrics and music, and shared the consumerist ethos of blinged-up US Hip-hop and R&B, grime tended towards choppier beats and synth stabs, MC rhymes rather than singing voices, and localized shout-outs in its east and south London 'street' commentaries and beefs between rival MCs. Mediated in pirate radio, mix CDs, DVDs, mp3s and countless blogs and forums on the web, grime features MCs flowing with local and outernational accents (including Jamaican patwah) over beats that recall the retro-futuristic soundscapes of computer games. Most of the commentary on grime is dominated by the discourse of territoriality: its definitions and boundaries as a genre ('Wot Do U Call It?', in the words of one of its elder statesmen, Wiley[19]), as well as its postcode localism and turf battles between and within crews. Grime is hardwired as 'a technology of the self' and is an exemplar of the governmentality of a British music discourse obsessed with genre divisions, new market categories and geographical origins. This makes it a compelling cultural arena in which to see how subjects imagine themselves as the objects of surveillance.

One relatively high profile example is Dizzee Rascal's single 'Sirens' from his third album *Maths + English* (2007).[20] A heavy rock guitar tone rather than a riff is used for its dissonance. Produced by Dizzee and his manager Cage, the track has a 1980s hip-hop sound with sampled snare drums, reminiscent of the rock–rap crossover of Aerosmith and Run-D.M.C.'s 'Walk This Way' (1986). A police siren is a recurring refrain and Dizzee repeats the chorus 'I can hear them sirens coming'

---

[17]   This exchange can be seen in the following video clip: 'Obama Won Because of Hip Hop – Go Dizzee Rascal', at http://www.youtube.com/watch?v=sRTe4q-vR0g, accessed 1 May 2010.

[18]   *NME*, 'Estelle: Paxman Treated Dizzee Rascal Like an Idiot'.

[19]   On Roll Deep, *Roll Deep Presents Grimey, Vol. 1*, 2004.

[20]   Dizzee Rascal, *Maths + English*, 2007. W.I.Z.'s video for 'Sirens' may be viewed at http://www.youtube.com/watch?v=IPpxxrl0xhM, accessed 1 May 2010.

and the need for the protagonist to run. The narrative recounts a chaotic crime gone wrong in Limehouse in East London. Dizzee's character and a mate commit a robbery and beat up an unfortunate man and woman. Dizzee is identified by a witness to the crime, so he is now on the run, though he continues to proclaim nihilistically, even as the track fades out, that 'I break the law, I will never change'. It's another articulation of the classic Afrodiasporic tale of the trickster on the run from white power, ironic but less comedic in its scene setting than another grime MC Lethal Bizzle's timely reworking of The Clash's cover of The Equals' 'Police on My Back'.

The director W.I.Z.'s music video for 'Sirens' seems primed for semiotic readings of race and class. It's a knowing kind of 'concept' video demonstrating that the hermeneutics of cultural studies have been internalized by media producers, and is somewhat discomfiting for this reason. Dizzee is hunted down at night in an inner-city landscape by white, red-jacketed foxhunters who for extra racial scariness have their faces painted white. One gentleman on a white horse breaks into a flat where Dizzee chats to a young black boy who wears a sweatshirt with the word 'England' printed on it. The foxhunter wrecks the place as the horse stomps around the flat. A momentary close-up shows a framed photo of a black man (Linton Kwesi Johnson!) falling to the floor, its glass shattered by the horse's hooves. Dizzee runs out of the house and through the streets. A street sign reads 'Orgreave Estate', alluding to the Battle of Orgreave in Yorkshire in 1984 when police on horseback fought with coal miners during the protracted strike that 'broke the back' of the union movement in Thatcher's Britain. Dizzee is eventually cornered in an alley by a group of uniformed foxhunters, including young women. They smear their faces with fox blood ready for the kill. Bloodlust and erotic lust for the black body are caught together as a young woman licks her lips and Dizzee chucks off his hooded parka to stand topless and defiant. The video does not offer 'positive images' to counter negative representations and stereotypes. It celebrates the glamour of the black outlaw as erotic spectacle and cannot help reproduce the representational tropes it critiques.

In the response to young people's knife and gun deaths during the 2000s, a succession of government officials and media outlets have predictably 'blamed' music, videos and films as causal agents in gun culture.[21] Musicians are still prepared in the context of these sensitivities to respond with in-your-face statements that in turn cause little outrage or controversy. Even in Dizzee Rascal's 2009 number 1 pop hit 'Bonkers', produced by Armand Van Helden in the United States, Dizzee shouts out, 'All I think about is sex and violence / A heavy bass line is my kind of silence'. The songs often preach to the already-converted constituencies of fans and followers who may or may not see how, or care if, 'sex and violence' are in quotation marks or hip-hop cliché. But the rhymes are often directly addressed to the state authorities and the idea of the criminal in the media.

---

[21]   Barry Didcock, 'Who Takes the Rap for Gun Culture? When Two Teenage Girls were Shot'.

Another track that makes this explicit is 'What You Know' (2008) by Two Fingers featuring Sway. Two Fingers is a collaboration between Brazilian electronic musician Amon Tobin and British producer Joe 'Doubleclick' Chapman, released on the Big Dada label based in London.[22] Sway (Derek Andrew Safo) is an MC from North London who won a MOBO award (Music of Black Origin) in 2005. The beat and the vocals were recorded in Montreal where Tobin was based, but describe life in London with some comparisons with gang culture in Brazil and Ghana. The dominant beat is a bhangra-style rhythm suggested by a processed 'Indian' drum sound, layers of percussion following this dominant pattern, short synth melodies, shards of bassy grunting electronic interference and occasional police sirens. In some respects, it is a dirtied-up version of the influential production styles of Timbaland and the Neptunes that moved away from the sampled funk snares of earlier hip-hop to a more techno-influenced sound in the late 90s and early 2000s. Sway repeatedly tells the listener that the police are coming but he's not running because he hasn't committed a crime. The refrain 'What you know about gangster life' suggests both an angry question to the listener and a statement about the limitations of the media's claims to truth. Sway's narrative takes us to a police station where his mugshots are taken. He says that the police detain suspects because they want to impress the newspapers that they're making an effort to fight crime. He switches from this dramatic encounter to talking about gang crime in London, how it has caused deaths in his family, and how he avoids carrying a gun despite the temptations.

Like other recordings addressing this issue, 'What You Know' negotiates between a critique of violent crime in the community and a critique of policing. One of the founders of Rinse FM, a pirate and now online radio station crucial to grime and dubstep's development, the DJ and producer Geeneus recorded 'Knife & Gun' with the MCs Riko, Wiley and Breeze in 2008, which more directly addressed the (potential) perpetrators of violence. The label of one side of this 12-inch single shows a photograph of street graffiti tags where an EN3 sign has been crossed out and replaced with E5 and also by S8, indicating some of the territorial competition. The label on the other side features a sign that reads 'No Spitting' in English with Devnagari script underneath, alluding to Indian signage but also punning on the term 'spitting' used to describe rapping.[23]

Even if South Asia and the Middle East are not mentioned in lyrics, the music and associated images suggest those places are close to home. The name Two Fingers has several connotations but the Dutch designer Karol Lasia's artwork bears a resemblance to the silhouettes of the World Trade Center's Twin Towers.[24]

---

[22]   Two Fingers, *Two Fingers*, 2008.

[23]   The labels for Geeneus ft. Riko, Wiley & Breeze, *Knife & Gun (Blackdown Mixes)*, 2008, at http://www.boomkat.com/item.cfm?id=146976 and http://www.boomkat.com/item.cfm?id=172533, accessed 3 May 2010.

[24]   Selected works of Karol Lasia at Khomatech, http://www.khomatech.com/, accessed 3 May 2010.

In grime, there are more direct references to terror. The producer Terror Danjah has composed beats for many grime MCs. A collection of his instrumentals from 2003–2009 is titled *Gremlinz* after an evil synthetic cackle that is a signature on most of his recordings. The cover of this release features a photograph of him with an African mask.[25] With their stuttering minimal beats, lumbering bass lines and titles such as 'Creeper', many of the tracks evoke monsters stalking the urban landscape. Wiley and Trimbal (Javan St. Prix), who both once belonged to the Roll Deep Crew have invoked terror bogie men in two versions of the track 'Taliban' produced by Scratchy/DVA. Wiley's version finds him greeted by Trimbal, 'Assalaamalaikum', after which he sends shouts out to his 'soldiers' around London, and confesses to the attractions of converting to Islam.[26] In Trimbal's solo version he describes fictional or real Muslims in London, and in one striking line says he will put 'nail bombs in Christmas gifts'. Trimbal goes by many names, including Taliban Trim.

This provocative theatricality is well established in hip-hop's tradition of daring antipathies and role playing, but is more charged in a political climate sensitive to such public statements. Many of the most visible Islamists in the UK have been identified as recent English converts, and musicians may also be at risk for their work being taken literally. For example, Samina Malik, the 23-year-old 'lyrical terrorist' from Southall, west London, was arrested under Section 57 of the Counter Terrorism Act in October 2008 after police found written notes with rhymes about martyrdom and beheading alongside other Islamist literature. She was acquitted on appeal in June 2009.

In the midst of widespread terror discourse, a pop song with young girls chanting 'All I want to do is go boom, boom, boom' (the booms backed up with synchronized gunshots) reaches number 1 on the iTunes charts in 2008 and is nominated for a Grammy as Record of the Year in 2009. M.I.A.'s 'Paper Planes' (2007) could allude to the first attack on the World Trade Center: 'we crash and deliver like UPS trucks'. On the David Letterman show, the gunshots were removed from M.I.A.'s performance. 'Paper Planes' comes from M.I.A.'s second official album *Kala* (2007). US DJ Diplo and M.I.A. produced the track in Brooklyn, with additional production from the UK dance music producer Switch. The song was released as a single in February 2008, and in several mixes on the *Homeland Securities* EP. It gained a higher profile in the US when it was used in the promotional trailer for the film comedy *Pineapple Express*, released in August 2008. It became ubiquitous in 2009 after its use in Danny Boyle's multiple Oscar-winning film *Slumdog Millionaire* (2009). Its invocation to gunplay was underlined by the missile whine of Mick Jones's lead guitar sampled from The Clash's 'Straight to Hell' (1983).

M.I.A.'s music and the visuals of record sleeves, promotional photographs and videos (often designed and directed by her) have animated the figures

---

25   Terror Danjah, *Gremlinz: The Instrumentals 2003–2009*, 2009.
26   Trimbal, *Soulfood Vol. 1*, 2007.

of the refugee, asylum seeker, immigrant, slum dweller and terrorist. Her first widely distributed release was *Piracy Funds Terrorism Vol. 1* (2004), a mixtape with Diplo that was released without clearance for the use of sampled copyrighted material. It became a viral mp3 phenomenon and promoted her first tour of North America in 2004 and debut album *Arular* (2005), released by XL Recordings, one of the UK's most influential independent labels. *Arular* was well-received, and M.I.A. (Maya Arulpragasam) became a focus for professional journalists and bloggers to debate and arbitrate the ethics of cross-cultural exchange. A cluster of positive and negative types and tropes emerged in countless blog entries and comment threads, major and minor music publications. M.I.A. was a refugee-immigrant done good; a postcolonial pimp and whore; a cultural thief; Arundhati Roy with a drum machine; Mowgli with a spray can; hip-hop punk Situationist; prole art threat and bourgie fetish; terrorist bitch and slumming ragpicker; an average talent with skilled (male) producers pulling the strings. Music journalists also tended to determine her authenticity or lack of it based on signs of middle-class privilege, the veracity of her transnational experience as a Sri Lankan refugee, and whether or not she was an apologist for Tamil terrorism. Much of the commentary was geared to putting M.I.A. 'in her place'.[27] Ironically her music seemed to be highly mobile in the cultural economy, though it also reflected on the limits of mobility for goods and people.

'Paper Planes' uses the registers of children's voices to articulate media connectedness and satirize xenophobia. The protagonist of the song can easily reproduce visas for entry into the nation, celebrates guns, and may even consume illegal drugs. 'Hit me on my burner, prepaid wireless', sings M.I.A. in her nasal West London accent in 'Paper Planes', tapping into transnational hip-hop's associative techniques for capturing and connecting objects, brands and accessories such as laptops and phones. 'All I wanna do is take your money', she and the Brooklyn girls chant, satirizing one vein of anti-immigrant sentiment as well as her own position as an artist selling difference, a 'bona fide hustler making my name'. Several of her songs, including '10 Dollar' and '20 Dollar', involve financial transactions in which she plays the trafficked commodity.

Occupied Territories

From these characters, I want to turn now to dubstep in which human voices are less prominent, or where the spatial imaginaries and sound effects dominate human subjects. In many cases the voices are often present as brief samples, chopped, processed or faint in the mix. In dubstep, the average tempo is around 140 beats per minute, with sub-bass frequencies below 90 Hz to the fore, though there is considerable variation. The peculiarly British frenzy for policing dance genres and renaming them to create novelty is a distraction from some of the specific energies of this formation as it develops like a rhizome to produce different strains. Dubstep has a shared history with early grime, jungle, drum 'n' bass and UK garage, but also a longer Afrofuturist genealogy linked to Detroit and Eurotechno, electronic funk and Jamaican sound system culture and studio aesthetics. It relies on the media assemblage of independent labels, clubs, pirate and public radio stations, and websites that post tracks and archive the scene.

Dub is a vital if sometimes buried precursor of dubstep. Dub is inherently a 'ghostly' technique as it relies on the incomplete spectral presences of previous recordings as they are versioned. Dub's use of echo, reverb and the movement of sounds across the stereo audio-scape have also made it ideal for articulating madness and otherworldliness. The genre also carries with it the multivalent notion of 'dread': the historical weight of racism as it has defined subjects; a sense of crisis; and an ever-present danger.[28] Michael Veal has suggested that dub's 'structural uncertainty resonates with an age of the refugee, the nomad, the displaced person, the de-centered inhabitant of the culturally exploding megapolis, the liminal terrorist, and a historical period in which the old seems to be giving way to an uncertain new at an unprecedented rate.'[29] The website of Steve Goodman's (aka Kode9) Hyperdub label describes 'a world trembling in an echology [*sic*] of fear'.[30] Goodman has also written about the use of low frequencies as weapons of 'sonic warfare'.[31] Contemporary British music like dubstep transplants the echoes of paranoia found in Jamaican music and hip-hop. Simon Reynolds noted of jungle and drum 'n' bass in the 1990s that it registered 'late capitalist economic instability, institutionalized racism, and increased surveillance and harassment of youth by the police'.[32] The aesthetics of many recent records, such as The Bug's *London Zoo* (2008) use sub-bass frequencies within an aesthetic that evokes war more aggressively with amplified low frequencies that may also be painful.[33]

---

[28]   Peter Hitchcock, 'It Dread Inna Inglan: Linton Kwesi Johnson, Dread, and Dub Identity', pp. 7–8.

[29]   Michael Veal, *Dub: Soundscapes and Shattered Songs in Jamaican Reggae*, p. 256.

[30]   Kode9 & the SpaceApe, *Memories of the Future*.

[31]   Steve Goodman, *Sonic Warfare: Sound, Affect and the Ecology of Fear*.

[32]   Simon Reynolds, *Generation Ecstasy: Into the World of Techno and Rave Culture*, 1998, p. 354.

[33]   See also the military video for The Bug feat. Warrior Queen, 'Poison Dart', 2008, at http://www.ninjatune.net/videos/video.php?type=flv&id=136, accessed 3 May 2010; and their collaboration about the London terrorist attacks of 7 July 2005, The Bug feat. Warrior Queen, 'Dem A Bomb We', 2005, at www.youtube.com/watch?v=4k5hNwfUe4M, accessed 3 May 2010.

The techno influence in dubstep encourages 'cinematic' readings that elaborate spaces associated with sound. The blog Woebot (Matt Ingram) suggests that 'perhaps Dubstep is a kind of contemporary Exotica foundered [*sic*] on recycling old Jamaican music?'[34] Producers also use voices, string refrains and percussion that betray an interest in Indian, Chinese, Middle Eastern and African soundscapes. Websites that market and comment on this music usually encompass it all under the term 'ethnic'. Woebot uses 'Exotica' here as a gentle insult because it signals not just a genre but also an improper appropriation of the other. This may be a limitation of music criticism that polices the ethnic boundaries of music looking for 'bad objects' without taking the fantasies and contradictory desires of exoticism seriously.[35] If popular culture offers a 'phantom history of race relations', as Dick Hebdige once put it,[36] then we need to be more attentive to its *phantoms* and other fabulist sonic figures, spaces and temporalities. They offer a respite from and a challenge to ethnographic modes of knowledge. The belief in 'authentic' musical identities and the anti-racist critiques that underpin the disavowal of exotica as bad object sometimes reveal a deeper-rooted desire to control and mark off the other. The gestures of some dubstep, however, imagine the orient as if it's right here.

These orientalist citations appear in more than one modality, though they do include many musical clichés. Dusk and Blackdown's *Margins Music* (2008) is a concept album that takes the listener on a tour of London's African, Caribbean and Asian neighbourhoods and combines the influences of Hindi film music, bhangra, grime and dubstep, using local MCs, vocalists and documentary sound-bites. *Margins Music* celebrates the convivial multiculture, 'beyond the corporate finance of the City, the anodyne bars of the West End and the affluent riches out west', according to its CD packaging, which also notes that '[i]f we have our hoods up, maybe we're cold?'[37] Bristol recording artist Pinch samples a cluster of harmonium chords with the stuttering drum slaps and rolling sub-bass pressure on 'Qawwali' (2006). But in many examples of sub-bass culture, the Muslim references are more elliptical. An Arabian melody emerges through the fog and crackle of Burial's recordings; sometimes an R&B female vocal has been treated so that it floats up in the mix and then decays without us understanding what it has said, but it sounds vaguely eastern. More recognizably Arabic voices are sampled in tracks by Shackleton whose recordings for the Skull Disco label include Asian and African percussion, wind instruments and drones, and have titles like 'Hamas Rule' and 'El Din' that point to the Muslim world. Zeke Clough's artwork for a raft of these and other Skull Disco releases on 12-inch singles and compilations feature comic-book and day-of-the-dead grotesques with skeletons exposed to torture (as in *Soundboy's Suicide Note*, 2008), ancient Egyptian figures with animal heads (as in *Soundboy's*

---

34   Woebot, 'Farewell', 4 January 2008.
35   Phil Ford, 'Taboo: Time and Belief in Exotica', pp. 107 and 128.
36   Dick Hebdige, *Subculture: The Meaning of Style*, p. 58.
37   Liner notes, Dusk + Blackdown, *Margins Music*, 2008. Blackdown (aka Martin Clark) also writes on grime and dubstep for Pitchfork at www.pitchfork.com

Ashes Get Chopped Out and Snorted, 2007), and piles of vegetable and animal matter (as in *Soundboy's Bones Get Buried in the Dirt*, 2006). Shackleton has also recorded with the label and artists at Mordant Music, exemplars of what Simon Reynolds has called 'haunted audio' to describe 'a genre-without-name: more of a flavour or atmosphere than a style with boundaries'.[38] This hauntological dimension might be emblematic of the postcolonial melancholia identified by Paul Gilroy, yet not just a mourning for an England or Britain that has disappeared or doesn't know what it is, but also an oblique registration of the troubling dead bodies and ghosts of Empire past and present.

It seems appropriate that a canonical example of 'haunted audio', the spaghetti-western reggae of the Specials' 'Ghost Town' (1981) would be versioned in the new century by Kode9 & the SpaceApe.[39] The latter recites the lyrics in even slower, heavier and more deliberate dread patwah deadpan than Linton Kwesi Johnson's over a slow sub-bass heartbeat, ghostly melodica and wind effects: 'This town comin' like a ghost town, this ya place is comin' like a wasteground'. In April 2008, the song's writer Jerry Dammers, members of his Orchestra, the Hypnotic Brass Ensemble, Damon Albarn, a clutch of grime and hip-hop MCs, and the SpaceApe performed the song at the end of the Love Music Hate Racism concert in front of over 110,000 people in Victoria Park, London. Dammers said the British National Party, which had been in the ascendancy, was like a mouth ulcer that you have to treat with Listerine and gargling. As the song began, en masse the crowd gargled the 'middle eastern' brass and keyboard melody. As he invited SpaceApe to the stage to finish the song and conclude the concert, Dammers dedicated it to 'Stephen Lawrence, Anthony Walker and all the hundreds and hundreds of people that have been killed in racial attacks over the years.'

Conclusion

At the end of the century's first decade, dance music multiculture continues to thrive in the UK. These music styles and cultures mediate and circulate the 'troubling' affects of a nation at war overseas and on the home front. Much of the commentary on these genres tends to dwell on 'placing it', situating it, marking its territory (usually as a genre), nationalizing it, and making claims about its authenticity based on its belonging. One of the most influential and controversial recent statements on much of this music comes from Simon Reynolds, who in 2009 compiled a set of articles that he had written on dance music in Britain for *The Wire* since the early 1990s. He argued for a 'hardcore continuum' that brought together Afrodiasporic and electronic musical influences as well as an economic and media infrastructure that had sustained this music over the last two decades.[40]

---

[38]   Simon Reynolds, 'Society of the Spectral'.

[39]   On Various Artists, *5: Five Years of Hyperdub*, 2009.

[40]   Simon Reynolds, 'The Hardcore Continuum: Introduction'.

Reynolds' effort to demarcate and delineate this musical formation at a February 2009 talk at FACT (Foundation for Art and Creative Technology) in Liverpool met with considerable resistance, particularly in the blogosphere.[41] A conference featuring music journalists and academics was organized subsequently at the Centre for Cultural Studies Research, University of East London in April 2009. This event emphasized the generational divide between older critics, academics and fans looking back at an apparent 'highpoint of origin' for this music in the early 90s and a younger constituency not wanting to be told their music was less radical musically and politically.[42] The problems of genre definition and the empirical status of this continuum were raised by Alex Williams.[43] A great volume of discourse has resulted from this attempt to put music in an enclosure fenced off by one or two critics.[44] The continuum described by Reynolds embeds black culture in Britain. But as a form of territorialism it might also distract us from more seriously considering the music's deeper roots, more diverse routes and contemporary political affects.

---

[41]   Simon Reynolds, 'The Hardcore Continuum, or (a) Theory and its Discontents'.

[42]   Jeremy Gilbert, 'The Hardcore Continuum?', pp. 18–22.

[43]   Splintering Bone Ashes, 'Invention or Discovery or, When is a Genre Not a Genre'.

[44]   Mark Fisher, 'The Abstract Reality of the "Hardcore Continuum"', pp. 123–6.

Bibliography

Adams, Ruth, 'The Englishness of English Punk: Sex Pistols, Subcultures, and Nostalgia', *Popular Music and Society*, 31/4 (2008): 469–88.

Ahmed, Sara, 'Affective Economies', *Social Text*, 79, 22/2 (2004): 117–39.

Alford, B.W.E., *Britain in the World Economy since 1880* (London–New York: Longman, 1996).

Anderson, Paul, and Nyta Mann, *Safety First: The Making of New Labour* (London: Granta, 1997).

Armitage, Simon, 'Foreword', in Armitage (ed.), *Great Lyricists: Alex Turner* (London: The Guardian, 2008).

Auslander, Philip, *Performing Glam Rock: Gender and Theatricality in Popular Music* (Ann Arbor, MI: University of Michigan Press, 2006).

Bailey, Peter, *Popular Culture and Performance in the Victorian City* (Cambridge: Cambridge University Press, 1998).

Baldwin, Laura, 'Why [i]t's Time for the "Battle of the Sexes" to End', *The F-Word*, July 2004, at http://www.thefword.org.uk/features/2004/07/why_its_time_for _the_battle_of_the_sexes_to_end, accessed 14 May 2010.

Banerjea, Koushik, 'Sounds of Whose Underground? The Fine Tuning of Diaspora in an Age of Mechanical Reproduction', *Theory, Culture & Society*, 17/3 (2000): 64–79.

Bannister, Matthew, *White Boys, White Noise: Masculinities and 1980s Indie Guitar Rock* (Aldershot: Ashgate, 2006).

Baxter-Moore, Nick, '"This is Where I Belong": Identity, Social Class and the Nostalgic Englishness of Ray Davies and the Kinks', *Popular Music and Society*, 29/2 (2006): 145–65.

BBC, 'Festival Fun Survives Crime Rise', 26 June 1999, at http://news.bbc. co.uk/1/hi/special_report/1999/06/99/glastonbury_1999/379088.stm, accessed 5 May 2010.

————, 'Bloc Party Blast "Stupid" Oasis', 29 March 2007, at http://news.bbc. co.uk/go/pr/fr/-/hi/entertainment/6505739.stm, accessed 27 January 2009.

————, 'Blair: In His Own Words', 11 May 2007, at http://news.bbc.co.uk/1/ hi/uk_politics/3750847.stm, accessed 12 May 2010.

Behr, Rafael, 'It May be a Golden Age for Pop Lyrics, but Is Amy Really That Good?', from *The Guardian*, 1 June 2008, at http://www.buzzle.com/ articles/198780.html, accessed 20 May 2010.

Bell, Daniel, *The End of Ideology: On the Exhaustion of Political Ideas in the Fifties* (Glencoe, IL: Free Press, 1960).

Bennett, Andy, '"Village Greens and Terraced Streets": Britpop and Representations of "Britishness"', *Young*, 5/4 (1997): 20–33.

————, 'Subcultures or Neo-Tribes?: Rethinking the Relationship between Youth, Style and Musical Taste', *Sociology*, 33/3 (1999): 599–617.

————, *Popular Music and Youth Culture: Music, Identity and Place* (Basingstoke: Macmillan, 2000).

————, 'The Forgotten Decade: Rethinking the Popular Music of the 1970s', *Popular Music History*, 2/1 (2007): 5–24.

————, Barry Shank and Jason Toynbee, *The Popular Music Studies Reader* (London: Routledge, 2006).

Bevan, Ian, *Top of the Bill: The Story of the London Palladium* (London: Frederick Muller, 1952).

Blake, Andrew, 'Re-placing British Music', in Mica Nava and Alan O'Shea (eds), *Modern Times: Reflections on a Century of English Modernity* (Routledge: London, 1996).

Booth, Alan (ed.), *British Economic Development since 1945* (Manchester–New York: Manchester University Press, 1995).

Brabazon, Tara, 'Robbie Williams: A Better Man?', *International Journal of Cultural Studies*, 5/1 (2002): 45–66.

Bracewell, Michael, *England is Mine: Pop Life in Albion from Wilde to Goldie* (London: Flamingo, 1998).

————, *The Nineties: When Surface Was Depth* (London: Flamingo, 2002).

————, 'I'm Surprised I Made it to 30', Arts Interview [with Brett Anderson], *The Guardian*, G2, 2 September 2008, pp. 26–7.

Bradley, Dick, *Understanding Rock'n'Roll: Popular Music in Britain 1955–1964* (Buckingham: Open University Press, 1992).

Bragg, Billy, *The Progressive Patriot: A Search for Belonging* (London: Bantam, 2006).

Brickell, Chris, 'The Transformation of Heterosexism and its Paradoxes', in Chrys Ingraham (ed.), *Thinking Straight: The Power, the Promise, and the Paradox of Heterosexuality* (New York, Routledge, 2005).

Bristow, Jennie, 'Blair's Other Babies', 9 May 2001, at http://www.spiked-online.com/Articles/00000002D0A5.htm, accessed 4 May 2010.

British Phonographic Institute, 'Yearly Best Selling Albums 1999', at http://www.bpi.co.uk/assets/../Yearly%20best%20sellers%20-%20albums.pdf, accessed 16 April 2009.

Bruce, Frank, *Scottish Showbusiness: Music Hall, Variety and Pantomime* (Edinburgh: NMS Publishing, 2000).

Bryant, Christopher, 'These Englands, or Where does Devolution Leave the English?', *Nations and Nationalism*, 9/3 (2003): 393–412.

Buckley, David, *Strange Fascination – David Bowie: The Definitive Story* (London: Virgin Books, 2000).

Butler, David, and Dennis Kavanagh, *The British General Election of 1997* (Basingstoke: Macmillan, 1997).

Cagle, M. van, *Reconstructing Pop/Subculture: Art, Rock and Andy Warhol* (London: Sage, 1995).

Cairns, Dan, 'Kings of the Road', *Times*, 27 March 2005, at http://entertainment.timesonline.co.uk/tol/arts_and_entertainment/music/article43731, accessed 14 November 2008.

————, 'The Prolific Kaiser Chiefs on Off with Their Heads', *The Times*, 12 October 2008, at http://entertainment.timesonline.co.uk/tol/arts_and_entertainment/music/article49153, accessed 14 November 2008.

————, 'Oasis: Roundhouse, NW1', *Sunday Times: Culture*, 2 November 2008, p. 40.

Cameron, Keith, 'Songs in the Key of Life', *The Guardian*, 23 June 2001, at http://www.rocksbackpages.com/article.html?ArticleID=13664, accessed 17 April 2009.

Cannadine, David, 'The "Last Night of the Proms" in Historical Perspective', *Historical Research*, 81/212 (2008): 315–49.

Cavanagh, David, 'Blur in the Studio', *Mojo*, 22 September 1995, pp. 68–77.

Chambers, Iain, *Urban Rhythms: Pop Music and Popular Culture* (Basingstoke: Macmillan, 1985).

Chang, Jeff, 'News from Nowhere?', *The Nation*, 17 November 2007, at http://www.thenation.com/doc/20071119/chang, accessed 3 May 2010.

Christgau, Robert, 'Burning Bright', *The Village Voice*, 22 February 2005, at http://www.villagevoice.com/2005-02-22/music/burning-bright/, accessed 3 May 2010.

Clarke, John, 'The Skinheads and the Magical Recovery of Community', in Stuart Hall and Tony Jefferson (eds), *Resistance through Rituals: Youth Subcultures in Post-War Britain* (London: Hutchinson, 1976).

Clayson, Alan, *The Beat Merchants: The Origins, History, Impact and Rock Legacy of the 1960s British Pop Groups* (London: Blandford, 1995).

————, *Hamburg: The Cradle of British Rock* (London: Sanctuary Publishing, 1997).

Cloonan, Martin, 'State of the Nation: "Englishness", Pop, and Politics in the mid-1990s', *Popular Music and Society*, 21/2 (1997): 47–70.

Clough, Patricia T., 'The Affective Turn: Political Economy and the Biomediated Body', *Theory, Culture and Society*, 25/1 (2004): 1–22.

Cochrane, Kira, 'The Dark World of Lads' Mags', *New Statesman*, 23 August 2007, at http://www.newstatesman.com/society/2007/08/lad-culture-cochrane-loaded, accessed 15 May 2010.

Cohen, Sara, *Rock Culture in Liverpool: Popular Music in the Making* (Oxford: Oxford University Press, 1991).

Collings, Matthew, *Blimey! From Bohemia to Britpop: The London Artworld from Francis Bacon to Damien Hirst* (London: 21 Publishing, 1997).

Collins, Andrew, 'Cello, Cello', *Q*, October 1996, pp. 28–30.

————, 'They're Big and they're Clever: the Success of the Arctic Monkeys Marks the Return of Brainy Pop', *The Times*, 20 January 2006, at http://entertainment.timesonline.co.uk/tol/arts_and_entertainment/music/article715358.ece, accessed 4 May 2010.

Connell, John, and Chris Gibson, *Sound Tracks: Popular Music, Identity, and Place* (London: Routledge, 2002).

Covach, John, 'Pangs of History in late 1970s New-Wave Rock', in Allan F. Moore (ed.), *Analyzing Popular Music* (Cambridge: Cambridge University Press, 2003).

Cox, Tom, 'West End Pearls: Scottish Bands used to be Pompous Arena Queens, but since Glasgow became European City of Culture, a Remarkable Renaissance in its Pop Scene has Occurred. Tom Cox talks to the quietly confident bands who live in Britain's Hippest Musical City', *The Guardian*, 16 January 1998, p. T012.

Crescent Canuck, 'So it's the Blacks Who Are at Fault?', April 2007, at http://crescentcanuck.blogspot.com/2007/04/so-its-blacks-who-are-at-fault.html, accessed 1 May 2010.

Davies, Ray, and Damon Albarn, Interview, *Mojo*, September 1995, pp. 78–82.

Davies, Rebecca, 'Banal Britishness and Reconstituted Welshness: The Politics of National Identities in Wales', *Contemporary Wales*, 18/1 (2006): 106–21.

Dee, Johnny, Review of 'Stutter', *NME*, 16 October 1993, at http://www.stutter.demon.co.uk/elastica/faq.html, accessed 19 April 2010.

Didcock, Barry, 'Who Takes The Rap for Gun Culture?; When Two Teenage Girls were Shot', *Sunday Herald*, 12 January 2003, at http://findarticles.com/p/articles/mi_qn4156/is_20030112/ai_n9626906/, accessed 1 May 2010.

Dougan, John, *The Who Sell Out* (New York: Continuum, 2006).

Dowd, Maureen, 'Labor's Love Lost?', *New York Times*, 23 April 1997, at http://www.nytimes.com/1997/04/23/opinion/labor-s-love-lost.html?sec=&spon=&pagewanted=all, accessed 23 April 2010.

Dowling, Stephen, 'Are We in Britpop's Second Wave?', *BBC News*, 19 August 2005, at http://news.bbc.co.uk/go/pr/fr/-2/hi/entertainment/4745137.stm, accessed 18 August 2008.

Downes, Julia, 'Riot Grrrl: The Legacy and Contemporary Landscape of DIY Feminist Cultural Activism', in Nadone Monem (ed.), *Riot Grrrl: Revolution Girl Style Now* (London: Black Dog Publishing, 2007).

Driver, Stephen, and Luke Martell, *New Labour: Politics after Thatcherism* (Cambridge: Polity, 2006).

Du Noyer, Paul, *In the City: A Celebration of London Music* (London: Virgin, 2009).

Eder, Bruce, 'Buddy Holly', at http://www.memorabletv.com/musicworld/halloffame/buddyholly.htm, accessed 16 April 2010.

————, 'Herman's Hermits: Biography', at http://www.allmusic.com/cg/amg.dll?p=amg&sql=11:kifuxqe5ld0e~T1, accessed 16 April 2010.

Edwards, Rebecca, 'Everyday, When I Wake Up, I Thank the Lord I'm Welsh: Reading the Markers of Welsh Identity in 1990s Pop Music', *Contemporary Wales*, 19/1 (2007): 142–60.

Ehrlich, Cyril, *Harmonious Alliance: A History of the Performing Right Society* (Oxford: Oxford University Press, 1989).

Eliot, T.S., *Selected Essays* (Faber: London, 1951).

Ellis, Iain, 'Alternative Rock Cultures: Lonnie Donegan and the Birth of British Rock', at http://www.popmatters.com/music/columns/ellis/060511.shtml, accessed 16 April 2010.

Emerson, Ken, *Always Magic in the Air: The Bomp and Brilliance of the Brill Building Era* (New York: Penguin, 2006).

Ennis, Philip H., *The Seventh Stream: The Emergence of Rocknroll in American Popular Music* (Middletown: Wesleyan University Press, 1992).

Erlewine, Stephen Thomas, 'Sgt. Pepper's Lonely Hearts Club Band', *Rolling Stone*, issue 507, 1987, at http://www.rollingstone.com/reviews/album/220919/sgt_peppers_lonely_hearts_club_band, accessed 18 April 2010.

————, 'Sgt. Pepper's Lonely Hearts Club Band' [n.d.], at http://www.allmusic.com/cg/amg.dll?p=amg&sql=10:difwxql5ldae, accessed 5 May 2010.

Everett, Walter, *The Beatles as Musicians: Revolver through the Anthology* (New York: Oxford University Press, 1999).

————, *The Beatles as Musicians: The Quarry Men through Rubber Soul* (New York: Oxford University Press, 2001).

Fast, Susan, *In the Houses of the Holy: Led Zeppelin and the Power of Rock Music* (Oxford: Oxford University Press, 2001).

Fisher, Mark, 'The Abstract Reality of the "Hardcore Continuum"', *Dancecult: Journal of Electronic Dance Music Culture*, 1/1 (2009): 123–6.

Fonarow, Wendy, *Empire of Dirt: The Aesthetics and Rituals of British Indie Music* (Middletown, CT: Wesleyan University Press, 2006).

Ford, Phil, 'Taboo: Time and Belief in Exotica', *Representations*, 103 (2008): 107–35.

Fortnum, Ian, 'The Stereophonics', *Vox*, June 1998, at http://www.rocksbackpages.com/article.html?ArticleID=354, accessed 18 April 2009.

Foster, Mo, *Play Like Elvis: How British Musicians Bought the American Dream* (London: Sanctuary Publishing, 2000).

Fricke, David, 'Off with Their Heads Review', *Rolling Stone*, 30 October 2008, at http://www.rollingstone.com/reviews/album/23506957/review/23589124/off_with_their_heads, accessed 14 November 2008.

Friedlander, Paul, *Rock and Roll: A Social History* (Boulder, CO: Westview, 1996).

Frith, Simon, 'The Suburban Sensibility in British Rock and Pop', in Roger Silverstone (ed.), *Visions of Suburbia* (London: Routledge, 1997), reprinted in Frith, *Taking Popular Music Seriously* (Aldershot: Ashgate, 2007).

————, 'Does British Music Still Matter?: A Reflection on the Changing Status of British Popular Music in the Global Music Market', *European Journal of Cultural Studies*, 7 (2004): 43–58.

————, 'The Industrialisation of Music', in Andy Bennett, Barry Shank and Jason Toynbee (eds), *The Popular Music Studies Reader* (London: Routledge, 2006).

————, *Taking Popular Music Seriously* (Aldershot: Ashgate, 2007).

————, and Howard Horne, *Art into Pop* (London: Methuen, 1987).

Fukuyama, Francis, *End of History and the Last Man* (London: H. Hamilton, 1989/1992).

Gilbert, Jeremy, 'The Hardcore Continuum?', *Dancecult: Journal of Electronic Dance Music Culture*, 1/1 (2009): 18–22.

Gilbert, Pat, 'Britpop Now!: Pat Gilbert finds that behind the hype, there are worries that Britpop may have already run its course', *Record Collector*, 194 (October 2005), pp. 24–5.

————, 'Whatever People Say I Am, That's What I'm Not', *Q*, March 2008, p. 89.

Gillies, Midge, *Marie Lloyd: The One and Only* (London: Victor Gollancz, 1999).

Gilroy, Paul, *There Ain't No Black in the Union Jack* (London: Unwin Hyman, 1987).

————, 'Joined-up Politics and Postcolonial Melancholia', *Theory, Culture & Society*, 18/2–3 (2001): 151–67.

————, *After Empire: Melancholia or Convivial Culture?* (London and New York: Routledge, 2004).

————, 'Multiculture, Double Consciousness and the "War on Terror"', *Patterns of Prejudice*, 39/4 (2005): 431–43.

Goodman, Steve, *Sonic Warfare: Sound, Affect and the Ecology of Fear* (Cambridge: MIT Press, 2009).

Gluck, J, 'Super Furry Animals', launch.com, Summer 2000, at http://www.rocksbackpages.com/article.html?ArticleID=4152, accessed 14 April 2009.

Grainge, Paul, *Monochrome Memories: Nostalgia and Style in Retro America* (Wesport, CT: Praeger, 2002).

Greer, Germaine, *The Whole Woman* (New York: Anchor Books, 2000).

Groom, Nick, *The Union Jack: The Story of the British Flag* (London: Atlantic, 2007).

Hall, Stuart, 'Introduction: Who Needs Identity?', in Hall and Paul DuGay (eds), *Questions of Cultural Identity* (London: Sage, 1996).

Harker, Dave, 'The Making of the Tyneside Concert Hall', *Popular Music*, 1/1 (1981): 27–56.

Harris, John, *The Last Party: Britpop, Blair and the Demise of English Rock* (London: Fourth Estate, 2003).

————, *Britpop!: Cool Britannia and the Spectacular Demise of English Rock* (London: Harper Perennial/Da Capo Press, 2003/2004).

Haslam, Dave, *Manchester, England* (London: Fourth Estate, 1999).

Hattenstone, Simon, 'Who Wants to be a Drug Addict at 41?', *Guardian Weekend*, 6 December 2008, at http://www.guardian.co.uk/music/2008/dec/06/noel-gallagher-oasis, accessed 20 May 2010.

Hawkins, Stan, *Settling the Pop Score: Pop Texts and Identity Politics* (Aldershot: Ashgate, 2002).

————, *The British Pop Dandy: Masculinity, Popular Music and Culture* (Aldershot: Ashgate, 2009).

Healy, Fran, 12 Memories: press release, October 2003, at http://www.saintedpr. com/pr/travis/Biog.doc, accessed 20 April 2009.

Heasley, Robert, 'Crossing the Borders of Gendered Sexuality: Queer Masculinities of Straight Men', in C. Ingraham (ed.), *Thinking Straight: The Power, the Promise, and the Paradox of Heterosexuality* (London: Routledge, 2005).

Hebdige, Dick, 'The Meaning of Mod', in Stuart Hall and Tony Jefferson (eds), *Resistance through Rituals: Youth Subcultures in Post-War Britain* (London: Hutchinson, 1976).

————, *Subculture: The Meaning of Style* (London: Routledge, 1979).

Hesmondhalgh, David, 'Indie: The Institutional Politics and Aesthetics of a Popular Music Genre', *Cultural Studies*, 13 (1999): 34–61.

————, 'British Popular Music and National Identity', in David Morley and Kevin Robins (eds), *British Cultural Studies: Geography, Nationality and Identity* (Oxford: Oxford University Press, 2001).

Hibbert, Tom, 'Manic Street Preachers: Pathetic...', *Q Magazine*, May 1992, http://www.rocksbackpages.com/article.html?ArticleID=13859&SearchText= hibbert, accessed 5 May 2010.

Hicks, Michael, *Sixties Rock: Garage, Psychedelic, and Other Satisfactions* (Urbana, IL: University of Illinois Press, 1999).

Hill, Sarah, *'Blerwytirhwng?': The Place of Welsh Pop Music* (Aldershot: Ashgate, 2007).

Hinsliff, Gaby, and Ned Temko, 'What I Really Mean about Liking the Arctic Monkeys, by Gordon Brown', *The Guardian*, 24 September 2006, at http:// www.guardian.co.uk/politics/2006/sep/24/uk/arts, accessed 3 February 2009.

Hitchcock, Peter, 'It Dread Inna Inglan: Linton Kwesi Johnson, Dread, and Dub Identity', *Postmodern Culture*, 4/1 (1993): 1–25.

Hobson, John Atkinson, *The Psychology of Jingoism* (London: Grant Richards, 1901).

Hoggart, Richard, *The Uses of Literacy* (London: Pelican, 1957).

Hoskins, Barney, 'The Third Invasion: Britpop Strikes!', *Musician*, July 1996, available on the web at: http://www.rocksbackpages.com.dbgw.lis.curtin.edu. au/article.html?ArticleID=1546&SearchText=britpop

Howson, John, *Songs Sung in Suffolk* (Stowmarket: Veteran Tapes, 1992).

Huq, Rupa, *Beyond Subculture: Pop, You and Identity in a Postcolonial World* (London: Routledge, 2006).

Hutnyk, John, 'Pantomime Terror: Diasporic Music in a Time of War', *Journal of Creative Communications*, 2/1–2 (2007): 123–41.

Hyder, Rehan, *Brimful of Asia: Negotiating Ethnicity on the UK Music Scene* (Aldershot: Ashgate, 2004).

Inglis, Ian, '"Some Kind of Wonderful": The Creative Legacy of the Brill Building', *American Music*, 21/1 (2003): 214–35.

Jackson, Stevi, 'Sexuality, Heterosexuality and Gender Hierarchy: Getting Our Priorities Straight', in Chris Ingraham (ed.), *Thinking Straight: The Power, the Promise, and the Paradox of Heterosexuality* (London: Routledge, 2005).

James, 'Famous Tales of the Formerly Young and Presently Stupid', 12 January 2006, at http://www.greenpeaness.org/2006/01/famous-tales-of-formerly-young-and.html, accessed 19 April 2010.

James, Alex, *Bit of a Blur: The Autobiography* (London: Little Brown, 2007).

Jha, Alok, 'Lad Culture Corrupts Men as much as it Debases Women', *The Guardian*, 30 March 2006, at http://www.guardian.co.uk/commentisfree/2006/mar/30/comment.prisonsandprobation, accessed 14 May 2010.

Johnson, Howard, Review of Sleeper, *Pleased to Meet You*, *Q*, November 1997, at http://vu.morrissey-solo.com/sleeper/2000/info/rev/pleased.htm, accessed 11 May 2010.

Jones, Cliff, 'Looking for a New England', *The Face*, 68 (1994): 40–46.

Kearney, Mary Celeste, 'The Missing Links: Riot Grrrl–Feminism–Lesbian Culture', in Sheila Whiteley (ed.), *Sexing the Groove: Popular Music and Gender* (London: Routledge, 1997).

Kiely, Richard, Frank Bechhofer and David McCrone, 'Birth, Blood and Belonging: Identity Claims in Post-Devolution Scotland', *The Sociological Review*, 53/1 (2005): 150–71.

Kift, Dagmar, *The Victorian Music Hall: Culture, Class and Conflict* (Cambridge: Cambridge University Press, 1996).

Kirkup, James, 'Profile: James Purnell – the Baby Faced Assassin', *Telegraph*, 5 June 2009, at http://www.telegraph.co.uk/news/newstopics/politics/5447924/Profile-James-Purnell---the-baby-faced-assassin.html, accessed 23 April 2010.

Kode9 & The SpaceApe, *Memories of the Future*, at http://www.hyperdub.net/memoriesofthefuture.html, accessed 3 May 2010.

Kumar, Krishan, 'Nation and Empire: English and British National Identity in Comparative Perspective', *Theory & Society*, 29 (2000): 575–608.

Kundnani, Arun, *The End of Tolerance: Racism in 21st Century Britain* (London–Ann Arbor, MI: Pluto Press, 2007).

Laing, Dave, *The Sound of Our Time* (Chicago: Quadrangle, 1969).

————, *One Chord Wonders: Power and Meaning in Punk Rock* (Milton Keynes: Open University Press, 1985).

————, 'Roll Over Lonnie (Tell George Formby the News)', in Charlie Gillett and Simon Frith (eds), *The Beat Goes On: The Rock File Reader* (London: Pluto Press, 1996/1972).

————, 'Cockney Rock', in Harris M. Berger and Michael Thomas Carroll (eds), *Global Pop, Local Language* (Jackson, MI: University of Mississippi Press, 2003).

————, 'Nine Lives in the Music Business: Reg Dwight and Elton John in the 1960s', *Popular Music History*, 2/3 (2007): 237–61.

————, 'Six Boys, Six Beatles: The Formative Years 1950–62', in Kenneth Womack (ed.), *The Cambridge Companion to the Beatles* (Cambridge: Cambridge University Press, 2009).

Larkin, Colin (ed.), *The Virgin Encyclopedia of Popular Music*, concise 3rd edn (London: Virgin Books, 1999).

Last.FM, 'The Gyres', at http://www.last.fm/music/The+Gyres/+tags, accessed 6 May 2010.

Lauder, Sir Harry, *Roamin' in the Gloamin'* (Wakefield: EP Publishing, 1976/1928).

Leach, Elizabeth Eva, 'Vicars of "Wannabe": Authenticity and the Spice Girls', *Popular Music*, 20/2 (2001): 143–67.

Lee, Edward, *Folk Song and Music Hall* (London: Routledge, 1982).

Leigh, Spencer, with illustrations by John Firminger, *Puttin' on the Style*: *The Lonnie Donegan Story* (Kent: Finbarr, 2003).

Lemish, Dafna, 'Spice World: Constructing Femininity the Popular Way', *Popular Music and Society*, 26/1 (2003): 17–29.

Leonard, Marion, 'Rebel Girl, You Are the Queen of My World', in Sheila Whiteley (ed.), *Sexing the Groove: Popular Music and Gender* (London: Routledge, 1997).

Leys, Colin, *Politics in Britain: An Introduction* (London: Verso, 1983).

McCormick, Neil, 'A Little Bit Music Hall, a Little Bit Rock'n'Roll', *Telegraph*, 30 June 2003, at http://www.telegraph.co.uk/arts/main.jhtml?xml=/arts/2003/06/30/bmrob30.xml, accessed 16 April 2010.

————, 'How Keane, Snow Patrol, Kaiser Chiefs and Razorlight Followed Oasis to Revive Britpop', *Telegraph*, 23 October 2008, at http://www.telegraph.co.uk/culture/music/3562452/How-Keane-Snow-Patrol-Kaiser-Chiefs-and-Razorlight-followed-Oasis-to-revive-Britpop.html, accessed 5 May 2010.

McCrone, David, 'A Nation that Dare Not Speak its Name', *Ethnicities*, 6/2 (2006): 267–78.

MacDonald, Ian, *Revolution in the Head* (London: Fourth Estate, 1994).

MacInnes, Colin, 'Young England, Half English', in MacInnes (ed.), *England, Half-English* (London: Chatto & Windus, 1961/1986).

————, *Sweet Saturday Night* (London: MacGibbon and Kee, 1969).

McKay, George, '"I'm So Bored with the USA": The Punk in Cyberpunk', in Roger Sabin (ed.), *Punk Rock: So What? The Cultural Legacy of Punk* (London: Routledge, 1999).

McLaughlin, Eugene, 'Re-branding Britain', Open University 2002, at http://www.open2.net/society/socialchange/new_brit_coolbritainnia.html, accessed 5 May 2010.

McLean, Craig, '21st-Century Boy', *The Observer*, 27 January 2007, at http://www.guardian.co.uk/music/2007/jan/07/popandrock.features1/html, accessed 18 January 2009.

————, 'Hey, Hey it's The Arctic Monkeys', *Times*, 28 July 2007, at http://entertainment.timesonline.co.uk/tol/arts_and_entertainment/music/article 212396, accessed 9 December 2008.

Maconie, Stuart, 'Elvis Costello and Justine Frischmann: Pleased to Meet You', *Q*, October 1996, pp. 70–74.

————, 'The Death of a Party', *Select*, August 1999, p. 3.

Mahoney, Elisabeth, 'Rip it Up, Start Again', *The Independent*, 30 April 1999, p. 11.

Maitland, Sara, *Vesta Tilley* (London: Virago, 1986).

Malik, Sarita, 'The Black and White Minstrel Show', at http://www.museum.tv/archives/etv/B/htmlB/blackandwhim/blackandwhim.htm, accessed 16 April 2010.

Mander, Raymond, and Joe Mitchenson, *British Music Hall*, rev. edn (London: Gentry Books, 1974).

Mandler, Peter, 'Two Cultures—One—Or Many?', in Kathleen Burke (ed.), *The British Isles since 1945* (Oxford: Oxford University Press, 2003).

Manzoor, Sarfraz, 'Sarfraz Manzoor Asks What "Englishness" Means Today in a City Like Bradford', *The Guardian*, 5 July 2009, at http://www.guardian.co.uk/stage/2009/jul/05/bradford-englishness-jb-priestley, accessed 1 May 2010.

Marten, Neville, and Jeff Hudson, *The Kinks: Well Respected Men* (London: Sanctuary Publishing, 1998).

Martin, Gavin, 'Rings around Cardiff: Super Furry Animals', *Daily Mirror*, 2003, at http://www.rocksbackpages.com/article.html?ArticleID=4988, accessed 14 April 2009.

Mason, Stewart, Review of The Kinks, 'Dandy', at http://www.allmusic.com/cg/amg.dll?p=amg&sql=33:fpfqxct0ldse, accessed 16 April 2010.

Mellers, Wilfrid, *Twilight of the Gods: The Beatles in Retrospect* (London: Faber, 1973).

Melly, Jim, *Last Orders Please: Rod Stewart, the 'Faces' and the Britain We Forgot* (London: Ebury, 2003).

Middleton, Richard, *Studying Popular Music* (Milton Keynes: Open University Press, 1990).

Miller, Andy, *The Kinks Are the Village Green Preservation Society* (New York: Continuum, 2003).

Miller, W., 'Furry Cool: Super Band are Animal Magic', *The Daily Mirror*, 7 September 2001, p. 16.

Moore, Allan F., *Rock: The Primary Text: Developing a Musicology of Rock* (Aldershot: Ashgate, 1993/2001).

Morley, David, and Robins, Kevin, 'Introduction: The National Culture in its New Global Context', in Morley and Robins (eds), *British Cultural Studies: Geography, Nationality and Identity* (Oxford: Oxford University Press, 2001).

———— (eds), *British Cultural Studies: Geography, Nationality and Identity* (Oxford: Oxford University Press, 2001).

Myers, Ben, 'Stereophonics: Three Local Boys Go Global', *Kerrang!*, April 1999, at http://www.rocksbackpages.com/article.html?ArticleID=10583, accessed 5 May 2010.

NME, 'Glasgow Garage', 10 May 1999, at http://www.nme.com/reviews/travis/1098, accessed 5 May 2010.

————, 'Nicky Wire says Glastonbury "Shithole" Comment was a Joke', 20 June 2007, at http://www.nme.com/news/manic-street-preachers/29067, accessed 5 May 2010.

————, 'Tony Blair was Worried Oasis would Trash Downing Street', 10 July 2007, at http://www.nme.com/news/oasis/29600, accessed 23 April 2010.

————, 'Manic Street Preachers' Richey Edwards Officially Dead', 24 November 2008, at http://www.nme.com/news/manic-street-preachers/41236, accessed 5 May 2010.

————, 'Blur: are Shite Once Again', 12 December 2008, at http://www.nme.com/news/mogwai/41622, accessed 4 May 2010.

————, 'Estelle: "Paxman Treated Dizzee Rascal Like an Idiot"', 18 December 2008, at http://www.nme.com/news/dizzee-rascal/41727, accessed 1 May 2010.

Norris, Clive, Mike McCahill and David Wood, 'Editorial. The Growth of CCTV: A Global Perspective on the International Diffusion of Video Surveillance in Publicly Accessible Space', *Surveillance & Society*, 2/2–3 (2004): 110–35.

Nostalgia Central, 'Variety, News and Sport', at http://www.nostalgiacentral.com/music/music_60.htm, accessed 3 July 2008.

Nott, James, *Music for the People: Popular Music and Dance in Interwar Britain* (Oxford: Oxford University Press, 2002).

Noys, Benjamin, 'Into the "Jungle"', *Popular Music*, 14/3 (1995): 321–32.

O'Brien, Lucy, 'The Woman Punk Made Me', in Roger Sabin (ed.), *Punk Rock: So What? The Cultural Legacy of Punk* (London: Routledge, 1999).

O'Reilly, John, 'Tunespotting: The New Offering from Young Scottish Band Mogwai is a Masterpiece of Understatement', *The Guardian*, 2 April 1999, p. T017.

Oakley, Kate, 'Not So Cool Britannia: The Role of the Creative Industries in Economic Development', *International Journal of Cultural Studies*, 7/1 (2004): 67–77.

Oliver, Paul, 'Introduction to Part Two: From the 1950s to the Present', in Oliver (ed.), *Black Music in Britain: Essays on the Afro-Asian Contribution to Popular Music* (Milton Keynes: Open University Press, 1990).

Osley, Richard, 'Britpop is Back … and This Time even the US Charts Can't Ignore it', *Independent*, 22 April 2007, at http://www.independent.co.uk/news/uk/this-britain/britpop-is-backand-this-time-even-the-us-charts-cant-ignore-it-445737.html, accessed 5 May 2010.

P., Steve, 'Every Day I Love the US Less', *BBC*: *Top of the Pops*, 27 February 2006, at http://www.bbc.co.uk/totp/news/news/2006/02/27/29919.shtml, accessed 5 May 2010.

204   *BRITPOP AND THE ENGLISH MUSIC TRADITION*

Palladino, Grace, *Teenagers: An American History* (New York: Basic Books, 1996).

Parekh, Bikhu, *The Future of Multi-Ethnic Britain: The Parekh Report* (London: Profile, 2000).

Parsonage, Catherine, *The Evolution of Jazz in Britain, 1880–1935* (Aldershot: Ashgate, 2005).

Pearsall, Ronald, *Edwardian Popular Song* (Newton Abbot: David & Charles, 1975).

Peirce, Gareth, 'Was it Like This for the Irish?', *London Review of Books*, 10 April 2008, at http://www.lrb.co.uk/v30/n07/peir01_.html, accessed 1 May 2010.

Percival, J. Mark, 'Making Music Radio: The Record Industry and Popular Music Production in the UK' (unpublished PhD thesis, University of Stirling, 2007).

————, 'Time, Space and Identity and Indie Music Production in West Central Scotland', unpublished conference paper, presented at the EMP Pop Conference, 20 April 2007, Seattle, WA, USA.

Peters, Guy, 'Trainspotting: Music from the Motion Picture (1996)', at http://www.guypetersreviews.com/trainspotting.php, accessed 19 April 2010.

Peterson, Richard A., *Creating Country Music: Fabricating Authenticity* (Chicago: University of Chicago Press, 1997).

Petridis, Alexis, 'CD of the Week: Stereophonics, Language. Sex. Violence. Other?', *The Guardian*, 4 March 2005, at http://www.guardian.co.uk/music/2005/mar/04/popandrock.shopping6, accessed 5 May 2010.

————, 'This is Going to Look Really Bad', *The Guardian*, 7 October 2005, at http://wwwguardian.co.uk/music/2005/oct/07/popandrock.blocparty, accessed 9 September 2009.

————, 'The Soundtrack', *The Guardian*, 2 January 2008, at http://music.guardian.co.uk/0,3319287620122428,00.html, accessed 5 May 2010.

Phillips, Caryl, 'Kingdom of the Blind', *The Guardian*, 17 July 2004, at http://www.guardian.co.uk/books/2004/jul/17/featuresreviews.guardianreview1, accessed 5 May 2010.

Pickering, Michael, *Blackface Minstrelsy in Britain* (Aldershot: Ashgate, 2008).

————, and Emily Keightley, 'The Modalities of Nostalgia', *Current Sociology*, 54/6 (2006): 919–41.

Pieterse, Jan Nederveen, 'Global Multiculture, Flexible Acculturation', *Globalizations*, 4/1 (2007): 65–79.

Pinch, Emma, 'Travis: New Album's Creative Process was Liberatingly Unstructured', *Liverpool Daily Post*, 29 August 2008, at http://www.liverpooldailypost.co.uk/liverpool-life-features/liverpool-arts/2008/08/29/travis-new-album-s-creative-process-was-liberatingly-unstructured-92534-21630243/, accessed 5 May 2010.

Porter, Charlie, 'Songs for the Soul, Not for the Sales List', *The Times*, 29 November 1997, p. 15.

————, 'Balancing Act', *The Times*, 13 June 1998, p. 10.

Q, 'Ten Years in a Nutshell', October 1996 (decennial edn).

Quinn, Steven, 'Rumble in the Jungle: The Invisible History of Drum'n'Bass', *Transformations*, 3 (May 2002), at http://www.transformationsjournal.org/journal/issue_03/pdf/quinn.pdf, accessed 5 May 2010.

Randall, Annie J., *Dusty! Queen of the Postmods* (New York: Oxford University Press, 2009).

Raphael, Amy, *Never Mind the Bollocks: Women Rewrite Rock* (London: Virago Press, 1995).

Regev, Motti, and Edwin Seroussi, *Popular Music and National Culture in Israel* (Berkeley: LA–London: University of California Press, 2004).

Reynolds, Simon, 'Manic Street Preachers', *Melody Maker*, 20 July 1991, at http://www.rocksbackpages.com/article.html?ArticleID=994, accessed 18 April 2009.

———, 'Suede: The Best New Band in America?', *Melody Maker*, 19 June 1993, at http://www.rocksbackpages.com/article.html?ArticleID=1032, accessed 16 April 2009.

———, *Generation Ecstasy: Into the World of Techno and Rave Culture* (Boston: Little, Brown, 1998).

———, 'Piracy Funds What?', *The Village Voice*, 15 February 2005, at http://www.villagevoice.com/2005-02-15/music/piracy-funds-what/, accessed 3 May 2010.

———, 'Reasons to Be Cheerful', *Frieze Magazine*, issue 25 (November–December 2005), at http://www.frieze.com/issue/article/reasons_to_be_cheerful_3, accessed 15 May 2010.

———, 'Society of the Spectral', *The Wire*, 273 (November 2006), pp. 26–33.

———, 'The Hardcore Continuum: Introduction', *The Wire*, 300 (February 2009), at http://www.thewire.co.uk/articles/2009/, accessed 3 May 2010.

———, 'The Hardcore Continuum, or, (a) Theory and its Discontents', 27 February 2009, at http://energyflashbysimonreynolds.blogspot.com/2009/02/hardcore-continuum-or-theory-and-its.html, accessed 3 May 2010.

———, and Joy Press, *The Sex Revolts: Gender, Rebellion and Rock 'n' Roll* (Cambridge, MA: Harvard University Press, 1995).

Richards, Jeffrey, *Imperialism and Music: Britain 1876–1953* (Manchester: Manchester University Press, 2001).

Riis, Thomas L., 'The Experience and Impact of Black Entertainers in England, 1895–1920', *American Music*, 4/1 (1986): 50–58.

Robinson, Peter, 'All Killer No Landfiller', *The Guardian*, 17 January 2009, at http://www.guardian.co.uk/music/2009/jan/17/florence-and-the-machine-indie, accessed 15 May 2010.

Rogan, Johnny, *Morrissey and Marr: The Severed Alliance* (London: Omnibus Press, 1994).

Rojek, Chris, *Brit-Myth: Who Do the British Think They Are?* (London: Reaktion, 2007).

Rolling Stone, Review of The Beatles, *Sgt. Pepper's Lonely Hearts Club Band*, at http://www.rollingstone.com/reviews/album/220919/sgt_peppers_lonely_ hearts_club_band, accessed 7 July 2008.

Russell, Dave, *Popular Music in England, 1840–1914: A Social History* (Manchester: Manchester University Press, 1997).

Sabin, Roger (ed.), *Punk Rock: So What? The Cultural Legacy of Punk* (London: Routledge, 1999).

Sadie, Stanley (ed.), *New Grove Dictionary of Music and Musicians* (London: Macmillan, 2001).

St Michael, Mick, *Oasis* (London: Virgin Publishing, 1996).

Sandbrook, Dominick, *Never Had It So Good: A History of Britain from Suez to the Beatles* (London: Little, Brown, 2005).

Sanhera, Jasvinder, *Shame* (London: Hodder & Stoughton, 2007).

———, *Daughters of Shame* (London: Hodder, 2009).

Scheurer, Timothy E., 'The Beatles, the Brill Building, and the Persistence of Tin Pan Alley in the Age of Rock', *Popular Music and Society*, 20/4 (1996): 89–102.

Schuster, Liza, and John Solomos, 'Race, Immigration and Asylum: New Labour's Agenda and its Consequences', *Ethnicities*, 4/2 (2004): 267–300.

Scott, Derek B., '(What's the Copy?) The Beatles and Oasis', in Y. Heinonen, M. Heuger, S. Whiteley, T. Nurmesjävi and J. Koskimäki (eds), *Beatlestudies 3* (University of Jyväskylä Department of Music, Research Report 23, 2001).

Segal, Victoria, 'Kaiser Chiefs: Yours Truly, Angry Mob', *The Times*, 24 February 2007, at http://entertainment.timesonline.co.uk/tol/arts_and_entertainment/ music/cd_reviews/, accessed 5 May 2010.

Senelick, Laurence (ed.), *Tavern Singing in Early Victorian London: The Diaries of Charles Rice for 1840 and 1841* (London: Society for Theatre Research, 1997).

———, and David Cheshire, *British Music Hall, 1840–1923: A Bibliography and Guide to Sources, with a Supplement on European Music-Hall* (Hamden, CT: ACLS History, 1997).

Shaar Murray, Charles, 'The Social Rehabilitation of the Sex Pistols', *NME*, 6 August 1977, at http://www.rocksbackpages.com/article.html?ArticleID=11778, accessed 16 April 2009.

Sharma, Sanjay, 'Noisy Asians or "Asian Noise"?', in Sharma, John Hutnyk and Ashwani Sharma (eds), *Dis-Orienting Rhythms: The Politics of the New Asian Dance Music* (London: Zed Books, 1996).

———, and Ashwani Sharma, 'White Paranoia: Orientalism in the Age of Empire', *Fashion Theory*, 3–4 (2003): 1–17.

———, John Hutnyk and Ashwani Sharma (eds), *Dis-Orienting Rhythms: The Politics of the New Asian Dance Music* (London: Zed Books, 1996).

Sharp, Cecil J., *English Folk-Song: Some Conclusions* (London: Novello, 1907/1936).

Shelley, Jim, 'Oasis', *Independent, Magazine*, 20 January 2000, pp. 10–16.

Sherwin, Adam, 'Arctic Monkeys Race to Top of the Tree', *The Times*, 30 January 2006, at http://entertainment.timesonline.co.uk/tol/arts_and_entertainment/music/article7222745, accessed 9 December 2008.

Simpson, Dave, 'We're Bigger Now than Ever', *The Guardian*, 12 October 2007, p. 6.

Simpson, Mark, *It's a Queer World: Deviant Adventures in Pop Culture* (London: The Haworth Press, 1999).

——————, *Saint Morrissey* (London: SAF Publishing, 2004).

Smith, Andrew, 'A Tour of the New Pop Landscape', *The Sunday Times: The Culture*, 1 September 1996, p. 4.

Smith, Patricia Juliana (ed.), *The Queer Sixties* (London: Routledge, 1999).

Smithers, Nigel, 'Herman's Hermits: British Pop Band of the Sixties Who Enjoyed Enormous Stateside Success', at http://www.hermanshermits.com/articles/musicmags/mar87_rc_p2.html, accessed 16 April 2010.

Snow, Matt, 'Gang of Four: Hard (EMI)', *NME*, 10 September 1983, at http://www.rocksbackpages.com/article.html?ArticleID=5826, accessed 16 April 2009.

Spencer, Neil, 'Here at Last. Oasis Break the Drought', *Observer*, 10 August 1997, p. 1.

Splintering Bone Ashes, 'Invention or Discovery – or, When is a Genre Not a Genre', 30 April 2009, at http://splinteringboneashes.blogspot.com/2009/04/invention-or-discovery-or-when-is-genre.html, accessed 3 May 2010.

Starpulse, 'Liam Gallagher Hates "Wonderwall"', 31 August 2008, at http://www.starpulse.com/news/index.php/2008/08/31/liam_gallagher_hates_wonderwall_, accessed 27 April 2010.

Stedman-Jones, Gareth, 'Working-Class Culture and Working-Class Politics in London 1870–1900', in Barry Waites, Tony Bennet and Graham Martin (eds), *Popular Culture Past and Present: A Reader* (London: Croom Helm, 1982/1973).

Stewart, Alexander, '"Funky Drummer": New Orleans, James Brown and the Rhythmic Transformation of American Popular Music', *Popular Music*, 19/3 (2000): 293–318.

Stokes, Martin, 'Introduction: Ethnicity, Identity and Music', in Stokes (ed.), *Ethnicity, Identity and Music: The Musical Construction of Place* (Oxford: Berg, 1994).

Stratton, Allegra, 'James Purnell: I Lost Faith in Gordon Brown Months Ago', *The Guardian*, 17 July 2009, at http://www.guardian.co.uk/politics/2009/jul/17/james-purnell-gordon-brown-reform, accessed 12 May 2010.

Stratton, Jon, *Jews, Race and Popular Music* (Aldershot: Ashgate, 2009).

Sullivan, Caroline, 'Never Mind the Bo***cks – Here's the Heart and Soul', *The Guardian*, 12 August 1997, p. 2.

Sullivan, Patricia Gordon, '"Let's Have a Go at It": The British Music Hall and the Kinks', in Thomas M. Kitts and Michael J. Kraus (eds), *Living on a Thin Line: Crossing Aesthetic Borders with the Kinks* (Rumford: Rock 'n' roll Research Press, 2002).

Sutherland, Richard, and Will Straw, 'The Canadian Music Industry at a Crossroads', in Daniel Taras, Maria Bakardjieva and Frits Pannekoek (eds), *How Canadians Communicate 2* (Calgary, AB: University of Calgary Press, 2007).

Swanwick, Keith, *Popular Music and the Teacher* (Oxford: Pergamon, 1968).

Taylor, Jodie, 'Playing it Queer: Understanding Queer Gender, Sexual and Musical Praxis in a "New" Musicological Context' (unpublished thesis, Griffith University, 2008).

Taylor, Paul, 'Are Rock's Big Hitters now Simply Quoasis?', *Manchester Evening News*, 9 October 2008, p. 10.

The Elastica Connection, 'FAQ', at http://www.stutter.demon.co.uk/elastica/faq. html#who#who, accessed 19 April 2010.

'The Empire Gobs Back', *Rolling Stone, Yearbook 1995* (New York: Wenner Media, 1995).

The Internet Movie Database, 'Memorable Quotes for The Rolling Stones Rock and Roll Circus', at http://www.imdb.com/title/tt0122689/quotes, accessed 5 May 2010.

Thompson, Ben, 'Super Furry Animals', *Mojo*, August 1996, at http://www. rocksbackpages.com/article.html?ArticleID=1567, accessed 6 May 2010.

————, 'Come on, Feel the Noise', *The Independent*, 19 March 1999, p. 12.

————, *Ways of Hearing: A User's Guide to the Pop Psyche from Elvis to Eminem* (London: Orion, 2001).

Tilley, James, and Anthony Heath, 'The Decline of British National Pride', *The British Journal of Sociology*, 58/4 (2007): 661–78.

Times, The, 'Kaiser Chiefs Talking Point', 2005, at http://entertainment.timesonline. co.uk/tol/arts_and_entertainment/music/article52875, accessed 14 November 2008.

Tomlinson, John, *Cultural Imperialism: A Critical Introduction* (Baltimore, MD: Johns Hopkins University Press, 1991).

Vaughan Williams, Ralph, and Albert Lancester Lloyds (eds), *The Penguin Book of English Folk Songs* (Harmondsworth: Penguin, 1959).

Veal, Michael, *Dub: Soundscapes and Shattered Songs in Jamaican Reggae* (Middletown, CT: Wesleyan University Press, 2007).

Wald, Gayle, *Just a Girl? Rock Music, Feminism, and the Cultural Construction of Female Youth* (Chicago: University of Chicago Press, 1998).

Weinstein, Deena, 'All Singers Are Dicks', *Popular Music and Society*, 27/3 (2004): 323–34.

Wheaton, Robert, 'London Calling – For Congo, Colombo, Sri Lanka…', in Mary Gaitskill (ed.), *Da Capo Best Music Writing 2006* (New York: Da Capo Press, 2006).

Whiley, Jo, 'The '00s', *Q*, March 2008, p. 83.

White, Livingston A., 'Reconsidering Cultural Imperialism Theory', *Transnational Broadcasting Studies*, 6 (2001), at http://www.tbsjournal.com/Archives/ Spring01/white.html, accessed 17 April 2010.

Whitehead, Stephen M., and Frank J. Barrett (eds), *The Masculinities Reader* (Cambridge: Polity Press, 2005).

Whiteley, Sheila, *Women and Popular Music: Sexuality, Identity and Subjectivity* (London: Routledge, 2000).

————, *Too Much Too Young: Popular Music, Age, and Gender* (London: Routledge, 2005).

————, '"A Boy in the Bush": Morrissey, Sexuality and Dialogical Meanings', in Sean Campbell and Colin Coulter (eds), *Essays on The Smiths* (Manchester: Manchester University Press, forthcoming [2010]).

Williams, Raymond, *The Long Revolution* (Harmondsworth: Penguin, 1965).

————, *The Country and the City* (St Albans: Paladin, 1975).

————, *Culture* (London, Fontana, 1981).

Williams, Tryst, 'Is it Cool Cymru – Again?', *Western Mail*, 25 May 2006, at http://www.walesonline.co.uk/news/wales-news/tm_objectid=17127849&met hod=full&siteid=50082&headline=is-this-the-second-coming-of-cool-cymru- -name_page.html, accessed 6 May 2010.

Willis, Paul, *Learning to Labour: How Working Class Kids Get Working Class Jobs* (Farnborough: Saxon House, 1977).

Wintour, Patrick, and Vikram Dodd, 'Blair Blames Spate of Murders on Black Culture', *The Guardian*, 12 April 2007, at http://www.guardian.co.uk/ politics/2007/apr/12/ukcrime.race, accessed 1 May 2010.

Woebot, 'Farewell', 4 January 2008, at http://www.woebot.com/index2.html, accessed 3 May 2010.

Wolfson, Sam, 'The Last Shadow Puppets, the Age of Understatement', *The Observer*, 20 April 2008, at http://www.guardian.co.uk/music/2008/ apr/20/popandrock, accessed 6 May 2010.

Young, Toby, and Tom Vanderbilt, 'The End of Irony', *The Modern Review*, April–May 1994, pp. 6–7.

Youngs, Ian, 'Sound of 2005: Kaiser Chiefs', *BBC News*, 3 January 2005, at http://news.bbc.co.uk/2/hi/entertainment/4.html, accessed 20 October 2007.

Ziff, Bruce, and Pratima V. Rao, 'Introduction to Cultural Appropriation: A Framework for Analysis', in Ziff and Rao (eds), *Borrowed Power: Essays on Cultural Appropriation* (New Brunswick, NJ: Rutgers University Press, 1997).

Zuberi, Nabeel, *Sounds English: Transnational Popular Music* (Urbana, IL: University of Illinois Press, 2001).

Discography

Blur, 'Girls & Boys', *Parklife*, EMI (1994).

Cameron, Keith, and Owen Morris (compilers and eds), *Oasis Interviews*, Creation Records CCV001 (1996).

Manic Street Preachers, 'A Design for Life', *Everything Must Go*, Epic (1996).

Oasis, 'Wonderwall', (*What's the Story) Morning Glory?*, Creation Records (1995).
Oasis Interview, March 1995, Sound and Media SAM 7023, 1996.
Pulp, 'Common People', *Different Class*, Polygram (1995).
Roll Deep, *Roll Deep Presents Grimey, Vol. 1*, DMC (2004).
Terror Danjah, *Gremlinz: The Instrumentals 2003–2009*, Planet Mu (2009).
The Beatles, Interview CD, Sound and Media SAM 7001 (1995).
Trimbal, *Soulfood Vol. 1*, Trimbal (2007).
Two Fingers, *Two Fingers*, Big Dada Recordings (2008).
Various Artists, *5: Five Years of Hyperdub*, Hyperdub (2009).

Select Videography

BBC, *Later with Jools Holland 2 – Cool Britannia 2*, Warner (2005).
Dizzee Rascal, 'Sirens', at http://www.youtube.com/watch?v=IPpxxrl0xhM, accessed 1 May 2010.
Elastica, 'Stutter', at http://www.youtube.com/watch?v=mwNfiB4zBQo, accessed 19 April 2010.
The Bug featuring Warrior Queen, 'Dem A Bomb We', 2005, at www.youtube.com/watch?v=4k5hNwfUe4M, accessed 3 May 2010
The Bug featuring Warrior Queen, 'Poison Dart', 2008, at http://www.ninjatune.net/videos/video.php?type=flv&id=136, accessed 3 May 2010.
YouTube, 'Obama Won Because of Hip Hop – Go Dizzee Rascal', at http://www.youtube.com/watch?v=sRTe4q-vR0g, accessed 1 May 2010.

Index

Alison Scores

South Wales Echo.